rolling away

Rolling Away

my agony with ecstasy

Lynn Marie Smith

ATRIA BOOKS

New York   London   Toronto   Sydney

ATRIA BOOKS
1230 Avenue of the Americas
New York, NY 10020

ISBN: 0-7434-9043-6

First Atria Books hardcover edition May 2005

10 9 8 7 6 5 4 3 2 1

ATRIA B O O K S is a trademark of Simon & Schuster, Inc.

Manufactured in the United States of America

For information regarding special discounts for bulk purchases,
please contact Simon & Schuster Special Sales at 1-800-456-6798
or business@simonandschuster.com

For Kelley McEnery Baker and Kate Patton
And to all mothers, like my own, who love unconditionally.

contents

part 5 ∗ coming clEan

I never wanted to be an addict. I don't think any of us do. It just happens. One day you think you are normal, living a normal life, and then one day there is concrete proof that you are not.

rolling away

The dark night of the soul
Comes just before revelation.

When everything is lost,
And all seems darkness,
Then comes the new life
And all that is needed.

—Joseph Campbell

This is a true story, although some names and details have been changed to protect the guilty.

Am I Dead?

As I rise from the couch, something inside my mind snaps. My thoughts begin to race as I fight for air. *Am I having a heart attack?* I stare at the bodies around me. *How the hell did I get here?* Everything seems strangely familiar. My skin begins to itch. I stagger into the bathroom and plunge my fingers down my throat. Nothing.

I plead to Mason. "Get me out of this. Make it stop, please."

From the stunned look on his face he has no idea what is manifesting inside of me. Neither do I.

"Have a cigarette," mutters Kelly, "get some rest."

They don't give a shit about me. The last thing in the world I can do is rest. I pace frantically in my bedroom, changing in and out of clothes, believing it will alter my state. I stumble into my pajamas, clench my eyes, and plead for sleep. My heart feels like it's beating for a thousand people. The decay of the apartment charges through my nostrils as I inhale months of cigarette smoke that clings to the walls. My head throbs with confusion. Voices, footsteps, and sirens scream in my ears. I begin to pray, something I have not done in years. I have deprived myself of so many things that I once loved. I want to fall asleep instantly, wake up, and feel normal . . . *whatever the fuck that is.* If I could just split my skull open and reach inside to turn the switch off, I could make it stop. This is hell. I suddenly glimpse myself from above. I must be dying. *Am I dead?*

I rush to the mirror and stare at a grinning skeleton. I look to Mason for comfort, but I envision the devil instead. I picture myself running and never stopping.

"Are you mad at me?" whimpers Kelly.

I force her out of the way and grab the phone. It is four o'clock in the morning. My mother answers.

"Mommy, I am dead and in hell, please rescue me."

"Lynn . . . Lynn, relax, everything is going to be fine. What's going on . . . Lynn?"

"I don't know, please, please, please, come get me."

"Lynn, what is wrong? Are you using drugs?"

"Yes, no, I don't know, help me please," I am moaning.

"I'm on my way, Lynn. Is Mason with you?"

" I think, yes, yes, he's here . . . I am going to his house . . . I'll be there."

"Stay with him . . ." pleads my mom.

I drop the phone on the ground and run to my room.

"Make sure you hide the bong if your mother is coming here," yells Kelly before slamming her door.

I seize my wooden rosary beads from my dresser drawer and dart downstairs out into the street. I sense danger hunting me. Mason clutches my arm and pulls me back onto the sidewalk, as cars swerve to dodge me.

"Am I dead? Are you not telling me something, Mason?"

"No, babe, you're not dead. You are right here with me."

"I don't believe you, you're lying."

Mason stays by my side. I sense my existence creeping away. Time is blurry, but it seems I haven't slept in years. Today I am being punished for all of the bad choices that I have made. I still wish to make it right, but I guess my time is up. Standing outside, agitated, I gaze at my neighbors as they leave for work. One seems familiar. I stare directly into his eyes, his gaze passes through me. I am an illusion.

Mason flags down a taxi and pulls me inside. As we cross the

Manhattan Bridge, I peer out the back window and witness the orange sky rising behind me. In this moment I am protected. The rays of warmth grant me a sense of calm and serenity that my soul has been needing. I desperately cling to it as it slips away. I insist that we take the cab to the Roberts House, a building that I lived in during my first year in the city. I might find something there, a valuable clue. I jump out only to see that it is no longer open. *Did it ever exist?* I am in a fucking nightmare. Where the hell is the alarm clock to pull me out? I race down Third Avenue to Mason's parents' apartment. The glaring daylight is burning my eyes and stinging my skin. I am exposed to the world, as every pedestrian I pass stares right through me. At his parents' place, I shiver with fear as I peel my clothes off in the bathroom. I force myself into the shower. The lights are blinding and the water reeks of bleach. The hammering of my heart is all I can hear. Slithering back into my pajamas, I rush outside, searching for relief, only to find none. Mason chases after me as I plot my escape. I am darkened, confused, delirious, and mad all at once.

It is nine o'clock in the morning and I am now terrified that my mother is coming. When she pulls up to the curb, I spot my little sister Stephanie sitting in the backseat. For the first time, the sight of my mom does not relieve me. I turn to flee, but Mason forces me into the car and I fight to get out.

My mother grabs my hand. "Do you trust me?"

I say yes, but I am lying.

We speed off, leaving Mason frozen on the curb. The Lincoln Tunnel is my birth canal and I am being torn out of the city, the womb I have known for so long. I listen to my demons yelling for me to come back. I sob and shake as Stephanie holds on to me. Thrusting my legs, unable to sit still, I begin running in place. I am paralyzed with thirst, so we stop at a gas station. My mom hands me two bottles of water and I begin to guzzle them. It does not satisfy me. I plead to her for reassurance. We drive past a big rock painted with dull red letters, JESUS SAVES.

"See that, Lynn, what does it say?" I hear the fear in her voice.

I want so much to believe it, but I am powerless. Coming to a standstill in traffic, a woman in a hideous green car smiles and winks at me. She must know something that I don't. Paranoia has set in. I scrutinize each expression on my mother's face, searching for the key. If I am clever enough to solve this riddle, I will survive.

When we arrive in Pennsylvania, where I grew up, we rush immediately to the hospital. The emergency room becomes my confessional. I purge all of the dirty secrets that I have kept locked away. I own up to my sins, exposing my love affair with the pretty poison I call ecstasy. I can't stop biting the skin off my fingertips. I tell the doctor about my friends, the clubs, the drugs, and the lies. All the lies. My mother sits speechless in her chair. A drop of blood falls from my thumb onto my pants. The doctor discusses substance abuse treatment facilities with me as if I were completely lucid. Now I know I am crazy. No one seems to realize the shape of my mind. All I can smell is the doctor's rotten breath as he hands me two sleeping pills and tells me to go home and take them before bedtime.

"Come back if your condition worsens. Take care."

Worsens? How can I get any fucking worse? Thanks, doc.

We silently pull into the driveway of the house that haunted my childhood. My mother insists on offering me tea, as if it is some kind of magic potion. The thought of ingesting anything makes me ill, but Mom copes with trouble the only way she knows how. She avoids it, confident that this episode will simply disappear. She draws me a bath, but I refuse to get in it. I disintegrate over the next few hours. My mother guarantees me that I will be fine after getting some rest and hands me the two tiny pills with a glass of water. I stare into my hand. Music suddenly begins thrashing in my head. Chills surge through my core as familiar voices invade my ears.

Are you feelin' it, babe? Oh my God, this shit is good . . . I love you.

Are you feelin' it? Are you feelin' it? Are you feelin' . . . ?

I will not fall for these tricks. I reject Mom's invitation and place the pills on the counter. *This is only a test. A simple test by your emergency broadcast system.* Here is the perfect opportunity to just say no. I am certain these are no better than the shit I was popping in the city. No one will convince me of their lies. My sister Stacey seems to think that this is all an act. *Lynn trying to hog the spotlight . . . again.* Frustrated by my behavior, Stacey gets a nurse on the phone to assure me that the pills will provide me with rest. As if I am going to listen to another person in the medical field. *Yeah, right.* The whole time my father continues watching television as if nothing is wrong.

"Just swallow the pills, Lynn. Stop making such a big deal of it," he mutters before going to hide in his room. The usual supportive advice from father of the year.

I crawl into my mother's bed as she holds me in her arms. Stacey and Steph bring blankets into the room and lie on the floor. Stephanie, wise beyond her years, lies in front of the door, sure I will try to escape. With eyes wide open, hallucinations creep in as I watch my mother's face morph into Mason's. I'm a bomb set to explode. I stumble past Stephanie and dart outside. My mother chases after me, sobbing, pleading with me to stop, as if I have control over this.

"Let me go, Mom. Please let me rest in peace so I can move on to the next world."

"Lynn, I love you. You are alive! I am your mother, I am telling you the truth."

"You are keeping me here in this life and I need to leave. I know this is hard for you, but I can't go on like this. I am dead."

Having no other choice, they pull me into the car and take me back to the hospital. It is morning again, the days have melted into each other and I have lost all sense of clarity. My father is already at the hospital, where he works as a nurse. He enters the room showing no emotion and avoids looking at me. *Great bedside manner.* We all sit in a dark, windowless holding cell. It is the first time we have sat together as a family to confront anything. I am instructed to sign papers to commit myself to the psychiatric ward of the hospital. If I do not cooperate, my parents or the state will be forced to commit me. Tasting the barrel of a gun in my mouth, I scribble my name and it is done.

part 1

*

thE drop

No Place Like Home

From the outside my house looks like every other one on Bloom Street. A ranch home, two-car garage, groomed shrubs lining the front of it, and a rose bush by the entrance. But we have something that the others didn't. In our front yard stands a giant, old oak tree. No matter how many times my father trimmed it back, the tree seemed to grow bigger and bigger each spring. It shaded everything and prevented the sunlight from ever shining through the front windows. Driving past 1320 Bloom Street, you might not even know there is a house there because it is always hiding behind that big oak.

When I was in high school, I stayed away from the house as much as possible. If I wasn't in class, I was rehearsing for a play. I lived in the school's theater. The stage was my one true home. I felt safe there. My mother, friends, and teachers told me that I had a gift, a real talent. But I knew the only reason that I excelled in acting was because I had spent my whole life doing it. Practice makes perfect. I performed every day, putting on a show free of charge, for my family, friends, and teachers. If there was ever a lull in conversation or an uncomfortable silence, you could always count on me to chime in with a joke or kooky observation, anything to avoid the tension in the air. I could read a room, get a laugh, and work a crowd with my eyes closed. Acting was my survival and my greatest defense.

From my earliest memories I remember my mother crying. My

father had yelled at her for buying clothes for us that he thought we didn't need or she was upset that he was too hung over on Christmas morning to open gifts with us. There was an endless supply of reasons for her to cry and that's what she was always doing, at least to my young ears. I would crouch down in the hallway outside her bedroom door and listen to her sniffling. She didn't want my sisters and I to see her like that. She was protecting us, but it only made me more scared and distrustful to live in that house.

There was a routine that she and my father had perfected: he would bring something up, asking for an argument, throwing a lit match on the gasoline, and then came my mother's yelling. My father would just sit in his chair with his leg crossed, nodding at her like she was a child. Then he would go outside to mow the lawn or disappear to the bar. My mother would rush to her bedroom, and later magically resurface with a big smile, lie on the floor, and play Chutes and Ladders with us. The whole time I would stare at her glossy eyes and watch little bits of mascara crawl down her cheeks.

My sisters and I dealt with it very differently. Stacey, the oldest, was the good girl, straightening and cleaning her room. Stephanie, the youngest, would become even more introverted and quietly hold onto my mom's leg. I took center stage. I would do a crazy dance or impression and watch my mother's face light up. I learned early on that laughter is more like Novocain than real medicine. I was the comic relief. So this "gift" that people said that I had was actually a survival strategy, although later it became a tool of manipulation.

Growing up in chaos, in a home where any second the floor could give way, I learned to dodge bullets and keep on movin'. It was every man for himself. If I stood still I was an easy target. I wanted to be a kid and have fun. Instead I was busy worrying about when the next disaster or argument would break out between my father and any one of us.

My father is not what you would call a cruel man. He kept his distance both emotionally and physically from all of us. He never asked me or my sisters questions about life, school, boys, the weather, or anything, ever. He simply didn't care. The only time he did communicate was to tell us something was wrong. "Jesus Christ, Kathy, why didn't you pay this bill? . . . Lynnie, clean up your room . . . Stacey, move the car into the garage . . . Stephanie, did you take my goddamn brush again?" He spewed negativity, and we absorbed every drop.

My father never laid a finger on any of us: no hitting, no hugging. Nothing. Mentally he knew how to hurt us, though, always knowing what button to push at just the right time. My mother, sisters, and I became daily obstacles between him and his beer. He would do whatever it took to clear his path to get to that bar stool. He was an alcoholic. This was obvious to me, but no one dared talk about it, especially my mother.

He was different when people came over to visit. He was on his best behavior, laughing, making jokes, talking to me like he cared. He'd brag about me to his friends. I was the shiny Corvette covered up in a dark garage, only shown off when there was an audience. We always kept up appearances and I was a fake and a phony just like him, playing along with the charade. I loathed the idea of anybody knowing how my family truly lived behind closed doors. Once the friends left and the party was over, it was back to status quo—cold, distant, and tense. I was more comfortable with that anyway.

My father never told me that he loved me, so my mother said it every chance she got. She thought she could love us enough for both of them. When you're little you know where the love is because you gravitate toward it. The affection only came from my mom, so I found myself in competition with my sisters to get it. I knew there was only so much to go around and I wanted as much as I could get.

I never understood why my mother stayed with him for so long. She married him at nineteen. She was young, naïve, and wanted nothing more than to be a mother. My father made that simple, by being neither a husband nor a dad. She was determined to make it last. My mom enabled and ignored, putting on a show for every-one. She spent so much time pretending. No matter how bad it got, and it got bad, she wasn't going to leave him. My mother took her vows very seriously, as she grew up in a strict, Catholic household where she was taught to stick it out. My father didn't cheat or leave her black and blue, so he was a fine husband. They slept in different rooms and when they weren't arguing they were nowhere near each other. In my entire life, I never once remember seeing them hug, kiss, or show any sign of affection toward each other. I must have been the only kid in grade school that begged her mommy to get a divorce.

By the time I got to high school, I had so much rage inside of me I thought I was going to explode. Not knowing how to deal with this, I threw myself into all the extracurricular activities I could. I landed the lead in each school theater production, was on the forensics team, was on the homecoming and prom courts, and earned straight As. I tried to be the best at everything, but acting was all that I really loved. I knew that I had some talent and beyond that, it was a great escape. I was a big fish in a small pond. In any case, I planned to get the hell out of Dodge as soon as high school was over. I grew up watching my father drink his life away and see-ing my mom wasting away with him, both of them rotting in that town. I told myself day after day that I would never be like that. I knew that after graduation if I didn't leave when I had the chance, I would be stuck in Danville. I felt the wet cement drying around my feet and needed to get away before it was too late. *Drivers, start your engines.* So I began running and didn't stop. I had no idea at the time what I was running to or from, but I knew that if I moved away and went to the big city, nothing or no one could catch me. Not my small town roots, not my alcoholic father, not even myself. I was going to live in New York City and start a new life.

Gee, I Think I'm Gonna Like It Here...

I clutched my mother's arm as our car entered the Lincoln Tunnel. *Is this actually happening?* After all the tears, arguments, phone calls, and preparation, the time had come for my arrival in the Big Apple. I couldn't wait to study theater, drink espresso, wear black, and dance on top of taxicabs like the kids in *Fame*. Everyone was going to see my name in lights.

My knees were shaking, I looked at my mother and saw the discomfort in her eyes. There weren't too many tunnels, traffic jams, or cabs in good old Danville, Pennsylvania, population . . . really small. Lots of cows, pickup trucks, and green pastures, but you wouldn't find any of this kind of excitement. The possibilities were endless for me now.

As we exited the tunnel, my mom hesitated at a fork before making a right onto Forty-second Street. A taxi's horn rang in my ears as the driver passed, flipping us the bird.

"Well, isn't that just sweet," said my mom. "You better not start acting like that once you live here."

"Mom, I don't think I will ever grow chest hair or drive a cab, don't you worry."

Driving through Times Square, we passed countless street vendors selling hot dogs, nuts, and pretzels. The smell made my tummy rumble. The sights and sounds were intoxicating. Purses, watches, and jewelry sparkled under the neon billboards. Each storefront seemed to be inviting me in. A group of boys danced on the street corner. I watched one of them spin on his head and flip back up onto his feet. The crowd around him roared with applause. I wanted to jump out and join the celebration.

"Lynn, pay attention, look at the directions. Am I turning left on Thirty-sixth Street?" my mom asked.

"Yes, the building is on Thirty-sixth Street, mom, so we will turn left there," I reassured her.

I was going to board at the Roberts House, It's a women's Christian housing dormitory. Living there was my only option. Getting my own apartment was too expensive and living with a stranger was out of the question. It would have given my mother nightmares every minute. There were also other girls from the Academy of Dramatic Arts staying there, so I would be connected to my school. I couldn't count the number of times my mom said, "The Roberts House will provide a secure environment for your transition to urban life." I would have my own room, but have to share a bath. Having grown up with three other females in a house with one bathroom, I was going to have no problem adjusting.

There was no parking outside the building, so we began to circle in search of a spot. "What do they expect me to do, just throw you out the door?" said my mom.

There was not a single space anywhere. It was February and my mom was glistening with sweat. She had worked so hard to make this possible. We couldn't even afford a state school, let alone a private acting conservatory that cost twenty grand a year to attend, but my mom knew how badly I wanted this and was determined to make this happen. So after remortgaging our house and several loans later, here we were, moving me into the life of my dreams.

After an hour of driving in circles, we knew it was time to call it quits and decided to find a parking garage.

"*Hola, senoritas,* how long are you staying?" said the young man attending the garage.

"All day, at least." My mom's voice was shaky.

He took the keys, gave us a wink, and handed her the slip. I grabbed my suitcases from the back of our reliable old minivan and gave my mom a hug.

"Well, you made it through the drive, that's a good sign," I said to my mom.

She squeezed my hand and said, "I love you."

I watched the tears forming in her big brown eyes.

"Mom, not yet, please, we still have to get through the day."

She took one of my many bags and we began to walk down Third Avenue. The smell of the streets filled my head. It was a mixture of gasoline, winter, smoke, and possibility. I was floating on air. The noise of the sirens, horns, and speeding cars welcomed me in. *I am not in Kansas anymore.*

We walked through the large, wooden doors of the building. I saw two girls sitting on a couch, reading aloud from a script in the room on the left. We were greeted at the front desk by a woman named Julia. She was warm, friendly, and smelled like vanilla. She gave me a hug.

"I am so excited you are going to be staying with us. I believe you are on the third floor, just let me check." She scanned her notebook. "Yes, Smith, Lynn, room three oh one. Let me show you upstairs and then I will give you the grand tour."

I looked around for an elevator, but instead she opened a door to a stairwell. *I am certainly going to get my exercise today. Welcome to New York, baby.* My mom and I shared a laugh as we took a break between floors. In Pennsylvania, walking anywhere, and I mean anywhere, was thought of as strange. If you were going to say hello to your neighbor, you drove.

We approached the room and I was shocked by how close the doors were to one another. Julia opened the door and my mother and I both gasped. My closet at home was bigger. It reminded me of a miniature display room in a museum. There was a twin bed up against one wall. A small dresser and desk were smashed together along the other wall, not an inch between them. We had to step all the way into the room in order to shut the door. I didn't care. I was thrilled. It wasn't a five star hotel, but this eight-by-ten space was all mine. There was one window that looked out at the city. I could see the top of the Empire State Building, the red and green lights shining bright. *Not bad, a room with a view, and it's not staring at a cemetery like our house in Danville.*

"I'll leave you ladies alone and then we can meet downstairs for the rest of the tour," Julia said before shutting the door.

I sat down on my bed and wondered if my entire body would fit on it. *Hell, I like to sleep in the fetal position anyway.* My mother began to sob. "Lynn, I can't believe this. I can't leave you here."

"Why? What's wrong, Mom?"

"Oh, nothing," she said, moving my long, sandy blonde hair away from my face. "I know this is what you want, but this room is so small, and oh . . . I love you, I just need some time to process this."

"Mom, look out my window. I mean, did you ever think this could happen? This is the beginning for me. I start school next week and I bet I'll have this city figured out by tomorrow!" We both laughed at the absurdity of it all. *Three hours ago I was in little old Danville, PA, and now I'm standing in the center of the universe.*

"I am so proud of you, Lynn," she said, kissing my forehead.

She had said those words so many times before that she could have been saying "pass the salt," but I knew how much she meant it. What a woman, my mother. A full-time job, raising three girls, and married to my father. If she would just leave him, pack up, and move here with me, my life would be complete. But she would have to explain that to Stacey and Stephanie. That definitely wouldn't go over too well.

My mom and I have always had a magical connection. She noticed a sparkle in my eye early on and encouraged my creativity. Whether I was doing an interpretive dance in the living room or sitting on her lap talking about the latest drama with my boyfriend, she was a captive audience. We had a special bond and understood each other, even without words. My biggest fan to this very day.

We glanced at my cubicle one more time and my mom shook her head as I locked my door. We found Julia downstairs and she took us into the dining area. It was a vast room with several antique tables and chairs. There was also one wide-screen television on the back wall. She explained that there were only two meals provided a day. "Breakfast is served from seven until eight in the morning and dinner is from six until seven-thirty in the evening," Julia explained. "No exceptions." *I guess no one has time for lunch in this town.*

She took us outside to a courtyard. There were two red picnic tables surrounded by frozen ground and groupings of dead plants. I was hoping it turned into a garden once the weather changed.

"It is too frigid to sit out here now, but once spring arrives, it is delightful. Girls often congregate outside to study and rehearse," said Julia.

It hit me at that moment that this was not a weekend visit. I was actually going to live here and experience the changing seasons. I pictured myself lying outside on the grass with my latest script in hand. I'd always loved the feeling of finding out which character I'd been chosen to play. I would run home from school and scour the pages to count how many pages I was on. My drama teacher, Ms. Cronrath, would always insist, "Read the script in its entirety and please abstain from jumping ahead to your scenes." *As if.*

We walked into the living area and Julia pointed out the endless supply of literature on the wall, everything from Hemingway to Nancy Drew. A beautiful old piano sat in the corner by the window overlooking the street. *I wish I knew how to play.* A song from the musical *Annie* was echoing in my ears. *Gee, I think I'm gonna like it here . . .*

"There is no noise in the common areas after ten o'clock. The doors are always locked at eleven in the evening, so if you arrive after that, ring the bell and someone at the front desk will let you in. Also be sure to sign in and out so we know if you are here." She directed the next comment to my mom. "If you are unable to contact Lynn or if there is some kind of emergency, we always keep track of the girls, so please don't worry."

Although I imagined this was somewhat like a minimum security prison, I saw the relief on my mother's face and didn't give it a second thought.

"Well, I am sure you want to get settled and spend time with your mother," she said. "Where are you staying, Kathy?"

"Oh, I'm just spending the day and then heading back to Pennsylvania. I have another daughter at home waiting for me."

I wanted my mom to stay the weekend to help me get settled and prepared for school, but she never trusted leaving Stephanie at home with my father, even though she was fifteen. Besides, my mom couldn't afford to spend money on a hotel and I knew not to push the issue. I was both angry and sad. Angry that my father wouldn't come to see me off, and sad that he refused to accompany my mom on this trip. He used his usual excuse that had to do with a "buddy" needing him to help out with something. His friends always came before us. I learned long ago not to expect anything from him, but I knew my mother still held out hope.

We climbed back up the three flights to my room and began to unpack my clothes. Unable to stuff them all into the tiny drawers and closet, I gave up and left the rest stacked on a small patch of floor. My mother opened her purse and handed me a little red box and a green journal with a white ribbon tied around it.

"This is just the beginning. I know you are going to do great things. Hold on to your faith," she said with such conviction. "Keep track of your experiences."

I sat down on my bed flipping through the blank pages of the journal and then opened the red box. Inside was a set of wooden rosary beads. I held them in my hands. "They're beautiful, Mom, where did you get them?"

"They came from Italy. A friend from work bought them at the Vatican and got them blessed by the pope."

The wooden beads felt so smooth on my fingers. "Thank you so much. I will try to use both of these gifts every day," I said.

The hours passed and the reality of my mother's departure

caused a knot to form in my stomach. I didn't want her to leave. We decided to grab a bite before she headed off. There was no shortage of choices in this town, it was a bit overwhelming. We settled on a deli; it was a cafeteria, grocery store, and coffee shop all rolled into one. I had never seen such a massive salad bar—hot meats, cold salads, Jell-O, what appeared to be raw fish, and countless other strange combinations. I was so excited to be in a different setting, I would have eaten mud if it was being served. *Good-bye to the dirt roads, the endless silence, the small town gossip, and the boredom.* I was getting my first taste of freedom along with some interesting foods. We sat down with our potpourri of salads and two Snapples. The butterflies in my stomach made it hard to eat anything. I was amazed at the broad assortment of people filtering in and out. They walked fast, ate fast, and talked fast. I felt right at home.

My mom glanced at her watch. "I should get moving since it's already dark and I have a long drive ahead of me."

We threw away our barely touched plates and slowly headed back to my new home. Holding hands in silence, we were both unsure of what the future held. My mother stopped in and said good-bye to Julia, asking her to keep an eye on me. I was embarrassed and comforted at the same time. We turned the corner and walked up Third Avenue toward the parking garage.

"Don't worry about me, Mom, I'm going to be all right."

"There is no doubt in my mind . . . but I am still going to worry, that's my job," she said, smiling as tears rolled down her face.

My mom handed the attendant the slip and he went to retrieve the car. I embraced my mother and she began to sob. No amount of good-byes made it any easier. Her warmth permeated through my thick winter coat. The overpowering scent of her perfume comforted me. I was ready to let go and someday my mother would be, too, just not today. She got into the van and grabbed the box of Kleenex that she strategically placed there before we left. I blew a kiss and watched her drive away before making my way back. The daylight had vanished, but the city refused to get dark. The bitter air wrapped itself around me and I braced myself. *My life has begun.*

Back in my room "Free Fallin'" was playing on the radio. That's exactly how I felt. I pulled out my new journal . . .

Feb. 1, 1997: I am lying on MY bed, in MY new home. I can hear the wind, the cars, the sirens; a beautiful orchestra of noise. The sweet smell of the city is sneaking through my cracked window and filling the room with excitement. I feel my life unfolding. I don't know a single soul here, but I know that I fit, even though I've only been here for a few hours.

I came from a small town filled with a lot of small minds. I crave stimulating conversations and new cultures. There is no diversity in Danville. The only dark-skinned people are families returning from a summer vacation at Hilton Head. Everyone is white. I want to learn about different cultures, taste new foods, and study great playwrights. I want to learn, grow, and expand my world. This is not just a city of skyscrapers and millions of people. It is the place that holds my future.

Midnight in the Big Apple, all alone but not lonely. I lie back on my new bed and look over at the old chest of drawers. I see the initials A.H. carved into the front. I wonder who inhabited this space before me. Was she from a small town? What dreams led here? Where was she now? Did she make it? Was she a star? I know when the next young girl enters this room she will know that I was here. She will feel it in the room, that the one before her did what she came here to do. I close my eyes. The city surrounds me and listens to all of my thoughts and secrets. I can't wait to start acting school. I am ready for anything.

Good night from NYC,
Lynn

It Was Because of Chuck Taylor

The people I gravitated toward at school were the mysterious, heroin-chic-looking types, straight out of a Calvin Klein ad. This was all new ground for me. As much as I stood out in a small town, in NYC I felt I was fresh off the turnip truck. There were only so many choices in Danville where the biggest (and busiest) store was Wal-Mart, but somehow I managed to make do. Although I knew I owed it all to a *Cosmo* article entitled "Look Like a Million Bucks for Twenty." As the weeks passed the final cut had been made and we were now a tight group of four. Lucy, Brian, Manny, and I. Lucy had the height and frame of a model with a face to match. I met her the first week I arrived in NYC.

I was sitting at the school bar, Desmond's Tavern, it was kind of like the Peach Pit from *90210,* but with liquor. An older bar, dark, stale, simple, no frills. *So not New York.* Tony was our "Nat," the bartender and the owner. He called us all by name and never asked for an ID. I knew why it had been labeled the school hangout. It could have been a post office—as long as they served us beer and didn't card, it would do. Tony could have been anywhere from forty to sixty years old. The thick glasses and thick Irish brogue made it hard to tell. He definitely was no stranger to the bottle. The red cheeks and occasional drool that found its way out of his mouth onto his shirt when he was talking were telltale signs, but he was sweet as hell.

I was with Krista, a girl that I had met the first night at the

Roberts House. She was short, thin, simple looking, and the only thing I had gathered from our few conversations was that she was in love with the Gap. Yes, the clothing franchise. I knew people had their favorite brands, but she talked about the store like it was a prospective husband. She wanted to own one, work in one, and someday star in their commercials. Her words not mine. She was from Indiana and had that grating midwestern twang in her voice. I prayed that my small town roots weren't that obvious. She was chatty, agitated, and slapped her knee really hard every time she laughed. It reminded me of something grandfathers or obnoxious uncles do at family gatherings, but I still found her odd and endearing.

So there we were. I noticed a group of girls in the corner at the front of the bar, none of whom were familiar. Evidently, everyone that went to Desmond's was from the academy so they must have been "Octobers," which was how we were labeled at acting school. I arrived in February so I was a "Feb," and those that came in October were "Octobers." I guess "Oct" didn't have the same ring to it. Not terribly complicated, but I had never been nicknamed a month, so it was kind of strange to be labeled that way.

One of the girls caught my eye. She was standing in the center of the group, very animated, and her voice was loud and melodic. I thought I heard an accent but it was hard to be sure with "Hard to Handle" blasting from the jukebox behind me. *I love that song.* The music selection was pretty unusual for an Irish pub. Sublime, Fleetwood Mac, the Femmes, Billy Joel, No Doubt, Elvis, a great mix of old and new. I'd already had two Budweisers so I was feeling pretty good. My wool sweater must have reeked. Everyone seemed to be smoking, including the animated girl with long, thick red hair, who looked like a movie star.

She was wearing a long, black leather jacket, tight, beatup jeans, and a red tank top, stunning yet approachable. *Bitch.* The most striking thing about her was that she was the center of attention, a fact of which she seemed oblivious—unlike the other girls around her who were smiling, laughing, talking at each other, like they were waiting for their closeups. Like any minute Scorsese was going to walk through the door with a camera crew. But not that girl, she was smoking, laughing, and buying rounds for her friends. She seemed to be having a good time without trying to get discovered like her pals.

Krista was chatting it up with some guy named Z or T, something with one letter, I don't remember, but I knew he was from our class. Having only been at school a week it was clear to me that the Febs were a big group of lame-os, minus a few of us, of course, who thought we were the shit. *Ha!* The funniest thing about Krista Dubois was that when I first met her she introduced herself as "Krista Dooboys, I mean, Doobwah," which she pronounced like Blanche in *Streetcar*. I laughed out loud because most people don't fuck up the pronunciation of their own names. She smiled and said, "My parents told me to pronounce it like Doobwah, because it sounds more cultured, more like a movie star, ya know?" I thought to myself, *It's gonna take a little more than that, sweetheart.* So I imagined she and T or Z were having quite the conversation over there. Most likely about their names, but one could only guess.

I walked over to the jukebox to stretch my legs. I really didn't know what I was looking for when I felt someone's presence next to me.

"Hello." It was the girl in the leather jacket and it was clear to me then that she had a British accent.

"Are you going to bloody play something or just stand there looking pissed?"

I was a little startled by the question, but the first thing that flew out of my mouth was, "I'm sorry, are you speaking English?"

Neither of us could keep a straight face and we both started laughing.

"I'm Lucy," she said putting her hand out.

"Lynn," I said while shaking hers. I noticed we both had big hands. I used to be so self-conscious about mine. It wasn't very ladylike to be able to palm a basketball. Somehow I felt validated knowing I wasn't alone.

"You must be a Feb," she said like she smelled it on my clothes, like it was some kind of a disease.

"That's what the word on the street is." *Did I really just say that?* "Are you from Manchester?" I said quickly, hoping she wouldn't remember the last comment.

"Good guess. . . ." she said while scouring the song choices.

"My father's relatives are all from England close to Manchester and when I heard you say 'bloody' and 'pissed' I knew you had to be . . ." I was rambling. She cut me off. *Thank God.*

"I think I saw you at the house, where are you staying?"

"The Roberts House, on Thirty-sixth Street, room three oh eight."

"Fuck you!" she said turning to hit me on the arm. She sounded so crass and proper at the same time. "I am in three ten right across the hall."

"Wow. Small world. The bedrooms are so roomy, aren't they??"

"Awful, just bloody awful." She pushed some buttons on the jukebox and said, "Well, I am sure we will run into each other soon, maybe I will pop by tomorrow to say hello. Nice trainers, by the way," and she walked away.

I must have appeared so obviously perplexed because she turned and yelled, pointing down at my feet, "Your shoes. I like your shoes!"

I looked down to remind myself, like I wasn't quite sure what my mother put me in that day. *What a dork.* Oh yeah, my Chucks. She liked Converse All Stars, I knew we were definitely going to be friends.

Uncovering Ecstasy

My stomach quivered with anticipation. The call had been made, the order had been placed, and tonight was the night. All that was left to do was wait. I had seen my friends roll once before. I chickened out at the last minute and decided to be a spectator instead. I watched Lucy swallow a tiny green pill in the shape of a four-leaf clover. She paced around in her apartment rambling away, straightening the rugs on the floor, organizing books on her shelf, and checking her watch every couple of minutes like it was some kind of timed science experiment. I guess it was, in a way. What if she turned into the color of the pill and grew large, rippling muscles that tore through her dress? What then? Just as I was pondering this absurd scenario, it was like watching her get hit by a tidal wave, her eyes glossed over and she was slammed in a matter of seconds. She floated over to me and began massaging my arm. Her head lolled as if it weighed a hundred pounds and then she let out a very loud moan. Just think of Meg Ryan in *When Harry Met Sally* and you get the picture.

"Oh Lynnie, you've gotta try this . . . it is fucking brilliant . . . brilliant," she said in that great Brit accent of hers. I was very curious, to say the least.

The buzzer rang and brought me back to the present moment. I pressed the intercom to let the dealer in. He was nothing like I expected. I remember in eighth grade health class there was a special day when our teacher "taught" us about drugs. Mrs. Turner was her name and she read out of a book the names of the "killers" and their effects. She could have been reading down her grocery list for all I knew, that was the level of emotion she evoked. She also stated that when a big, scary man cornered us in a dark alley and offered us drugs that we should "just say no" and run the other way. She must have been reading straight out of the Nancy Reagan handbook. But what really stuck with me was that she pronounced "marijuana" wrong, actually emphasizing the J.

So here he was, the big, scary drug dealer. Justin was his name. He shook each of our hands and actually introduced himself like he was about to sell us a refrigerator. He had boy-next-door good looks and couldn't have been that much older than we were, twenty-five at most. He was wearing a red winter coat, nice denim jeans, and a pair of Adidas shell toes. His slick hair was short, black, and wavy and his eyes were a dark shade of green. If I hadn't already known his occupation, I would have guessed he was either a J. Crew model or a member of a boy band. He stepped into Lucy's tiny living room. It was so much nicer now that she had her own apartment in the Village. It was small but nothing compared to the cramped quarters I was still living in. I was here more often than not, so it worked out great. He sat down on the futon, opened his black North Face book bag, and pulled out a large Ziploc full of what looked like hundreds of pills.

"I don't know what kind of roll you guys are looking for, but the Mitsubishis are what's hot right now. Not too speedy, not too mellow, a nice high. I also have Nikes, Smurfs, Supermans, Tellatubbies; you know, the usual mix," he said nonchalantly.

Umm. No, I don't know about the usual mix. I had no idea that ecstasy came in so many different names, shapes, and colors. But I felt surprisingly excited and delighted to have so many choices in front of me, *it's about fucking time.* I could pick the kind of pill and high I wanted, it was like shopping for a pair of jeans, the kind that fit just right and made your ass look small. *And I love shopping.*

"We will take the Mitsubishis." Lucy had seniority, so it seemed

only right to let her make the decisions. Oh yeah, and she was paying. She offered to pay pretty much for everything. She didn't have a
job but her daddy clearly did. She showed me a picture of her house
when she was talking about her "mum and dad" one night. I had to
pick my jaw up from the floor. Her "house," as she called it, looked
like Cinderella's castle at Disney World, maybe a little bigger. I
barely had enough money to get on the subway, let alone pay for
drugs, so I had no trouble graciously accepting her handouts.

"How many would you like to have for the evening?" asked
Justin.

"There're going to be four of us, so two each should do it. This
is Lynn's first time, so she might just need to take a lick of one; I
will finish hers," she said laughing.

"Okay. I usually charge thirty bucks a pill, but I will give them to
you ladies for twenty-five a pop tonight. It's a good deal," he said
assuring us.

She handed him two crisp hundred-dollar bills out of her black
leather Coach wallet without batting an eyelash. Justin gave her a
tiny little bag with the eight pills and patted me on the head and
said, "Congrats, this will be the best night of your life."

"Thanks." *I guess.* The pressure was on now.

Lucy and I planned on meeting Manny and Brian at McSwiggans
Pub on Second Avenue. It was a little hole in the wall that we fre-
quented because, like Desmond's, they never carded. I was beginning
to like Irish pubs. Lucy and I hopped in a cab on Sixth Avenue to
waste no time getting there. I was nervous, excited, scared, and
happy knowing that I would be with Lucy, Brian, and Manny for my
first time. It was like knowing you're going to lose your virginity with
someone you really loved, someone that really cared. The cab ride
seemed to take forever.

We walked into the bar and found Brian and Manny playing
pool in the back room. Lucy whispered to Brian that she had their
pills and handed him one of the tiny Baggies while planting a kiss on
his mouth. Speaking of virginity, Lucy had just given hers to Brian

the week before. Brian looked a bit like Ewan McGregor in *Trainspotting,* but with a little more meat on his bones. He had nice eyes, but never seemed to look in anyone else's when he talked. I hadn't figured him out yet, nor would I ever.

"Follow me to the bathroom," said Lucy.

I asked no questions and followed her. It must have looked odd that the two of us were going in there together, but I was sure we weren't the first to do so. The bathroom was so tiny, obviously made for one person. Once inside, she put the toilet seat down and reached into her wallet. She pulled out the Baggie with the other four pills inside it. The bathroom smelled of urine and stale beer, but I didn't mind. Lucy handed me a white pill and we tapped them against each other to make a toast.

"Cheers," we quietly said in unison.

"I love you, Lynnie, here's to a good night."

We put the pills on our tongues, scooped water into our mouths from the faucet, and swallowed. I had no idea what to expect. We walked out of the bathroom and were met by a fat lady rolling her eyes at us.

"It's about fucking time," she said.

Once again, this wasn't a classy joint, we didn't come here for the ambiance. The crowd could get a bit rough at times. It seemed to be the perfect atmosphere for a little bit of criminal behavior. Brian and Manny waited at the bar with a beer for each of us, smiling like two Cheshire cats. Lucy asked them if they had dropped, but we already knew the answer.

I sat on a bar stool while Manny rubbed my back. I'd had a crush on Manny since the first night that we met at Desmond's. He'd asked what my favorite band was. I told him I liked Radiohead and wanted to marry Thom Yorke. He shook my hand saying that I'd impressed him. It took a very small compliment from a guy to make a very big impact on me. Manny was nothing like the guys I usually dated, he was skinny as all hell and not terribly good looking. He had sharp features, small brown eyes, and a slight space between his front teeth. He wore a beard, which I loved, because it made him look like a cowboy. Sometimes he bleached his hair blond, which was awful, because it made him look like Dennis the Menace.

He always had the same damn shirt on, too. It was a long-sleeved baseball T, with yellow arms, a white body, and *You've got a friend in California* written across the front of it. Showers weren't much of a priority for him, either, but we both shared the same dry sense of humor and he made me laugh. He had nicknames for me like Lyndon B. Johnson, or just Lyndon B. for short. He made fun of me in a loving kind of way, similar to when you get your hair pulled by a boy in the third grade that has a crush on you. He was complicated, but I was positive he liked me in some twisted way. I was such a sucker for emotionally retarded guys.

As Manny was rubbing my back, my toes began to tingle. I was analyzing every feeling that I had in my body, anxiously awaiting my dinner guest. I started rubbing my legs. There was a knot in my stomach, maybe from the nerves or the pill, I was not sure which. I began peeling the label off of my cold Bud. We were all silently looking at one another, waiting for someone to make the first move.

I went to take a drink of my beer and as the coldness trickled down my throat, I was suddenly standing underneath a waterfall. A beautiful air passed through my entire body. My eyes slowly closed and I was in slow motion. Like I was actually in a beer commercial where they zoom in and slow down when the person takes a swig. Then suddenly I was being shot out of a cannon. My limbs were light and heavy at the same time. I forced myself to stand up because I thought I was going to fall off the bar stool. My body was Jell-O. They all began to laugh and nod their heads, like they knew exactly what was going to happen, like they had seen this movie before and this was their favorite part.

Lucy grabbed my arm, "Lynnie, are you all right?"

Her touch was fucking amazing. I grabbed her hand and started squeezing.

"Oh my God, oh my God, oh my God." Even talking felt good.

I was Dorothy stepping into Oz for the first time. My life was in Technicolor. Only I was not trying to find my way home, or was I? The bottles of liquor behind the bar shimmered like lights on a Christmas tree. I pushed my hair out of my face. It was silk and I wrapped it around my finger. I began to sigh, I had never felt so good in all of my life. I was overwhelmed. I knew that I couldn't stay in the bar for much longer or I would explode. I wanted to rip my clothes off and run down Second Avenue. I was free and liberated, oozing with love for all of mankind. While I was rubbing the bar down like it was a puppy, they made the decision that we should get a cab back to Lucy's place immediately.

Lucy held my hand. "We are going to go back to my place so we can chill."

We walked outside and the wind wrapped around my body, like sex but only better. Manny put me into the cab first, Lucy and Brian sat in the back with me and Manny took the seat next to the driver. I began rubbing my legs and touching the leather of the seat. My feet were dancing. I rolled down the window and let the cool air blanket my face. My eyes were closed. I was surrounded by good energy. Lucy began to rub my leg and I looked over at her and she was beaming. She had finally joined my party and suddenly looked like a *Playboy* centerfold to me.

"Oh Lynnie, I told you this would be fucking *brilliant*. This is fucking *brilliant*."

We didn't say much to each other after that, we just stared. I didn't see her as my best friend or even a girl, but as a fellow soul.

By this time, everyone was feeling it. Manny had struck up a conversation about religion with the driver and I was expecting them to hug any minute. Brian's eyes were closed, his head was resting on the back of the seat, and he was mumbling. I could feel everyone, each of their highs were merged with mine. Like we all swallowed the same pill, one cohesive unit. The drive could have taken three minutes or three hours. All I knew was that we all spilled out of the cab onto Bedford Street like hot, gooey liquid. Lucy paid the cabbie with a fifty and told him to keep the change. We all had our arms around each other, letting out sighs and laughter with few words.

Lucy fumbled with her keys, stopped, took a deep breath, and tried to obtain a moment of focus so that we could enter her apartment building. We filed in one by one. The hallway leading to her apartment was narrow. Thank God she was on the ground floor. The yellow walls were like spun gold, glistening like the morning sun. I never recalled her hallway being so beautiful. We got into her apartment, shut the door quickly, and kicked off our shoes. Lucy went right to the stereo and put on something mellow, like Sinead O'Connor. She lit a stick of incense and let her coat drop to the floor. It was an emergency drill, but instead of hurrying to leave, we were hurrying to stay. It was as if we were racing to see who could get comfortable the fastest.

I went into the bathroom, sat down on the cold toilet, and lay my head in my lap. No words could describe this feeling, no worries, no anxieties, I was surrounded by love. I felt every breath that came in and out of my body, every breeze that passed was a part of me. I began to cry. I wished that I could scream or sing at the top of my lungs, but all I could do was cry. Lucy walked through the door into the bathroom, shutting it quickly behind her. She sat down on the edge of the bathtub and lit a cigarette. I started to pee. The warm stream was heavenly. A huge release. I felt an outpouring of emotion.

"I love you, Lynnie," she said as smoke danced out of her mouth.

"I love you, too. Oh my god, Lucy, I can't fucking believe this. I don't even know what to say. This is fucking amazing."

"Here, take a drag," she said, passing the cigarette to me.

I put it to my lips and inhaled. Boom! I was being shot out of a cannon again. The smoke coated every inch of my lungs with what felt like a layer of ice.

I pulled up my pants and washed my hands. The cold water

running over them ignited waves of pleasure inside me. I had just been given the sense of touch for the very first time. I imagined this was how a baby must feel. Everything was new and just now opening itself up to me. I ran my wet hands through my hair, drenching it in water.

"Can I wear one of your tank tops? I need something that will let my body breathe."

"Don't leave, I will be right back."

My heart was as light as a feather. Lucy came back into the bathroom with two black tank tops, one for each of us. They were from Marks & Spencer in London. Soft and supple, I couldn't wait to get it on my body. I ripped my sweater off and Lucy followed. For once, I viewed my body as a friend, a beautiful extension of myself. Lucy's breasts were fucking amazing. Round and perfect. Her flesh was glowing like a star. I was staring at her like I was staring into the sun. I was stimulated, but not in a sexual way. I didn't want to get my brains fucked out. That was actually the farthest thing from my mind. I wanted to rub my body against Lucy's and merge our souls. I wanted to mix with her like hot wax, melt, and come together. We were not saying much at that point, just communicating with moans and smiles. She told me that this was one of the best rolls she'd ever had, and she'd had a lot.

We put our lacy tanks on like we were about to stroll down a catwalk. I was a goddess. Like the queen of fucking Sheba. Sexy, confident, and full of power. We went into the dark living room and I saw Manny and Brian sitting on the floor, talking intensely to each other. The music was massaging my ears. I looked around and realized they were my family. I would know and be friends with them for the rest of my life. We would celebrate birthdays, weddings, births, and thank one another in our Oscar speeches. We were all so beautiful. The stream of smoke billowing from the incense was as comforting as a thousand chocolate chip cookies right out of the oven. I crouched next to Manny and he wrapped his arms around me.

"Lynn, Lynn, Lynn."

He called me by name so I knew he was definitely feeling it. His hug was warm honey drizzled all over my body. This was how a hug should feel. All I could do was sit there, dumbfounded by every mixed emotion. I didn't know life could be like this.

Rain began falling outside and tapping against Lucy's windows. I crawled outside into the tiny courtyard and stood in the center with my head thrown back, letting the rain coat my tongue. *This must be heaven.* I was the only person in the world. I peeled my shirt off and leaned against the brick wall on the side of the building. I spread my wings out like I was about to take flight. This was the stuff of dreams. My life had greater meaning and I was part of something much bigger than myself. I was finally one with the world.

The rain was kissing my body over and over. I was pure and innocent. I was a pink sunset, ice-cream sundae, curtain call, rainbow, waterfall, and roller-coaster ride all rolled into one. All alone yet connected, I had just stumbled into the center of the universe and found the hidden treasure. The prize at the bottom of the cereal box was all mine.

When I was five or six years old I asked my mom what heaven was. I had heard the word at school and I was curious. She told me that it was a beautiful place where all of life's questions were answered. I now knew what she was talking about. For once I was speechless, free of questions, and full of answers. One pill and my whole life had changed.

Academy 101

Walking through the halls of the academy you could sense the history that lived in the building. It was over a century old and still counting. A six-story brick structure with classrooms, dance studios, dressing rooms, rehearsal halls, a library, a costume department, three large theaters, and a student lounge. It had a lot of character. Pictures of alumni lined the walls, everyone from Kirk Douglas to Grace Kelly, to Robert Redford to Danny DeVito to Kim Cattrall, the list went on and on. Whenever I used the bathroom inside the school, I often wondered if Lauren Bacall, or another starlet, sat on that same toilet. I somehow hoped their celebrity would rub off on me.

The "professional two-year training program" that I was enrolled in included classes in acting, acting styles, voice and speech, vocal production, movement, theater history, fencing, acting for the camera, makeup, cold reading, and Alexander technique. I was so on my way to being one of the kids from *Fame*. The first year was divided into two eleven-week periods; after the first eleven weeks, we were reassigned to different sections, which meant new classmates and new teachers. At the end of the school year we would be evaluated on our performances in a set of examination plays. Admission to second year was by invitation only. Members of the faculty and administration would meet and discuss each student, and "invitations were extended to those who were considered ready to master and benefit from the advanced second-year work." This was serious stuff.

My classes began at nine every morning and went until two each day. Each week I was stepping into different characters, studying playwrights, and retraining my vocal cords to articulate. For me, attending school was equivalent to going to recess or my best friend's house: constant play. I was learning how to use my "instrument" in a new way. The purpose of first-year acting classes was "to achieve relaxed, free, truthful use of self, in imaginary circumstances." Every day consisted of exercises for relaxation, concentration, sensitivity to other actors, and to external and internal stimuli.

One day I would be asked to bring in a picture of someone special to me and sit in front of the class and be "present in the moment," with whatever I was feeling. Another day I might have to stare into a fellow actor's eyes for the duration of the class and let myself be "affected" by that person. At times it felt more like therapy than school, but I loved it. I also loved the grading system; Excellent, Acceptable, Unacceptable, or Failing. My kind of place, no messy GPAs.

My teachers liked me, especially Peter Jensen. Girls fell all over him. He reminded me of Harrison Ford, rugged and good looking. He had a strength and intelligence that I loved. He critiqued me without bashing my shortcomings. I learned more from him than any other teacher. We had a mutual understanding that the students in my class were lacking in focus and drive. I think he liked having me around. I appreciated that he always gave me challenging scenes and good partners. He made me want to be an actor and really live out my dream. I felt strong in his class. I was fearless. I gave it my all and the teachers and students saw that. But while the teachers appreciated it, my fellow Febs were annoyed and thought I was the teacher's pet.

Jackie B. was a teacher that every student feared. She reminded me of Penny Marshall with that annoying whiney voice, but with ninety times the attitude. She took the tough love approach, or maybe just the tough approach. She said she wanted to break us down and mold us into finely tuned instruments. I didn't buy it. I thought she was a jealous and sick woman who got her kicks watching students run out of the room crying. I never did. If there was one thing I knew, it was that no one was going to break my ass down again. She was a picnic compared to my dad. I was paying her to teach me, not make me an insecure actor. I may have been an insecure person, but while acting I was a rock of confidence.

I was finally living the life that I had only dreamed about. I had a clean slate in an exciting city and a world of new possibilities. I was no longer the little farm girl from Pennsylvania, I was evolving. Acting school during the day, hanging with my friends at night. Life was good and I had a feeling it was only going to get better.

Lust for Life

Cocaine. I was seeing it for the first time. Lucy and I were together again in another shitty little bathroom stall. Do you sense a pattern? She had a vial full of white powder that she promised was "great blow." At this point I had tried E a few times, which I loved, and smoked pot, which I hated. I was tired and out of control on it. I also peed my pants in the middle of Second Avenue because I couldn't control my laughter or my bladder, but that's beside the point.

The little bottle was made of glass and inside was the world's tiniest spoon. It looked like it came right out of Barbie's Dream House. I watched Lucy gently scoop up some powder and place the spoon under her right nostril. She inhaled it hard, like she was trying to suck a booger back up into her head. Her eyes began to tear and she handed the little vial to me. I was reminded of the time in high school when my best friend Jill and I skipped class and sat in my backyard, sharing a cigarette. We were both scared and didn't have the slightest idea how to smoke. I felt dangerous for the first time in my life. That was the wildest moment I had until I moved to New York City. Here I was about to put a strange substance up my nose that came from God knows where or God knows who, and I didn't care. Simple as that. I was not scared in the least, although I did feel a bit dangerous. I came to this city to shed my skin and experience life, not sit back and watch it pass me by.

"You should put it under the nostril that you breath easier from, so it goes straight up," said Lucy.

She was full of wisdom. I scooped a little mound onto the spoon and placed it under my left nostril. I must have blown out before I inhaled, because the powder flew into the air, causing a small snow squall.

"Fuck, I am so sorry," I said, like I had just broken her grandma's precious vase.

"No worries. Breathe in fast. Don't blow air out or you'll lose it," she said, as she wiped her finger over the spoon, gathering the coke that had survived my nasal blunder. She rubbed it onto her upper gums.

"What are you doing?" I asked.

"It's called a numb-er. It feels really fucking good."

"Oh," is all I could say.

I was determined to succeed this time. I scooped, snorted, and felt the burn. My nostril was on fire and my nose and eyes began streaming water. It was dripping down my throat. I was swallowing bathroom cleaner. I began to hack.

Lucy patted me on the back. "You'll be all right once you get use to it."

I would?

"It's the coke drip that makes you cough." She had an answer for everything.

Someone had just cleaned my head out with a vacuum. I was suddenly clear and focused. "Let's get the fuck out of this dingy bathroom," I said to Lucy.

We went out to the bar and she bought us two cold ones and we were off. My heart was racing and my mouth began to dribble nonsense. I talked about school, my acting class, my new scene, my teacher Thelma, the shoes I wanted to buy, the night I slept with Manny, and the warm weather, all in one breath. My mind was working overtime and my mouth was desperately trying to catch up. I could have accomplished anything. If someone asked me to build them a house or direct traffic, I would have hopped to it, or rather sprinted to it. Lucy's mouth seemed to be rambling away over there, too. We might have been talking at the same time. It was hard to tell because all I could concentrate on was the high. It felt so fucking great. I was licking my lips, nodding my head, scratching my arm over and over and over again.

"We need to put tunes on . . . and fast," said Lucy.

Good old Desmond's jukebox. I took my Bud with me, it was so light. I looked down and realized it was empty. *When did that happen?* Lucy's hand was shaking as she shoved quarter after quarter into the machine.

She was mumbling about something. "We must play tunes . . . no one else will choose the bloody tunes . . . the tunes."

I was shuffling back and forth next to her like I was practicing a new dance move, but I wasn't. I just couldn't seem to stand in one place. My knees were tapping against each other and I suddenly had to go to the bathroom. My stomach and bowels were churning. I flew back to the stall, luckily it wasn't occupied, and I sat down on the toilet instead of crouching above it like usual. Everything, and I mean everything, left my body. Not pretty at all. Beads of sweat were trickling down my head. I finished my business and went over to the sink. Under any other circumstance I would have thought that I was sick, maybe even dying, but now I didn't. I stared into the mirror. My pupils were taking over my eyes. I leaned in farther and smiled at myself. I felt good, really, really good. This was the person I'd always wanted to be. I was my truest self. I looked into the reflection and felt sexy, fuckable, and fierce. I washed my hands and made my way back to Lucy.

"Luce," I whispered in her ear. "I've just taken the biggest shit of my life."

"Right, that usually happens. Sometimes there's laxative cut with the coke."

I nodded my head, like this was normal. Snort powder, feel like Xena the Warrior Princess, and shit your brains out. This was just your run-of-the-mill, Friday night fun.

"We are going to have a little bump soon, so we don't lose our high."

At that point I had lost everything but my high. I was still reeling, but not for long. Lucy and I were dancing to "I'm Just a Girl." We were on our third beer, but I was the farthest thing from drunk. I was alert and wanting more. Lucy and I began taking turns using the bathroom to shovel more coke into our noses.

She put the vial in my front pocket and whispered, "Only one scoop at a time and alternate nostrils. Stretch it out . . . make it last."

I didn't listen to her. All I could hear was the voice in my head. So I cheated and did both nostrils at once. *Why keep coming back if I can kill two birds with one stone?* I didn't care about the music or the people or even Lucy.

We stood at the bar talking about our high, like if we ignored it, it might run right out the fucking door. All I could think about was coke. I wanted more, needed more, now. We guzzled beer like it was water. I might have been on my fifth, maybe sixth one. Lucy and I continued boogeying down, there was by no means a dance floor in this shit hole, just a little space in front of the jukebox that we made into our stage. We had drawn a crowd at that point, lots of people from school and strangers were staring. We were straight out of *Flashdance*. Sweating, grinding, and bouncing up and down. Two sweaty girls that were obviously fucked up sure could please a crowd. I could have cared less who was watching as long as I felt like this. I was going with it.

Grady, a guy from school, stopped me on my eighth or ninth trip to the bathroom. "Lynn you're not a cokehead, are you? You seem like such a sweetie," he said, laughing. *Am I that obvious?*

I shrugged his hand off of me, along with his comment. Sweet? Fuck that. I was sexy, strong, and fierce. Good-bye to the fresh-off-the-field look. I was going to make my mark in this town, I didn't know how, but this seemed like a fine start. I went into the bathroom and saw that the vial was almost empty, maybe two scoops left. I wanted to cry. I snorted. Lucy was right, I was getting used to this. There was no question we needed more. I continued our little game of Ping Pong and passed it back to her.

"It's almost gone," I said.

"I will just page the dealer and get more."

She paged the guy who sold her the stuff and we were going to meet him somewhere. I had crossed into a strange world, but I was right at home with it. If there was one thing I had mastered, it was adapting to my surroundings. Read the room and morph into what I needed to be to survive. Dealers, pagers, powder, pills, it seemed perfectly logical. I was in a new city and my life was in my hands. I could sleep late or not get any sleep, like in tonight's case, get drunk, dance, make out with strangers, skip down Broadway, I would do it all. Fuck, I felt crazy, wired, and ready for anything.

Lucy and I hopped in a cab to meet Sam, the dealer, at a little coffee shop that his family owned on Great Jones Street. Seemed only right, sell coke and coffee, the two went hand in hand. I waited in the cab, Lucy jumped out, and in five minutes was back with the goods. If this was anywhere else we would have looked suspicious, but not here, we blended right in. She was so in control. I loved that about her. We both sat in the cab tapping our legs and biting our nails. We needed to get back to her place *now*. She threw money at the driver and we raced into her apartment. It was always a race when you're fucked up, always a mission. Hurry up and get high.

We got inside and Lucy started cutting lines on her kitchen counter, using one of her many credit cards. She got an eight ball of coke, whatever that was. Eight ball, ten ball, what's the difference, as long as we were talking about coke, you could call it a basketball. I was ready. The lines on the counter looked big, really big. She rolled up a crisp twenty-dollar bill for me to use as a straw.

"That one is all yours," she said, pointing at the thick line that resembled a train track. "Take it in all at once. That will make the high last longer."

I took in a deep breath, like I was about to dive underwater. I placed the tight twenty under my left one, that was my coke nostril. Who knew? I sucked in with all of my might and the train track disappeared. I couldn't believe it. I did it. I was proud of myself, like I had just finished first in a competition and won a fucking medal. From that point on, the smell of money would forever remind me of cocaine. I watched as Lucy did hers. She was a pro. No hesitation and it was gone. Boom! We were slammed, rocking now.

Lucy and I took our coats off and took turns using the john. Yep, coke made you shit. Small price to pay, in my mind. We sat on her living room floor and chatted about acting school. What we liked, what we hated. Who we liked, who we hated. Basically we came to the conclusion that we only loved each other, which had already been established. She asked me about my family and I spilled my guts. I was so open on coke. No pretenses, I let it all hang out. Told her about my home life, about my alcoholic father, and about growing up poor. I didn't fucking care, all I cared about was this high and being there with her.

I listened to her talk about growing up rich and privileged. She rambled on about her Jewish upbringing and how much her parents expected from her. She told me about Katie, her little sister, who was my age and handicapped. We both cried, hugged, and did more coke. I thought I was falling in love with her, or maybe with the cocaine, I wasn't sure which.

The phone rang over and over. Manny and Brian left a dozen messages, threatening to kill us if we didn't call them, and we didn't. We delved into each other. I had never known anyone like her and never would again. We drank gallons of water because it was pointless to waste beer. We were high as kites and couldn't taste anything and besides, it had no affect once the coke had control. Lucy and I hugged and kissed. A little more than a peck, but no tongue, just two best friends high on coke kissing each other. Normal stuff, but all we could really seem to do on coke was more coke. So we did, until it was gone. We finished it.

It must have been five or six in the morning, the room was getting brighter and the lights were off. Lucy and I began to crash, hard. We knew that we could've gotten more, but we didn't. We paced, fidgeted, drank more water, and tried to relax, but it wasn't the same coming down. The feeling was gone. The high was over and after that it got ugly. In fact, it was a nightmare. There's nothing worse than a coke crash. Talking took too much effort, sleeping was impossible, and watching TV completely freaked me out. All I could do was hold on and pray for relief. I was wired and exhausted at the same time. I waited for my eyes to drop and my body to stop twitching, to just let go. Lucy pulled out her futon and made the bed. No matter how high or how bad she felt, she always made her bed with nice sheets and always cleaned up after herself. We crawled under the covers and I stared at the shadows on the ceiling. I felt dirty.

"This is the worst part, Lynnie . . . but no matter how awful it feels . . . the next time we have coke, we'll forget all about this . . . forget all about this shit . . . the comedown . . . and just remember the high . . . that great fucking high . . ."

Truer words were never spoken.

What Trip?

It was July and the heat in my room was oppressive. There was no air-conditioning in my little jail cell and I could feel the walls closing in on me. It was impossible to rest in there. My door was always wide open to allow in what little air there was circulating through the halls inside. My free time was not the same without Lucy now that she was done with her first year and back in Manchester for the summer. It made me hate the fact that I was a Feb rather than an Oct even more. No laughing, no late-night talks, and more importantly, no drugs.

I looked up as Krista entered my room.

"Do you want to go to Rene's apartment with Lily and me tonight, maybe hang out, and drink some beer?" she asked.

Lily was also a Feb. I didn't really know her, but she had quite the nasty reputation. I didn't care what I did at that point, as long as it involved cool beverages, I was in. "Sure, just give me a minute to get ready and I'll meet you downstairs."

"Great, see you in a few."

I slid into the lacey black tank top that I'd inherited from Lucy and my Diesel jeans that I'd spent my whole month's allowance on. It was worth it, I loved those jeans. My hair was getting long and had lightened from the sun. I had a nice tan from walking around the city. I could just start strolling when I got antsy or bored and there was always something to see. People watching at its finest.

Krista and I shared a cab uptown to the East Side. Rene was

French Canadian and reminded me of Fabio, but with black hair. Conversations with Rene were always about himself. He also ended every sentence with "ehh," which annoyed the hell out of me. Taking speech class made me aware of every little accent and dialect, but Rene's was beyond obvious. He, like most of the people I knew at school, came from money, and I think he might have been some kind of prince. At least he thought so. His apartment was great. It was a cozy place with AC, hardwood floors, leather couches, a great entertainment center, and a bedroom that was ten times the size of mine. It had two large windows overlooking First Avenue and he even had a water cooler in his room. Even though he was pompous and had a Canadian accent, I would have given anything to be him, at least for the summer.

Lily arrived after us. She was as crazy as Krista, but in a different way. Lily was drop dead gorgeous. She was known for getting into fights with any girl that looked at her the wrong way. She had no problem throwing punches and breaking noses. She was tiny, five foot two, maybe a hundred pounds soaking wet, but she was fierce. Lucy and I never spent time with her. She partied too much, even for us. Plus, we liked our noses.

Rene suggested that we all go over to Brother Jimmy's. It was a place where people ate wings, listened to music, and got hammered. I had no problem knocking some cold ones back tonight, especially when Rene was buying. Rich friends were fun. Lily seemed to be in a good mood, no fists were flying, only hormones. I could tell she wanted to get in Rene's pants and vice versa. When she talked to or at me it was clear she was focused on him. Crazy flirts, both of them.

"We should all drop some acid tonight," Lily said. "I've got some with me."

Acid? I had no idea what it was. I had heard of it, but wasn't too sure of the details and I didn't think or care to ask. I hated being the odd man out and not having a clue about it. She said it was great stuff, mind blowing; *hmmm,* sounded familiar. Krista was down for it, but she was down for anything. She hadn't found a group of friends to call her own. She was a loner and I think she was jealous that Lucy and I clicked so quickly.

Lily handed little squares of paper to Krista and me. It looked like a shred of notebook paper. I watched Lily put it on her tongue and wink. She had huge brown eyes. Purple and green sparkly eye shadow was painted above them. They were beautiful, but filled with something that I didn't trust. Her brown hair flowed down to her tiny ass. She looked like a rock star's girlfriend.

I must have looked worried because Krista whispered to me, "I've done this before and it's fun." I didn't know why I was listening to her, considering she pronounced her own name wrong, but at the time it was good enough for me. I put it on my tongue and felt it dissolve.

Rene was not into the whole drug thing and graciously declined. Whatever, Fabio. Krista, Lily, and I moved to the end of the bar and began to talk.

Lily said, "I want to fuck Rene . . . don't you think he's fine?"

"He has a girlfriend, though . . . you know Claudia, don't you?" said Krista.

"Fuck that, I get what I want," she said and then she broke out into a song: "I fucked your boyfriend, I fucked your man, I fucked your boyfriend, he stuck it in!"

I'd never heard that song on Casey Kasem's top forty, but it was a catchy tune.

Lily went on to tell us all about her suitors. "Maccaulay Culkin is in love with me. We went to the High School of Performing Arts together and he had a major crush on me and still does," she said, licking drops of beer off her top lip.

I had a hard time picturing the *Home Alone* kid as her stalker, but I found her stories humorous.

We decided to leave the bar and walk around the neighborhood. My eyes and body started to feel strange. Nothing like ecstasy, this was tingly in a scary way. The hair rose up on my arms and neck, oncoming danger. There was no euphoria and I started to envision the cars speeding by backward, leaving trails behind them. Krista and Lily were staring up at the sky laughing. I couldn't seem to move my head up in that direction. I walked to the corner of the sidewalk and vomited into a garbage can. All liquid.

Lily came running over and said, "Sometimes that happens when your trip is coming on."

I had no idea what she was talking about. What trip? Where was I going? I didn't know that it wasn't a good idea to take acid without knowing what you were in for. One of the reasons I liked using drugs was the sense of intimacy I felt with other people. Acid was nothing like that, it made me feel isolated and detached from everyone. That was something I didn't need help with. I later found out that it was crucial to be around people that you trusted. I should have read the manual, but it was too fucking late.

I was going in and out of consciousness, and when I came to I was sitting outside Rene's apartment building on the steps. The girls were cuddled together smiling and I was fifty feet across from them, although I was sitting right beside them. I heard them whispering about me. I saw horns sprouting from Lily's head. There was no question she was evil. I must have blacked out again because we were no longer outside Rene's place. I was on his bedroom floor in the dark and I heard crying.

Krista was pulling her hair out. At least that's what it looked like to my fucked-up mind, and Lily was smoking what could have been a cigar, a cigarette, or a cat. I had no idea. But the ashes were flying up to the ceiling instead of down. I had different clothes on, men's boxers and an oversize T-shirt. My face was wet, the crying I heard was my own. I was completely out of my body with no control over any function. I was just along for the ride. I had no idea how much time had passed, it could have been five minutes or five days. But I knew that I blacked out a number of times.

I was now in another apartment. I guess it was Lily's. I was standing in her kitchen drinking water. I knew I was out of control.

It was morning outside. I kept refilling my glass but I began to spill it, I couldn't control my hands. I soaked water on my shoes, on my body, on the floor. The room was flooding. I unlaced my shoes and took them off. Lily had really had it with me. I guess I hadn't made the party much fun. This wasn't supposed to happen. I wasn't prepared for any of this shit. Next thing I knew, she and Krista were pushing me into a cab. I was begging to stay. I was scared and didn't know what was happening. Lily shoved my hands inside and slammed the door. She gave the driver money and told him where I lived, because I had no idea.

I was all alone, crying, shaking, and thinking that this was never going to end. I was bouncing around the back of the cab. I closed my eyes. The cabdriver had a soothing voice, I didn't understand his words, but I felt the vibration. He kept telling me that I would be all right. What did he know? I grabbed for the door handle and I heard the locks click all at once. I could see his eyes in the rearview mirror, they were all that seemed friendly right now.

I was scared, wet, and alone. We went through Times Square. It was empty and covered in white, like a blizzard had come through. I thought it was summer, but who knows, maybe months had passed. An airplane was frozen in flight, suspended in the air. I was a blur, I shrank, I expanded, I disappeared inside myself. I was locked inside this never-ending riddle. The voices, the laughter. I needed an antidote fast. I saw a homeless man on the street. I could see through his skin into his bones. He waved at me. I screamed and screamed. Any other cabbie would have thrown my ass out on the street. Thank God I had this one.

The cab stopped and the driver convinced me to get out. He was gentle as he walked me to the door of a building that he said was mine. I didn't recognize it. He rang the buzzer. Julia opened the door. She looked shocked and her eyes scoured over me and began to bulge out of her head. She told me to come in, but I heard screams from behind her. I knew if I crossed through that door I was never coming back out. The Hotel California. I was drenched in sweat. She grabbed at my arm and I ran away. The cabbie was gone, I didn't know where. Maybe he was never there, who fucking knows.

I heard sirens. Thirty-sixth Street between Lex and Third was blocked off. I stopped. I was confused. My feet were stinging and I looked down to see that they were bare. I heard sirens all around me. I began to run and one of the uniformed men grabbed my arm. It hurt and I told him to stop. He squeezed tighter and I started to kick him. Another cop grabbed my other arm and they carried me up into the Roberts House. I heard their thoughts, they began to whisper in my mind: *I would like to see what's under those little shorts.* I heard their laughter. I wanted to disappear. There were so many faces, lots of faces. Julia told me my mother was on the phone. I needed her. I was shaking. I went to hold the phone, but I was stopped by the handcuffs that were locked behind my back. I began to scream. The girls on their way to breakfast were getting quite a show. No shoes, half-dressed, sweaty, and surrounded by police.

I heard my mom's voice in my ear. It was soft and calming. "Go with the policemen. Listen to them, Lynn. Julia will stay with you, I am on my way."

I believed her, even though they had done nothing but hurt and laugh at me. She was the only one I trusted. The police told me that I was going for a ride in an ambulance. They talked out of both sides of their mouths. I closed my eyes, but there was no darkness or peace, just more of the nightmare. Death. I tried to run again and they picked me up off the ground and carried me outside. I yelled, screamed, cried, and kicked. I said that I was sorry and begged them to let me go. All I heard was laughter and then I blacked out. My eyes were open and I was in an ambulance on a stretcher. What was happening? I thought I was being arrested and then killed. I couldn't stop moving my legs. A black woman was sitting over me. She had a nice face, but only for a moment. It began to melt and I heard her cackling. My skin was crawling with fear. Everything went dark.

I was handcuffed to a bed in Bellevue Hospital. I was in a bright room, too bright, all white, blinding. Masked men were hovering above me. I couldn't see any faces, just eyes. One had a needle, which became a knife, and he began poking at my right arm. Even though I was handcuffed to the bed, I tried desperately to move my arm away from him. I felt a stabbing pain. I was just a little speck in the center of all of this. I had no control. It was like Lynn, the real Lynn, was locked inside, waiting to be let out. Another one of them told me to drink a cup of thick, liquid tar. I refused. They jabbed tubes into my nose that turned into snakes. Liquid flooded my head, my brain, and my throat. I gagged over and over and over until I passed out.

When I woke up my mom was holding my hand. "Where am I?" I asked.

"Bellevue Hospital."

"What?" I looked down at my wrists. They looked and felt like raw meat. My right arm was battered and sore from the struggle with the IV. I began to sob.

"What happened to you, Lynn? How did this happen?" she said, staring at the streaks of dried blood on my right arm.

"I tried acid . . . I didn't know exactly what it was . . . or what it was going to do to me," I said, trying to focus. "It made me sick and I don't remember much . . . I was shoved into a cab . . . I didn't want to get in . . . and . . . and then . . ." I said, trying to catch my breath. My mom leaned in and held me. A shrilling scream came from behind the purple curtain. It sounded like a dying animal.

"I am taking you back to Pennsylvania with me. I called your school and told them you needed some time away," she said.

I moved my limp arms off her. "Mom . . . no . . . please. I have exam plays next week. If I don't finish there is no way I will be invited back next year." My head throbbed. I had been hit by a truck. My thoughts were blurred, but I was sane enough to realize that if I went back to Pennsylvania, I wouldn't be coming back to New York. My mom's eyes were sad and empty. I knew this was killing her. "I am sorry, I'm so sorry . . ." I said over and over again. "I promise nothing like this will ever happen again. I messed up . . . never again, I promise."

She stared down at the stained linoleum. I knew she wanted to believe me. She looked up and said, "We'll see. You need to get some rest first." She didn't ask me any other questions. No more details about that night, my friends, the drugs, nothing. She didn't want to know, and I didn't want to tell her, either. She wouldn't understand. I looked up at the fluorescent lights. Warm tears fell past my temples onto the stiff, bleached sheets. Today I had learned my lesson. I was never going to use . . . acid again. That was for damn sure.

A Second Chance

When I returned to the academy I felt everyone's eyes on me. I missed my first set of mandatory exam plays, but the teachers urged me to come back to at least finish what I had started. I wanted to be invited back for second year, although I worried that after what had happened they would reject me. I thought I had tarnished the school's good name. I held my head up high, finished rehearsing, and performed in my final two shows.

I dreaded having to see Lily, Krista, and Rene, even though Rene came up to me and apologized. He said he hoped I was okay. He wanted to help, he just didn't know what to do. I didn't blame him for anything, it was his apartment and he didn't want us using drugs in it. Lily and Krista were a different story. I couldn't get the image out of my head of the two of them pushing me into that cab, using force because I was too scared to get in. In my mind there was an unwritten rule that when someone was fucked up and needed help, on or off drugs, you took care of them. Not in this case. Lucy, Brian, or Manny would have been right there for me. I knew who my friends were. It was crystal clear. Lily was one evil girl. I didn't blame them for anything other than not getting help for me. They could have called the hospital or taken me somewhere, but pushing me into a cab alone in that condition, I was lucky to be alive.

After the exam plays were over, it was just a waiting game. There was about a month and a half until second year started. We would only get a phone call if we had been invited back. On my last day of school I honestly felt that I would not be returning. I went to see the dean because I wanted my conscience cleared. Her name was Harrieta. She was thin, in her late fifties, and looked like she walked right out of the Victorian era. She had a quiet elegance that commanded attention. When I entered her office there were scripts and books covering every inch of the walls. It even smelled musty like an old library. Something about that office lifted my spirits. I felt comfortable.

"Please come in and sit down," she said, touching her beautiful silver hair.

"I'm sorry to bother you without an appointment, but I wanted to apologize for my actions that took me to Bellevue Hospital," I said while she sat motionless with her blue eyes fixated on me. "I took acid for the first time and I really didn't know what it would do to me. I was unprepared for the ride. My friends got scared, left me alone, and I ended up in the hospital. I didn't want to miss my first exam play, but I had to. I worked really hard to get to this school, financially and emotionally. I want nothing more than to study here and I wanted you to know that."

After a brief silence she said, "You have nothing to apologize for. You are not the first student to experiment with drugs. I wish your friends would have stayed with you. It saddens me to think you were left alone," she said as a single tear rolled down her face. "I know that you are a talented and hard-working young lady, but you need to take better care of yourself. Please be cautious of the people you allow into your life." She got up from behind her desk and gave me a hug. She smelled like musk. I wish I could've stayed with her all day and talked with her about life. She walked me to the door.

I left her office feeling calm and clear. My cards were on the table and I had nothing to hide. I said a silent prayer that if I were to be invited back next year, I would work harder and not get distracted. I would just have to wait and see. I walked out the front door, down the steps, and spotted Krista and Lily smoking outside. Lily turned away but Krista gave me a little smile. I knew she was a good person, but was scared and insecure. Lily took advantage of that. I felt sorry for Krista, but not that sorry. I turned and walked up Madison Avenue. The weather was hot and sticky. The city had that ripe smell that it gets in the summer. I could see the heat rising from the sidewalks.

I walked toward the Roberts House and felt sick. Ever since my acid episode, I couldn't look at it the same way. I glanced down at my arm. It still ached from where the IV had stabbed me. It was changing from red to black and blue, and it also had turned green in some places. It was a reminder of that night. As I walked in the front door I got chills. I could see myself handcuffed in the foyer and hear my screams as I walked up the stairs to my room. The wounds were still fresh. My phone rang as I was walking into my room.

"Hello?"

"Yes, can I please speak with Lynn Smith?" a man's voice said.

"This is Lynn."

"I wanted to tell you that you have been invited back to second year. Congratulations."

I was silent for a moment, "Thank you, thank you, oh my God! Could you tell me who else is coming back?"

"I can't give you names, but only eight of the forty-some Febs were invited back. It's a small group. You will have an intimate second-year class. Take care and congratulations."

I hung up the phone and knelt at my window. I looked out and saw the Empire State building lit up in red, white, and blue for the Fourth of July. I felt a huge relief, knowing that I was going to be in school again. I was determined to work hard and party less. I felt caged with excitement in my tiny room. I had to get out of there. I floated downstairs and walked outside. The sun was descending, but the heat was still hanging on. I loved this city. I felt a kinship with her and knew that she understood me. We were going to be friends for a very long time.

part 2

*

thE rush

On the Verge

We sat in orchestra seats of the Majestic Theatre in the same space *The Phantom of the Opera* inhabited every night, waiting patiently for our own unveiling. At the time I considered it the greatest show on earth, my graduation from the American Academy of Dramatic Arts. The velvet-lined seats held our teachers, families, and anyone else that wanted to get a sneak peak at the newest talent that was about to be unleashed into the acting business. I worked so hard to get to this moment. Focused a lot more and partied a lot less my second year. I was truly proud of myself for making it to the finish line.

I turned around and saw my parents sitting several rows back. I blew my mom a kiss as my father stared up at the ceiling. I know he was looking for imperfections, thinking that he could have done a better job painting and spackling the interior. By profession my father was a nurse, but he also painted houses on the side. He said it was to bring in extra cash, but by the end of each job he usually decided to come down on his price or accept a case of Rolling Rock as payment instead. It made my mother furious. All his "friends" knew this about him and took advantage of his lack of self-worth. I couldn't believe my father actually made the trip to see me. I wondered what my mom had to do to convince him to come.

I imagined she said, "Ken, if you go with me to Lynn's graduation, I will make sure the fridge stays stocked every night . . ." or maybe she said, "I won't scold you for a whole month when you come in the door at seven P.M. all googly-eyed and slurring . . ."

Well, whatever she did, it worked. I never told him how happy it made me that he showed up that day. I was beyond expecting a close relationship with my father, but appearances were still important to me.

My seat was next to Manny since we were all in alphabetical order. The tension between us made me pick nonexistent lint off my black satin dress. Somewhere over the last few months there had been a shift. My interest in our relationship, or whatever it was, disappeared, while his hard-on became bigger. Coincidence? I think not. I guess I was more attractive when I became a challenge. This was a good thing to know. Since we first met I wanted Manny to be the loving, interested, clever boyfriend. Instead we got high together, fucked at night, and avoided each other during the day. Our connection only happened in the dark. We both kept a guard up and neither of us wanted to put them down to see what lived behind them. I think we both needed our safety zone, at least I knew I did.

Alan Alda and Blythe Danner (Gwyneth Paltrow's mom) were our guest speakers. Alan Alda was inspiring. He had spent over half his life in the business and if anyone knew how to get and keep work, it was him. He urged all of us to be proactive by finding theater companies, staying close to each other, writing our own scripts, and producing and performing in them. Basically he urged us to "never to give up, even in the face of rejection." From what he said, there was going to be lots and lots of that. Yippee! I listened closely, but I thought I would be different. I would leave this theater, wake up tomorrow, find an agent, and star in a Spielberg film within the year. I had it all planned out.

Blythe Danner spoke the way she was dressed, elegantly. Her cream suit made her face glow like a full moon. Her niece Paige was one of my fellow classmates. At school we often heard rumors of celebrities in the halls. "Did you hear that girl is really a Nicholson, she just changed her last name?" "That's Lauren Bacall's grandson . . ." There were all sorts of tales, but Paige's was for real. Blythe Danner told us about first starting out in the business when she was very young. Determination was her backbone, and after the first job it became easier each time to get the next one. Momentum, momentum. She also said she had learned even more from Gwyneth. Watching how hard her daughter worked for everything and the professionalism she brought to the stage and screen inspired her. As much as I believed Gwyneth was hardworking, it couldn't have been that difficult for her to find a part or an agent. Couldn't she just walk out of her bedroom and knock on the door across the hall? "Hi, Mom, can you call Miramax for me and get me a meeting with Harvey? Thanks." I was waiting for Blythe to say something about Gwynnie and Brad. What was he like? Was he as hot in person as he was in *Legends of the Fall?* But she didn't get into any of that.

I stood in the wings, waiting for my name to be called. I smelled the mustiness, the sweat, the hard work that lived in this space. I loved being backstage. Such sweet memories. The little butterflies that danced, the expectations, the last-minute preps before my cue. The hum of the silent audience that waited for the curtain to rise. I pulled at the top of my strapless dress, making sure nothing would pop out. All I needed was my left boob to fall out as I was shaking Alan Alda's hand.

Manny touched my arm and winked. "I guess this is it, Lyndon B . . . see you on the other side," he said before walking across the massive stage.

"Break a leg, Manny . . ." I said to his back.

I felt a knot forming in my throat. My eyes were beginning to water. I took a deep breath. This was the end of a huge chapter in my life. I could sense the familiar slipping away. I was not the same person who had arrived here two years ago. I was wiser, experienced, cultured, and had finally finished something that I'd started. My dream, the one that was locked inside me for as long as I could remember, was now a living, breathing thing.

"Ms. Lynn Marie Smith . . ." the voice echoed.

I began my stride across the stage with my eyes looking straight ahead, listening to the sound of my high heels meeting the floor. The blaring overhead lights warmed my bare arms. The applause was loud enough to silence my nervous thoughts. I looked out at all of the familiar faces. Lucy was nodding her head up and down, with that great shit-eating grin of hers. I could read her lips from up here: "Right fucking on." My mom was standing, crying, and waving at me as if I wouldn't be able to pick her out of the crowd. This diploma was as much hers as it was mine. My mind was clear, my head light, and I felt a warm glow throughout my body. It was like being high without the drug. The stage was my one true home. I wanted to stay up there all day. If I had known it would be years before I would stand on one again, I would have taken a little longer up there. I took my diploma in my left hand and with my right went down the line, shaking the president of the school's hand, then Alan Alda's and Blythe Danner's. They were all so warm. I really had the feeling that they cared as they congratulated me and said "good luck."

I was reeling for the rest of the afternoon. Of course, my parents weren't staying the night in the city. My father was in a big rush, as usual, to go nowhere. I talked my mom into going back to the academy for the reception. I secretly hoped there would be alcohol. That way my dad would be comfortable and he wouldn't pester my mom, "Come on, let's get moving, Kath . . ." It was strange to see him in a city atmosphere, out of his element. His eyes darted around the room like he was plotting his escape. No baseball cap or Wranglers with dried paint on them. My mother made him wear a nice, striped button-down and a pair of black pants. Thank God. It looked like a costume on him. I watched how vulnerable he looked that day. It made me sad.

I drank my share of sparkling cider, trying to trick myself into a buzz. I think it worked. I floated around the room, talking to different classmates, their parents, and my teachers. I was excited to introduce my mom to Peter Jensen, who had remained my favorite teacher throughout my time at the academy.

"Lynn was a pleasure to have in class. She definitely kept things interesting," he said, running his hand quickly through his black hair.

"She certainly keeps me on my toes," my mom said in the high-pitched voice she uses when she meets someone new. It made me laugh out loud. I felt her pinch the back of my arm.

"You certainly have a unique niche in this industry, Lynn. Stick with it. Take care of yourself and don't be a stranger. Congratulations," he said, giving me a hug.

I felt secure with him. "Thanks, Peter. You're the best," I said, grabbing my mom's hand and walking outside.

" I told you he was great, Mom . . . isn't he cool?"

"He's nice. He's right, Lynn, you do need to stick with it. I am really proud of you. I know you are going to do so well . . . I love you," she said as the air shifted. "I am going to try to help you as much as I can . . . but I can't take out any more loans for your living expenses. So you are going to have to work really hard if you want to stay here."

"Mom, I know this. I've had a job since I was fourteen. I know what I need to do . . ." I said. "I know it won't be easy, but nothing ever is."

We sat silently on the steps outside my school and watched the steady stream of passing cars and people. I wanted to tell my mom how great I thought she was, how beautiful she looked, how she deserved to feel as proud of herself as she did of me, how she could find someone that treated her like gold, how she could find her passion . . . but all I could say was "thank you." Sometimes that's just easier.

She squeezed my hand and the red splotch began to form on her neck, the one she always got before she cried. I wrapped my arms around her and welcomed her familiar warmth.

Just then my father came outside. "Kath, we need to get movin', it's gettin' late and we should get on the road."

"Yeah, I guess you're right," she said, glancing at her watch but not really reading the time.

"Mom, call me when you get home so I know you made it there okay."

My father walked down the steps, leaned in, and pressed his cheek quickly against mine and darted away. Anything more would have been strange.

"I love you. You looked great up there today," my mom said, taking small steps backward up Madison Avenue. "Oh, let me get one more picture of you standing outside your school," she said fumbling in her purse.

I leaned against the brick wall and raised both hands in the air. *Flash.*

"I am proud of you . . . you're a star!"

"We'll see," I laughed. "'Bye, drive carefully. I love you. Thanks . . . for everything."

My mom turned around and began to walk toward Thirty-second Street, trying to catch up with my father, who was already halfway up the block. I'm sure he was praying that the bar would still be open when they got home. A whole Saturday afternoon without beer was unheard of. I can still hear the cracking open of that can in my head. Saturday morning oldies would blare from the tiny radio that sat on our kitchen counter. First came the sounds of the Temptations or Elvis, then came the sound of the refrigerator door, and then the cracking open of one can after the other . . . *crack . . . crack . . . crack.* Ahhhh, the sweet soundtrack of my childhood.

Well, this was it. I sat back down on the warm concrete and looked up at the clear April sky. Time seemed to move faster as I got older. It felt like yesterday I was walking up these stairs for the first time, wide eyed and ready for anything. Now it was over. Good-bye to school. No more Jackie B. screaming, "You want to fuck him" during a romantic scene, no more Jim DeMonic telling me I needed to pull my tongue back when making an S and that my glottal stops were a mess. No more fourth-wall exercises, no more guided relaxation, no more fencing, no more. The school was a safe bubble. It was easy, studying "the craft" surrounded by mentors, talent, and possibility. Now it was time for reality. The world was waiting.

I was going to exercise, save money, take singing and dancing lessons, and audition, audition, audition. I was going to have an agent, perform on Broadway, and star in a feature film within a year. I knew something big was going to happen for me. I could taste it.

Waiting

a.) to remain or rest in expectation;
b.) to remain temporarily neglected,
unattended to, or postponed.

I had a vision for myself. For my life. It brought me to New York and led me to the academy. But something happened to it. My vision began to blur after leaving the security of school. I didn't wake up knowing I was going to study Shakespeare that day or rehearse a scene with someone. There was no guarantee that I would be pursuing my passion on a daily basis. No teachers, no guidance, nothing. It was all up to me now. I felt the weight of the world on my shoulders. My bills were piling up, student loans were due, no more grants, and no more help with living expenses. I knew how to balance equations, but I couldn't balance a checkbook to save my life.

I was unprepared for the harsh reality of survival in New York City. Bouncing from sublet to sublet, trying to turn a closet or a couch into a home. I was always living in someone else's environment, in someone else's space. I moved from a share on Central Park West to a sublet in Jackson Heights, then to another share in Woodside for a month, then back into Manhattan on the Lower East Side with a psycho and her two cats. I was in a state of constant motion, with no rest or stability.

During my second year of school I had started baby-sitting and working the front desk at a sports club for minimum wage. But without the extra help from my mom, this just didn't cut it. I needed more money. It seemed that waiting tables was the only option left, so I started taking résumés into restaurants and bars all over the city. I even threw in my headshot for the added effect. It was not uncommon to do this since everyone waiting tables was an aspiring actor, musician, or writer. My "waiting" experience up until that point was minimal. Nonexistent, really. I'd worked at a sub shop in Danville called Jim's Place. As long as I remembered the extra side of mayo with every order, I was good to go, although if you'd looked at my phony résumé you'd have had no idea.

I thankfully landed a job at Grill's Restaurant and Café. The manager liked me and fell for my résumé. It was in the Village, on the bustling corner of Bleecker and LaGuardia. There was outdoor seating, an open kitchen, and a big cozy bar. It was overwhelming. I had to learn how to use the computer, remember sauces and daily specials, and describe different wines. I didn't even know how to open a bottle. I was scared to death, but deep down believed I could handle it. I pretended that I knew what I was doing, until I actually did and, as usual, the rest followed.

I was the cute, perky waitress with short blonde hair that the customers requested. I knew when to laugh, when to be professional, and when people simply wanted to be served. I was good, really good. But I was working so many hours to make ends meet my acting was not happening. I never seemed to make it to a backstage audition because I was always waitressing. If I didn't pick up every shift, I couldn't afford to stay in the city. It was a double-edged sword, a catch-22. I spent all my time at the restaurant and no time doing what I loved, what I came here to do. I thought struggling was my fate.

Since I didn't see Lucy, Manny, and Brian every day the bond between us began to grow weaker. In my mind everyone I knew from school was on their way to receiving an Oscar. I would bump into old friends on the street. They were dressed in trendy clothes, on the way to an audition, and I was in head-to-toe black with a rolled-up apron in my hand. The majority of them did not have to work to stay in the city. Their parents provided for them. Some of them even owned their own apartments. They focused on their craft, while I held out hope that I would be discovered by a famous director that came into the restaurant. She would love the way that I read the snapper special and stare at me in awe, hand me her card, wink, and say, "You got it, kid, be in my office by noon tomorrow." That never happened. My bitterness grew. I began to avoid my old friends. Instead, I stayed close to my fellow waiters.

Restaurants were holding tanks for struggling artists. A waiting room, a purgatory of sorts, all of us listening for our numbers to be called. I hung out with the restaurant crowd. Some were older, professional servers, "lifers." I was quite young at twenty-one compared to some who were in their thirties and older. They were funny, creative, and wanted more, like me. None of us wanted to be there. We wanted to be sipping mimosas with our artist friends at table number 22, not serving them.

Some nights after work we went to Club Life a few doors down. Wednesday night was gay night so there were lots of beautiful men. I got drunk, or high on coke, something I never seemed to get sick of. It was so easy to slip back into my old habits. It was great dancing with hot men who wouldn't lay a hand on me, or call me "baby" or "sweetheart." I loved it. I kept telling myself it could be worse. My headshots collected dust under my bed as I punched orders into the computer, and made thousands of espressos. I couldn't stop if I wanted to, struggling was my vocation. I felt victimized by life.

No scripts, no auditions, although I did my fair share of celebrity spotting, usually from inside the restaurant as some snobby NYU student was insisting that there was bacon on her sandwich and someone in the kitchen just took it off. "I can taste it, I know there was bacon on this. I specifically asked you for no bacon!" I wanted to press my nose against her ugly face and say

"Oink!" but instead I smiled and ordered her a new one. Pleasing customers came first.

I wanted this to be a temporary situation. Do it Vegas style, play the game, make the money, and then cash out. But in the back of my mind the little voice was telling me, *Just a little longer, come on. Keep at this, you're making money, you're good at this, and if you stop, what then? What are the odds that you will actually land a part? You have no safety net. Do you really want to go back to Pennsylvania and live with your folks? Ha.* Every time I thought of ripping my apron off and walking out the door, that voice would scream in my ear.

So I continued waiting tables and at the same time waiting for something else—my big break, my chance, my life to begin. I was trapped in a vicious circle, an endless state of readiness, like a fly stuck to glue. I traded in the costume for an apron, the monologue for a daily special, the audience for a customer, and a script for a menu. This wasn't part of my master plan, my dream. I was squandering my life. I felt cheated, angry, and bitter for all the things I thought I couldn't have. *Why me, God? Why me?* I think I was afraid of taking a risk, afraid of participating, afraid of rejection, ruled by fear—I knew how to struggle, how to complain, how to wallow—but what was it like to be truly happy, truly love myself and my life? Would I ever know?

On the Rocks

There were mirrors behind me and lights above. I stood on a raised floor in front of the crowd. I felt their presence all around me. My stomach fluttered with anticipation as I stretched my arm toward the sky and opened my mouth . . . "On the rocks or straight up?" I said, reaching for a glass. It was my stage. I was the central focal point in the room. I chatted with people and made drinks while making jokes. I always had something cute on. Tight but tasteful. My tips were great, much more than when I waited tables. I was the drink maker and the merry maker. I could make or break somebody's good time and found that everyone was always nice to the bartender. I concocted shots, snuck them to the servers, and gave free drinks to regulars. I felt powerful and confident in front of those shiny bottles. I was liked, loved, adored, and often seduced. But no one could get too close, not with the big slab of wood standing between us. Just how I liked it.

Bartenders were royalty in this business. I didn't have to share my tips, but the waiters did, with me. I was sick of waiting tables, so when Grill's closed down without any notice, I knew it was my chance to create a new opportunity for myself. I didn't realize that I was only trading one distraction for another.

Artie, a former manager at Grill's, was looking for a new bartender and wanted me to fill the position. He knew I had very little experience, but liked me and thought I would be great. My first day at Pisces was scary. I kept *The Bartender's Bible* close and was nervous about serving anything other than a pint of beer. I stared at the bottles behind me. There were so many different kinds of vodka, gin, whiskey, ports, et cetera. My first customer thankfully ordered a draft. I kept telling myself I was going to be fine. I could do this. My first night was slow. It was a Monday so I really got to study the drinks. Highball, snifter, dessert, wine, rocks, shot, flute—there were different glasses for every conceivable drink. I just kept thinking of Tom Cruise in *Cocktail,* if he could do it, so could I. Knowing how to shake martinis or fill snifters just right was a serious talent. There were schools and colleges to attend if you wanted to get a degree or certificate to verify that you were a professional mixologist. *The Bartender's Bible* was my saving grace. People just loved to order complicated drinks, even though they usually had no idea what was in them. I drifted off to sleep at night concocting slippery nipples up against the wall and sex on a desert beach upside down.

I quickly developed a group of regulars. There was Nick, a soft-spoken guy from the East Village, Maker's Mark manhattan, not too sweet. No matter what he ordered he always gave me a ten-dollar tip. Then there was Daniel, a gay playwright-slash-proofreader that lived on Seventh and B. Stoli martini, dry with one olive. He was in his fifties, but looked as if he were seventy. Severely depressed, but always sweet. I watched his sad, stinky little dog, Molly, when he went away. Mark was a beautiful thirty-something successful broker who drank whatever I poured, usually black and tans. He had a dark sense of humor that I understood. He told me a lot about his family, his suicidal brother, and his wealthy parents. I knew he was a player, but we remained strictly friends, although I think we both secretly wanted to hook up.

All of my regulars, mostly men, opened themselves up to me. It was sad and beautiful, but like everything else in my life, it involved a substance, alcohol. I watched their eyes gloss over and listened to their words blend together like a daiquiri. It seemed like the only time I could get close to a man, one or both of us had to be intoxicated.

I worked late hours and snuck shots to get me through the night. After my work night was over I needed to be on the other side of that bar. After every shift I went out to different bars with people I had met at work. I ordered one Amstel Light after another and let the cool liquid sooth my soul. I felt a release the moment I sat down and the substance entered my body. When it took over, when it took control, I liked it. I didn't have to listen to everyone else's story or entertain, or serve, or be something for everyone else. I would drink myself into a stupor. I thought it enhanced my outlook to see two of everything. I would black out and have no idea how I got home. I didn't realize at the time that the father I was always running from was the person I was slowly becoming.

I enjoyed this life, but at the same time knew I was selling out. So it went on like that. I worked, got wasted, slept off my hangover as best I could, and then started over again. I started to live only at night. Being surrounded by smokers and drinkers was a recipe for disaster. My job description entitled me to numb others from their own pain and frustration. I could always sneak a little of their medicine into my own glass. I became great at pouring Baileys into my coffee mug unnoticed. Perfect disguise and perfect combination. The stimulating affects of caffeine and the loosening effects of the alcohol. Always trying to be two places at once. I wish I could have concocted a winning recipe for my life as easily as I could a cocktail.

One night after work one of the waiters, Natalio, came with me to our hangout, the Cherry Tavern. Some guy was hitting on me and asked what I did for a living. I said that I was an actor and Natalio, who was wasted, burst out with laughter and told the guy the only role that I played was a bartender. It killed me. I was so pissed off that it sobered me up. I left the bar and walked around the East Village. I was furious and sad. He was an asshole for saying it, but it was the bitter truth.

Ruin

I slept with Brian one night. Yes, my best friend's fucking boyfriend. In the year since school ended I hadn't seen much of the old crowd. I didn't want to. One random night the four of us got together at Lucy's and took E. When we crashed Manny passed out on the floor. Lucy fell asleep on her bed while Brian and I were awake, lying next to her. It was a sticky August evening, or morning rather. The room had an orangish glow from the sun beginning to rise outside. Tiny rays of light were creeping in through the cream curtains. I was in and out of consciousness, feeling the effects of the pill draining from my body. I always crashed harder than anyone else, lying awake trying hard to find relief. My mind never allowed me to drift off to sleep.

I felt a moist hand lift my tank top and rest on my stomach. It didn't feel good or bad, it just was. I was numbed by Brian's touch or maybe I was already numb, I don't really remember. He slithered on top of me, sliding my underwear down and pushed himself inside me. It all happened so quickly. I didn't fight it. I couldn't really feel a thing. I was completely detached. I laid there with Brian inside me, Lucy asleep beside us, and Manny on the floor. Brian was sweaty and grinning above me. His pupils were huge, like he was still feeling the effects of the ecstasy. It didn't last long. It couldn't. It was over before it started. He pulled himself out of me, rolled off of my motionless body, and closed his eyes.

I wanted to vomit, rip my skin off, and run out the door. I felt paralyzed with a sick feeling. The walls were closing in on me and my chest began to burn. In that moment everything had changed. I knew I would never look Lucy in the eye again. The intimate feelings I had for each of them were gone. Nothing was sacred. I hated myself for not stopping him, for not screaming, for ruining it all. In five minutes I said good-bye to the only friends I had ever really known in New York City. I got up off the bed, put my jeans on, grabbed my bag, and walked out of Lucy's apartment onto Bedford Street. I passed a man jogging with his dog. He stared at me like he knew what I had just done. I didn't care that I was sweaty, that my hair was not combed, that my teeth were grimy, or that my eyes were burning from no sleep. All I cared about was leaving, getting far away, and never turning back. I felt like a whore. Why didn't I stop him? Did I want it to happen?

Instead of facing the music, being the bigger person and talking to Lucy, I just ran away and didn't look back. Our friendship had deteriorated and it killed me. Lucy was such a huge part of my life, starting out in New York City. She was like an older sister, best friend, guru, and fashion icon all rolled into one. But I never really felt good enough to be her friend. In my mind she had more looks, more money, more wisdom, and more experience. Why would she want to spend her time with me? I was ashamed of my past, my small town roots, and my lack of knowledge about everything.

I worked so hard at being someone else. Someone cooler, wiser, more sophisticated. I was a fake and a phony. It took so much goddamn energy and eventually I cracked. I was petrified of getting too close to anyone. Drugs and alcohol made things a lot easier. Snort a line, swallow a pill, and I could have instant intimacy with anybody. There were no questions.

After that awful night with Brian in Lucy's apartment, things were over, really over. I rarely talked with Lucy after that. We both felt the sourness between us. She went on with her life and I went on with mine. My past became this scary, dark monster that I had to get away from. Familiar faces and places were not comforting. They were thorns in my side, reminders of what was or wasn't, ghosts that haunted me. I needed to be around people who didn't know my story. A clean slate. I thought I craved stability, but I didn't. I never knew what it was like to be secure and comfortable in my own skin. I lived in chaos. Jumping from sublet to sublet, guy to guy, job to job. The motion, the movement, the drama kept me alive. If I stayed in one place too long I'd find myself out. This war was just beginning and it was every girl for herself.

part 3

*

thE roll

No Swearing

I walked into Liquids Lounge and made my way through the fog of smoke. The music was thumping, mellow with a nice beat. I felt and looked great. I had recently highlighted my short spiky hair to make it even blonder. I threw out most of my old clothes and bought new duds. I wanted a new style. When I wasn't bartending at Pisces I was working out at Crunch as much as possible and boy, did I have the abs to prove it. I was a new woman in my tight, black leather pants, high-heeled boots, and a blood red tank top. I was ready to work the room.

My job was to mingle, drink, and get people to sign a guest list. The first time I came to Liquids, I met Jake. He struck up a conversation with me at the bar. He had bleached blond hair, was skinny as hell, and at six foot five he towered above me. He was ghostly white and his left eye was slightly more closed than his right. He had the thickest Brooklyn accent I'd ever heard. "Hey, sweetheart, do ya wanna job?" he said, sucking the life out of his cigarette. He promoted parties and DJs at different clubs throughout the city and asked me if I wanted to help him out one night a week. He was definitely no stranger to the night life. He said he'd pay me cash and that I could drink for free. Needless to say, it was an offer I couldn't refuse.

The space was great. High ceilings, intimate, posh, and gothic. Big, cushy velvet couches and chairs lined the room. Candlelit tables held drinks and ashtrays. Behind the bar was an exposed brick wall and there was even a little VIP area to the side of the DJ. It was on the Lower East Side, but you would never guess it by the look of the crowd. Not too many piercings or tattoos. A lot of nicely dressed young people sipping cosmopolitans and martinis.

I grabbed an Amstel Light and made my way through the herd with my clipboard and pen in hand. I started conversations with complete strangers, most of them tipsy, and convinced them to give me all their contact info. I made it sound as if being bombarded with e-mails about parties, clubs, raves, and DJs was a great thing. Most of them were agreeable. It seemed so easy to talk people into things when they were intoxicated. I was getting hot, being scrunched between people in front of the bar, and my legs were beginning to stick to my pants. Leather doesn't breath too easy, but it looked damn good and that's what mattered.

I ordered another Amstel and moved away from the bar toward the tables and couches. The temperature got a lot cooler and I could breathe easier, even with the clouds of smoke floating above. That's when I saw him sitting in a chair a few feet away. His face was round, beautiful, and perfect. He had dark skin, maybe he was Spanish. Whatever he was, he seemed to glow. He was dressed in a gray shirt, dark blue jeans, and orange Adidas. Casual but sexy. His dark eyes met mine and I knew. In that moment I felt something. I had never believed people fell in love at first sight, but my mind was changing. He smiled at me and I was at ease with the world.

I walked over to him and asked, "Will you please sign the guest list?"

"Absolutely," he said with no trace of an accent. I handed him the clipboard and he began filling in his info. The guy sitting next to him was eyeing me up and down like a piece of candy.

I looked away and took a swig of beer. "My name is Lynn, by the way."

"Oh, I'm sorry, my name is Mason and this is Matt," he said, pointing the pen toward the ripped Mafia-looking guy sitting next to him in a wife beater. Matt gave me a quick nod. Mason handed me back my pen and clipboard. "Here you go, Lynn."

"Thanks." I liked the way he said my name. It sounded familiar coming from his mouth.

"Have you been working for Jake long?"

"You know Jake?" I asked.

"He's a friend of mine."

"Oh, I guess you didn't need to give me your info then," I said.

"That's okay, I wasn't going to pass up a chance to talk to you," he said, smiling. He had such a trusting face.

"Well, maybe I'll see you later, I have to get back to all of this hard work," I said, laughing.

The next couple of hours I drank more beer, conned people into signing the list, and kept a close eye on Mason without being too obvious. I was feeling really buzzed. The party was winding down but the DJ was still spinning. I saw Mason coming my way. Before he even opened his mouth, I asked him, "Do you know where I can get some ecstasy?" He seemed a bit stunned. I had no idea why I said it, it just flew out.

"Well, you certainly have no problem asking for what you want. How do you know I am not a cop?" he asked.

"Arrest me . . . but you're not a cop, so just give me an answer."

"Well, I just happen to have some pills on me tonight," he said, patting his pants pocket.

"How much?" I asked. I couldn't even remember the last time I had to pay for drugs.

"For you, free. They're dolphins. Nice and smooth," he said, smiling.

"I've never had them, but I'm not afraid to try something new."

He reached into his pocket, shook my hand, and I felt the pill in my cold palm. Without even looking, I faked a cough and washed it down with my beer.

"I'll be right back, I have to give this list to Jake."

I came back to find Mason in the same spot. "How come you're not rolling tonight if you have pills in your pocket?" I asked.

"I didn't want to," he said.

"Oh . . ."

"Until now. I just swallowed one."

"Where did your talkative bodyguard go?" I asked

"Matt? He warms up once you get to know him. He had to get home."

We smiled at each other and walked over to one of the couches and sat down. We began to talk and I immediately felt warm flutters in my belly. The rush was nothing like it used to be, but it still felt good. He told me his mom was Dominican and his dad was whitebread American. That explained his unique coloring. I told him a little about my family. I wasn't about to get into the messy details and ruin my high. It turns out we were both middle children, so we had an instant connection. It was so easy to talk with him. I felt like we had known each other for a lot longer than a few hours. It could be that the E was kicking in: the butterflies, the warm chest, the glow.

"How do you manage to walk in those pants?" he asked me, touching my leg.

I could feel my leg turning to mush. "That's none of your business."

"You look amazing, I must say."

I liked him, I thought I loved him. I wanted to marry this guy and I didn't think it was the drug talking. I had to get up and move. My body couldn't sit still any longer. The DJ was spinning trance. Smooth and fluid.

I moved and swayed on the dance floor. My body felt flexible and warm. My arms felt like they were moving through water, slow and graceful. Mason stayed on the couch watching, both of us beaming at each other. I touched my arm and a ripple of chills passed through me. I could have stayed there all night with Mason, swaying and dancing, but it was four in the morning and the lounge was closing.

A guy came up to us as we were getting glasses of water from the bar. He introduced himself. "Hey guys, I'm Bobby. I'm going to this after-hours place close by. It's kind of by invite only, but you guys are welcome to come," he said with a nervous tick that made his head tilt to one side.

I knew neither Mason nor I wanted this night to end yet so we decided to join him. "Sure, we'll go." I thought it would be great to spend more time with Mason, especially while I was feeling this good. The dolphin was fucking amazing, but E no longer knocked me on my ass like a tidal wave the way it did the first few times. I felt smooth, high, peaceful, and completely in control of my words and actions.

We grabbed our jackets from the coat check and followed Bobby out the door toward Avenue A. When we got close Bobby slowed down and said, "Don't tell anyone else about this place, it's very private." He knocked on a random door that certainly didn't look like it led to a club or bar. Mason held on to my hand. My warm feelings were beginning to fade because I sensed something strange about to happen.

A man wearing a cowboy hat and mustache opened the door, looked at Bobby and then gave Mason and me the once over without saying a word.

"They're fine, friends of mine," Bobby said. The cowboy nodded and waved us in.

A sign that read NO SWEARING hung just inside the entrance. Lightbulbs dangled from the ceiling and a pool table sat between the front door and the unattended bar. An overweight woman sat in the corner singing and murmuring softly. It was an eerie sound, like an old music box. There was a jukebox that only played one hit wonders and the sound was turned down so you could barely hear it. There were old pieces of furniture throughout the space. Mason and I sat on a couch that looked like something my grandmother had when I was younger. It had a farm scene on it, horses, cats, and people standing in a field. There was nothing normal about this place. I felt like I was stepping into someone's dream or nightmare. I didn't know places like this existed. Needless to say, it was quite the buzz kill. The last thing you want to do on ecstasy is sit on an old couch, in a strangely lit room, with a fat lady singing in the corner, and a sign reminding you not to swear.

I soon realized after looking a little closer that everyone was doing coke. This was a coke bar. A balding older man collected money from people who wanted beer. He then left and returned shortly with a case of canned beer.

Mason got up and walked over to a guy standing by the pool table. "Where can we get some coke?"

"Over there," he whispered, pointing to an older black man sitting at the bar.

The man at the bar had skin like parchment paper and a massive afro. There was a tray in front of him with a mound of white powder on it. He was scraping it into little Baggies with a razor. Mason walked over, gave him cash, and brought back a little Baggie filled with coke. So here I was with a guy who I had just met a few hours ago, having taken E, and now sitting on a couch in the strangest place I'd ever been. Mason began cutting up lines on the wooden armrest closest to us. I have no idea what you would call the people surrounding us besides freaky.

Staring at him across a line of cocaine, I was reminded of *Lady and the Tramp*. Instead of sharing a spaghetti strand, here we were sharing a line, and meeting in the middle. After that first line all I wanted to do was talk to Mason. We moved closer and chatted quietly. I slipped and said "shit" and froze up, thinking about that sign, NO SWEARING! How did they enforce that rule anyway? I was waiting for a midget to appear on a tricycle with a siren and tie me up. The rules were interesting, you couldn't swear, but you could cut lines of cocaine until your heart was content . . . or stopped.

When our high began to fade we were ready to leave that place. I was afraid to move off the couch so Mason led the way. The cowboy came over and unlocked the door that led out to Twelfth Street. It was morning and snowing. My heels were sliding around and Mason grabbed my arm to keep me from falling. We walked around the Lower East Side, reeling from our adventure, while white fell from the sky. I wrapped my fuzzy scarf around my chin and mouth. I didn't know how or what to think. Mason walked me back to my apartment on Sixth Street.

"Would you come to my parents' house for dinner tonight?"

I wanted to see him again. "Meeting the family so soon?"

"Just my mom and sister, my dad's away on business."

"I would love to," I said.

We stopped at my building and the thought of my fourth-floor walk-up made me cringe. I stared up at the winter sky. Mason pulled my scarf away from my face and kissed me gently on the lips.

"'Bye. Get some sleep. I will see you in a few hours." He turned to walk away and began to slip on the icy sidewalk.

"Be careful, don't fall," I yelled, laughing.

"I think I already have."

Feelin' It

After that first night with Mason my whole world changed. When he broke the news to me that he was only home on his winter break from the University of Vermont and would soon be going back to finish out the year, I was crushed. He flew back to school five days after we met. We talked every night on the phone. We both were going crazy not seeing each other. He told me how miserable he was at school, that he was doing poorly, and wanted to leave. As much as I wanted him to drop everything and come back to the city, I told him he needed to do what he felt was best. He said the only reason he was there was to please his parents and he hated it. He was determined to leave. He signed himself out of school only two weeks after returning.

He moved back into his parents' place in Gramercy Park. They were disappointed and I'm sure they partially blamed me for his decision to leave. His family put a serious emphasis on education, and he would be the only one without a degree. It was funny how unhappy both of us were with our upbringings. Me, with no guidance or structure and Mason having exactly the opposite, being spoon-fed the right way to live his life.

His parents owned a large three bedroom with a studio attached that Mason stayed in. His dad traveled a lot for business so it was just him and his mother living there. She was great, a dark-haired, dark-skinned beauty. She was warm, loved to cook, and really enjoyed having the two of us around. I rarely spent any time in my tiny share in the East Village. Just a few days after he'd returned from Vermont our relationship had already solidified and progressed to where we were living together.

Mason knew all the hot spots in the city. He took me to Twilo, where I had been before for a Christmas party. That night I had spent all my time waiting for a free drink. I was miserable and I had left early. But this night was different. Mason wanted me to meet some more of his friends. "The gang" he called them. He brought a bag of pills with him.

As we were waiting in line he told me, "Security is sometimes tight on weekends. They will probably pat us down. I usually hide the pills in my underwear."

"I guess something does come between you and your Calvins," I said, laughing.

"Very funny," he snickered.

We had already swallowed pills in the cab on the way to the club. "Holy shit, I can feel it coming on already," I said.

"They're Nikes. They usually come on quick."

"What are you, a drug dealer?" I asked jokingly.

He just smiled. I was surprised, but not shocked. Instead I was excited and intrigued. I felt special, like I was chosen to be part of this new world, or underworld, that Mason belonged to.

We worked our way inside. Mason grabbed my hand and led the way through the masses. The crowd was sweaty, smiling, dancing, and fucked up. Eyes rolling back. Heads lolling. The heat of everyone's bodies wrapped around me. Mason found a corner, his corner, and relaxed against the wall. The space opened up. I let go of his hand and started moving. Up and down, my limbs had taken over, and my body felt every beat of the music. I danced next to a speaker and disappeared inside of it. I was the music. I didn't even realize my eyes were closed when Mason shook my arm. I opened them and he was laughing.

"Feeling good?"

"Hell yeah," I said.

"I want to introduce you to my friends. Come on." He took me off the dance floor. "This is Vinnie."

Vinnie was tall, lanky, with bleached hair, kind of looked like Jake from Liquids, but cuter and younger. He cracked a smile and nodded his head. "Looks like you're having fun."

I could feel myself licking my lips and biting them a little. Vinnie touched my hand. "Hello, hello, is anyone in there?"

"Oh my God, that feels good."

"I'll take that as a no." He looked back and waved to a girl with short black hair. "This is my girl, Kelly."

She had sharp, edgy features, her ivory skin reflected the flashing lights. She was beautiful. "Hey mama," she said, laughing. "So you're the hoochie Mason has been talking so much about. Ya feelin' good?"

I gave her a hug. As we danced I felt all of our energies meshing together. I danced with Kelly face to face, smiling, bouncing around. She had a unique style of dancing, all hips, all sex. "Trance is good, but I like booty house."

I nodded like I understood. All I knew is that I felt so fucking good. I realized how moving made my roll so much more intense. I lifted my arms in the air and let my head fall back. The lights looked like meteors shooting through the sky. I wanted to dance forever, stay in this warm place around people who didn't want to know any more about me than what I told them. People who danced and didn't care about your salary, what degree you had, or your life goals. People who lived to have a good time. I looked around and saw girls wearing wings and glitter all around me, angels with colorful hair. I saw guys who were ripped, wearing no shirts, twirling glowsticks, and sucking on pacifiers. People wore face masks, bright colors, lots of orange. It was a circus, a party, a recess from reality.

Surrounded by new people with a great guy. His eyes were as dark as a moonless night. Mason took care of me, always bringing me bottles of water and rubbing my shoulders whenever I took a break. It was almost like being a boxer in between rounds. Getting refueled and massaged before going back out to battle on the dance floor.

We were surrounded by hundreds of people, but all I could see was him. We moved closer. His skin was smooth caramel. We began to kiss, his warm lips sending bolts of intensity through me. I could see the colorful strobe lights through my closed eyes. I was under a sky of fireworks, frozen in this moment. Life couldn't get any better.

I whispered in his ear, "I love you." It just oozed right out like molasses, with no hesitation.

He pulled his head away from mine and looked right into my eyes. "I know. I love you, too."

The words danced in my ear, caressing and tickling my brain, much like the pill I swallowed. We hugged, danced close, and talked about how good we felt. An "Oh my God" from him and an "Oh my God" from me. We spent the rest of the night dancing. We all decided to hit the Bubble Room upstairs. We entered a quiet room filled with couches and large white rubber balls. People were sitting, bouncing, and rolling around on them. Literally. We found some open balls, leaned back on them, and sat on the cool floor.

My limbs were heavy and I draped my legs over Mason's. Kelly was leaning into me, her back against mine, and Vinnie's head was on her lap. Everyone was touching in some way, an invisible current connecting us all. My head was light and free. All we could do was laugh, smile, and sigh. My ears rang in the quiet. I could still feel the bass beneath us.

Mason rubbed my hand and I closed my eyes. I wanted to be with him forever. I loved hanging out with these people. Everyone seemed so real, no pretenses. This scene was so new to me. I was used to doing drugs and sitting around an apartment talking about life, acting, family, technique, and playwrights. Talk, talk, talk. But now it was different—fuck the words, all we needed was music and a place to groove. I found my new home in this club with these people. I was free, liberated, and truly happy with Mason and his friends.

When we left the club, the daylight was blinding. We gave Kelly and Vinnie a hug. "See you guys soon, right?"

"Hell yeah, mama. We love you guys," Kelly said.

"Later," said Vinnie.

Mason and I slid into one of the cabs that were lined up outside the club. I looked at the time. It was ten in the morning. Had we really been there for ten hours? Where did the time go? Sober time was so different than high time. When I was sober I felt every second, every minute, but when I was high time disappeared, melting, just sneaking by unnoticed. My body was tired, but my mind was still thumping from the music and motion. I leaned my head onto Mason's shoulder as he told the cabbie to go to his apartment on Eighteenth Street.

"I had such a great time. I really like your friends. Twilo was amazing."

"Yeah, it's a blast. You just have to know which nights to go. Van Dyk is spinning on Friday. We will definitely come back."

I closed my eyes and smiled.

Stop, Drop, and Roll

Mason placed his hand over my mouth. I felt the capsule hit my tongue. I was ready to roll. The wall Mason was leaning against was vibrating. I could see it moving. I had no idea what pill I'd swallowed. Nike, Mitsubishi, dolphin, who knew and who cared. I trusted Mason. His warm hands rested on my hips as I led the way through the herd. My chest tightened and my stomach began dancing. I couldn't wait to do the same.

Mason rubbed my neck, goose bumps covered my bare arms. "I love you, babe."

His words pulled my ear closer to his lips. I needed to get inside before I exploded. I approached the huge, bald black man, flashed my ID, and he waved me past. Mason paid fifty bucks for both of us to get in. He always had a wad of cash on him. I never asked too many questions.

We rushed past coat check. Bringing as little as possible was key; freezing my ass off for a little while was worth it. I moved from side to side, turning my body to fit though the holes in the crowd. I grinned as I pulled Mason along behind me. The music filled the space. It was deafening.

Jungle, hard house, trance, et cetera, there was something for everyone. I burst apart with motion, my roll was on. I looked back and Mason nodded, knowing that I was hit hard. He was smirking and his lip was beginning to twitch. That was his E face. God knows what mine looked like. We claimed our space on the floor. The gang was all there. No words. Everyone spoke through movement, through touch, through eye contact. Sweaty bodies everywhere. The ground under us shook like an earthquake. I began to move, felt the music, connected with the beat. I felt sexy when I danced. Eyes were on me and I liked the attention. I got off on it. I bounced, thrashed, and swung my neck from side to side, which always intensified my roll. A guy with glowsticks appeared before me, waving them in front of my eyes. The light teased my pupils, I felt them shrink and expand. The green trails remained in my sight long after he danced away. I looked at my friends all around me. Nothing could go wrong. The world smiled at me. It was a dream.

Every weekend we did the same thing. Got the gang together and swallowed pills. Mason gave so much away, he was giving, not selling. The two of us were like Bonnie and Clyde, Mickey and Mallory. There was a sense of belonging and camaraderie, we were a tribe, all wanting to feel beautiful and peaceful. I stopped hanging out with anyone that didn't use E. I entered another world and it separated the users from the nonusers. I wanted to be dancing and rolling, not sipping cosmos, or pounding shots in an Irish pub. I felt like I was the shit. I was good at ecstasy. We were a community of young people wanting escape and creating our own private universe. I was accepted, uninhibited, alive. I was a child again, reliving the childhood I'd never had. Group hugs. Group dances. Receiving and giving love without hesitation or embarrassment. I craved it all. We were a family. A collective group of lost souls. An inner circle that traveled in a pack, always up for a great night, a good time. Add a pretty pill to that mix and it created a unique elixir.

Vinnie was the straight man with the driest sense of humor. He never finished high school. He grew up on Long Island and loved his sisters. He had a sadness and toughness about him that lived in his eyes. It made me adore him. Then there was Kelly. Crazy and tough, from Michigan, both street smart and naïve at the same time. Her parents were super religious. They were always sending

Christian gifts and cards to her and Vinnie. They wanted him to accept Jesus Christ as his personal savior or else the fires of hell would consume him, or something like that. She had been around the block, though, a bad kid, in trouble with the law when she was younger. Kelly owned a gun, but her most shocking trait was that she loved to cross-stitch. She'd go out all night rolling and then wake up the next morning and start cross-stitching *The Last Supper* for her parents' anniversary gift.

Jake, tall, skinny Jake from Liquids, was the ringleader, the godfather to us all. He was by far the oldest, almost thirty, and had been around the club scene for a long time. A country line dancing instructor turned party promoter. Not too sure how that happened. He'd grown up in a rough part of Brooklyn and had done more drugs than all of us put together. Even on E you couldn't get too close to Jake, but he loved having us around.

Mason was the smarty pants, the cool nerd who always had pills to give out. He was always calm, always steady. I was the wild card of the bunch. Everyone thought I had it together, since I talked about acting, partied with the best of them, and still held down a job. But no matter how deep into the scene Mason and I got, there was still something about us that didn't quite fit with the crowd. This seemed to be a comfortable way of life for them, a hardened lifestyle that they had been used to for a long time. Parties, clubs, drugs, guns . . . compared to these people, I was June Fucking Cleaver.

Then there were countless others who floated in and out of our group. And there were always new people to meet when we were out. There was a closeness, an understanding among us all, but what tied us together was a tiny pill.

After Hours

I loved the preparation of it all. The anticipation of the night ahead. Going down on Broadway and buying a new tank or loose pair of jeans or pants. Counting the hours until my shift was over at the bar. Checking my cell phone messages to see where the party was. Sparkling up my eyes and spiking out my short, wild hair. I would slip into a costume and get ready to take center stage. Listening for my cue, where I needed to be when the clock struck two, three, four, or five. Cabbing it to one of our spots. Mason would meet me outside, hand me a pill, and the night would begin.

There was no distinction between the days of the week. Maybe Twilo on Saturday, some hard house, possibly Baktun on Sunday for a little jungle, take Monday off, then Centro-fly on Tuesday for the atmosphere, Exit on Wednesday in the VIP lounge just because, Thursday was always Jake's trance party at Liquids, and Friday could be Limelight, depending upon the DJ. This wasn't written in stone or anything, but each night in the city there was always a loft party, a DJ, a pill, a reason to stay out. I had tunnel vision. The music, Mason, the friends, the clubs, the Ecstasy meshed together. This was my life.

No snorting, no injecting, no preparation. It was a free ride, all-you-can-eat buffet. My Ecstasy world lived up to everything that my real life couldn't. Living at night, sleeping all day. Mason, Vinnie, Kelly, and I were inseparable. The party only ended when I passed out. The next five months formed into a single solid moment. There were the clubs and then there were the after-hours places, the after parties that kept things going way past daybreak. One night it was Kelly's apartment in Brooklyn, another night it might be at some warehouse on the West Side, or maybe at a secret space that only a select few knew about. We left a club high, skied out, and wanted more. More drugs, more music, more, more, more. We would all swallow another pill after leaving the club, usually in a cab, on our way to the next venue. Superman had his telephone booths, we had our taxicabs. The scene was always the same no matter where we went. There would always be music, even if it was coming out of a shitty stereo in someone's shitty apartment. There was no space too big or too small to house our needs.

I didn't see any of this as strange or harmful. It all felt normal. Everything that surrounded me was a reflection of myself, a mirror image, and everything matched up. The high was different now, not as smooth, that's why it was crucial to have music to dance off the excess energy. I was crashing harder than ever. I would stay up long after everyone else passed out. Mason would drift off, his mouth hanging open and his breath slow and heavy. I would listen closely. It was my music after the CD player stopped. The clock would say one or two in the afternoon, but my internal one said something entirely different. I'd eventually pass out.

Some nights I would go right from a party to bartend a brunch. Those days behind the bar when I hadn't slept at all were hell. I'd have to drink alcohol, coffee, anything to get me through the shift. At this point I could make drinks with my eyes closed, no thinking involved. Mason would come in toward the end of my shift, having just woken up, looking refreshed, while I was a fucking mess.

My thoughts and inner hum were always louder the day after going out, and since we were always going out, they were becoming an annoyance. I ignored them. All of these little things seemed a small inconvenience for the great time I was having. The sight of Mason calmed my nerves and my worries. We were living in a fantasyland, a dream. We would lie on his bed and kiss and cuddle.

We never had sex when we were rolling or coming down. It was difficult for him to keep it up and my body didn't desire it like it used to. The physicality of the dancing took its place. It was the first relationship I was in where sex wasn't the central theme. I liked it that way. When we did manage to have sex, it was beautiful. Soft and gentle, just like Mason.

Mason became my best friend, my partner in crime. A steady. The rock. No matter how high we got, he always seemed in control. His personality was unaffected, his sweetness, his sincerity was always there, he was still Mason, even with the drugs. Not me, the higher I got, the more detached I was from everyone. In fact, I could be downright mean. I purposefully ignored Mason. I danced with other people and devoured as much attention as I could. No matter how fucked up I became, Mason was always there to take me home at the end of the night.

What I found in Mason was something I'd never had with any other person. I knew he was my soul mate. I knew our paths had crossed for a reason. When I looked into his eyes, I felt like I had known him my whole life. I was vulnerable and opened up to him, showing him my pain and ugliness. He didn't run away. He came closer and hugged me tighter.

A Pretty Poison

Numbness, tingling
It starts at my toes and
Works it way up to my head.
Projecting the self
I'd like to be
Sexy, talkative, mysterious
Carefree.
One pill has dissolved
Chills surge through my core
Before it wears off
I swallow one more.
My skin's not my own
So many faces to see
Before I know it
I'm on to number three.
Sweat pours off my brow
The world is my stage
Lashing and dancing
Unleashing my rage.
Four, five,
And six (on a bet)
But usually after three
I try to forget.
The music has faded

There is no one around
The lights are too bright
My thumping heart the only sound.
Open the door
Shield my eyes from the sun
Knees are throbbing
A cab
Not one.
My clothes tell a story
Of where I have been
My mind, racing with emptiness
My soul, dirty with sin.
I get home to my cave
And shed my night skin.
Clenched eyes while awake
The drug always
Wins.

Creep

Mason's father was back after weeks of travel and that meant we could no longer play house. His mother was fine with me sleeping there, but Mason told me that his dad would not be pleased with the setup. I completely understood, but I hated that I had to start spending nights in my tiny cubicle on Avenue A. My roommate Jen was strange and, to top it off, she never cleaned her cat's litter box. So our tiny apartment smelled foul. I am not a cat person, never was and never will be, but I couldn't be picky. I needed a place to live in Manhattan. It was affordable and close to work, but other than that, it blew, royally.

It was the first night I had spent in my apartment since Mason returned from Vermont. He was staying home to have dinner with his family. I was invited, but not in the mood for a family gathering. I decided to stay home and get some rest. No parties, no clubs, no drugs. I slept on a twin-size loft bed and kept all my possessions underneath it. There was no room for anything other than the bed. I think the space was even smaller than my room at the Roberts House, if that was possible. I stared at the blue walls I had painted a few months ago. My little space of pale blue. I intended for it to feel like I was surrounded by the ocean, but instead I was trapped in a fish tank. I lined my ceiling with tiny Christmas lights in an attempt to make it cozier. I missed Mason. The quiet was unfamiliar and I felt a cold void without him by my side. I began to think about him, his face, his eyes, his lips, and before I knew it, I was asleep.

My dreams were becoming more and more vivid. They were frantic, with lots of motion and movement. The veil separating dream life from waking life was disappearing.

I had no idea how long I was asleep, but suddenly my eyes shot open and I was paralyzed with fear. I felt something, someone in the room, hovering near me. I clenched my eyes shut and reopened them to make sure I was awake. My heartbeat began to race and my blood was hot. I heard heavy breathing and it was not my own. My spine tingled. I tried to move my arms but couldn't. I only had control of my head. Everything else was glued to the mattress. My eyes were adjusting to the dark. I turned my head to the side and there he was. At the end of my bed, staring at me. He was old, his pale skin luminescent, with a face full of deep wrinkles. His hair was a grayish green, thin and sparse. He was wearing long, heavy dark clothing. I opened my mouth to scream, but felt like something was choking me. It began to move slowly up the length of my bed. An awful smell invaded my nose, like he was rotting from the inside out. The next seconds were like hours. Slow motion. As he came closer, I tried to look into his eyes, but there weren't any, just two gaping holes. A hideous monster. In that instant, I sprang up and gasped for air, as if I had just emerged from underwater. He moved backward slowly. I jumped off the bed and started swinging my arms. I screamed and tears flew from my eyes. The wall swallowed him as I punched my hand into it. I fell to the floor and curled up into a ball. My hand throbbed, my chest ached, and I was drenched in sweat. I was dumbfounded. I knew I was awake. I saw that man, that creature, with my own eyes. I jumped up, ran to the phone, and dialed Mason's number.

"Hello," his groggy voice answered.

I tried to speak, but all I could do was cry.

"Babe, babe, oh my God. What's wrong? Where are you?"

"Mason, I don't know what just happened. There was a man in my room."

"A man? What . . . ?"

"A man, a ghost, a spirit. I don't know what the fuck it was. I woke up and felt it next to me. I couldn't move. Oh my God. I tried to punch it and it disappeared."

"Calm down, are you sure? Are you sure you weren't dreaming? Maybe you were sleepwalking," he said.

"No, no, no. I've never done that. I jumped off my bed. I saw it. I saw it. It was ugly, dead, a ghost. I know I must sound crazy, but it's true."

"Babe, you're not crazy. I believe you."

"What time is it?" I asked.

"Four in the morning."

"I'm sorry. I'm sorry that I woke you up."

"No. Don't say that. I am here for you anytime, always."

"I love you."

"I love you, too. Is Jen there?"

"No, she's out."

"Do you want to cab it up here? I can let you in."

"No. No, I'll be fine. I was just freaked out. I feel better already."

"Call me first thing in the morning."

"I will."

"Get some sleep, sweetie. Good night."

"Good night."

I hung up the phone and went to the kitchen to get a bottle of water. I closed the fridge and felt something sweep across my feet. I jumped.

"Meow."

"Fuck!" My heart began to race again. Thank God my roommate wasn't home. The last thing I wanted was to share this Kodak moment with her.

I walked back toward my room and peeked in before entering. Nothing. What did I think? That he would be lying in my bed, smoking a stogie? I climbed up the ladder and pulled the covers over me. I looked over at the wall and saw specks of white where my fist had hit it. I still felt numb from the strange visit. I thought about what had happened. Was he dead? Had I seen a ghost? Did he step into the wrong world or had I? I always believed in the spirit world and guardian angels. But I never really thought about the other kind. The darker side of it all. Where did the lost souls go? Did they wander the earth close to us, trying to find their place, their home? Two worlds yearning to reconnect. I started thinking about the movie *The Exorcist*. Demons, possession, green vomit, hell, death, death, death. My head was reeling with black thoughts. Had I opened a door into a different dimension? Would I have other visitors? Would he return?

I sat up in my bed. There was no fucking way I could fall back asleep. I brought my blanket out into the living room and sat on the couch. Television was usually the best sedative. I pressed the power button on the remote and started channel surfing. A guy selling the worlds sharpest knives. *Click.* An Aerosmith video. *Click.* News program. *Click. The Munsters.* Yeah, right. *Click, click, click.* Off. Fuck it.

I got up and turned the stereo on. I pushed play. *Ahhh.* Good old Radiohead. I sat back down on the couch and noticed Jen's American Spirits lying on the coffee table. I lit one and leaned back, inhaling the warmth, disappearing into Thom Yorke's voice.

'Cause I'm a creep, I'm a weirdo. What the hell am I doing here? I don't belong here. I don't belong here . . .

Rolling Away

It was always an issue where Mason and I would crash at night. I hated being away from him, but my tiny bedroom barely fit me, much less the two of us. If Mason's dad was away his mom didn't mind if I stayed over, but if he was home I couldn't and we'd have to sleep apart. So when Kelly's lease was up and she found a big two bedroom in Brooklyn and invited Mason and me to join her and Vinnie, we jumped at the chance. I didn't really want to move out of Manhattan, but the positives outweighed the negatives. I could save on rent and live with Mason, and our two closest friends. It was a perfect opportunity to have our own space. In my mind this was a step up, but in reality this move was the final nail in my coffin.

I pulled the U-Haul up to the curb. A bunch of black guys were huddled outside the apartment building. They had a boom box and were laughing and talking loudly. When Mason and I stepped out of the van, it was like the record suddenly scratched and stopped. They were quietly staring at us as we began pulling boxes out. Thankfully we didn't have too much. It was mostly my stuff, books, stereo, television, et cetera. No furniture. I left my miniature bed at my old apartment. I filled my arms, Mason relocked the van, and then picked up the rest.

They were standing in front and wouldn't get out of the way, so we had to maneuver around them. I smiled, but didn't expect them to be bringing by an apple pie anytime soon. I was uncomfortable, but pushed all of my concerns to the back of my mind. Something crunched under my feet. There were tiny chicken bones covering the steps. *Uhhhhhg.* I just wanted to get our stuff inside and have a glass of water.

By the last trip, the crowd got sick of staring and continued with their music and conversation. The building was dirty. It smelled strange. Stale, like an old folks' home and greasy, like Burger King. Our apartment was on the second floor. A two-floor walk-up, two less than my last one, thank God for small favors. As we got to the first floor a little girl opened the door on the right and stood outside. I could hear a baby screaming. The girl didn't have shoes on and her hair looked like it hadn't been combed in years. I could see inside, the place was a mess, and there was no visible floor because of all the junk strewn about. The baby's screams were constant, as if no one was around to comfort her. My stomach began to burn and twist. I smiled at the girl and we continued upstairs. I thought about my mom. She would freak if she saw this place. If she wanted to visit I would have to meet her in the city, she never stayed overnight anyway. We got all the boxes inside. Vinnie and Kelly had moved most of their stuff in the afternoon before. I ordered a bed to be delivered, but it wouldn't arrive for a day or two. Mason and I sat side by side, glistening on top of a large box.

"So when are we having our neighbors over for dinner?" I asked.

"This is their territory. They probably all grew up on this block. We are outsiders, you know?" Mason said.

"Great. Comforting thought. So is this a safe area?"

"We're close to Park Slope, but not that close. It changes from block to block. This area is a bit rough and you won't be walking anywhere alone."

"I won't?"

"No, I'll be with you at all times," he said.

"Well, if you're trying to calm my nerves, its not working."

"I'm sure it's fine. I just want to be safe."

"Did you see all the bones outside on the steps? What are they?"

"Probably the last couple of white kids who tried moving in here . . ." he said.

"Ha ha ha, you're such a fucking comedian," I said, hitting his arm. We laughed and kissed each other.

"So where are we gonna sleep tonight?"

"The nice cushy floor in our room."

The apartment was newly renovated. You would never think it existed in this building. Hardwood floors, new kitchen, fresh paint coating the walls. My room was bigger than any other space I had lived in in New York City. A nice closet, a real closet, and I wouldn't be sleeping in it. There was a big window and I could fit a full-size bed in it. WOW. There was also room for a dresser and a second person. Imagine that.

Within days of being there, 217 St. John's Place became our clubhouse, our cave. A revolving door of friends and strangers. People in and out. Since my rent was so much cheaper, I cut down my work schedule. I was only bartending two nights a week now. My schedule was wide open. The weekend never stopped. Music was thumping at all hours and ecstasy was flowing freely. We still went out occasionally, but now that we all had a place to hang out it became less important. None of us were trying to hide anything from our roommates because we *were* the roommates. All living in the dark. We could do whatever we wanted, whenever we wanted. No more searching for an after-hours place or party, this was it. No paying thirty bucks to get into a club, this was free. Drugs were everywhere. We never had to hide them, we were safe here.

I was lying to my mom every time she called, telling her I was great, auditioning a lot, had an upstanding boyfriend, and interesting new friends. Each time she would attempt to plan a visit to my new apartment, I would make an excuse. I was going out of town, Kelly's family was visiting, I was sick; I had an endless supply of lies to dish out.

Two for Jump

We still made it out to Liquids on Thursdays for Jake's party. The four of us swallowed E in the cab on the way into Manhattan. One pill just didn't cut it anymore, so we all started with two. Two for jump. The details are still foggy from that night, but I know I was gone. We got inside and I immediately started dancing. I didn't care who was around me, I needed to move. I was all speed, no euphoria, no warm fuzzies, just a hard, pounding energy that I felt in my bones. I remember this guy dancing close to me, touching my hips. At first I thought it was Mason, but then I realized it wasn't. I didn't stop him. I didn't stop dancing. It was unusually crowded for a Thursday. I had no idea where the others were. I didn't care. He stayed close to me, his big hands, his breath heavy on the back of my neck. I became dizzy. I moved to the bar and got a glass of water from Meg, the bartender, and walked to the bathroom.

There were several individual bathrooms. I pushed the door to one open without knocking first to see if there was anyone inside. I put my cup down on top of the toilet paper holder and held onto the wall. I was nauseous and disoriented. Air passed over me and there he was. I must have forgotten to lock the door. Before I could open my mouth to say something, his tongue was in it, forcefully jamming his wet lips over mine. He tasted like smoke and vodka. He was tall and black, but other than that he was a blur. I pushed him off me and took a breath.

"You're so sexy. I want to lick your cunt," he said. "Come on. Leave with me."

His hands were pressed against the wall behind me, holding me in place. I was scared and trapped. I was hovering over the toilet with each of his legs to the side of mine. He moved closer and I pushed him again, crouched down, slid between his legs and out the door. I ran out of the bathroom crying, panting like a crazed animal. I forced my way through the crowd and out to the street. I didn't look for Mason, Vinnie, or Kelly. I just kept running.

I hailed a cab, got into the backseat blubbering, and told the man my address. "I only have twenty dollars and I need to get to Brooklyn."

"No problem, no problem. You okay?"

"I'm sorry, just having a rough night." I rolled down the window to let the air hit my warm face. Streaks of tears hardened on my cheeks. I wasn't fucked-up anymore. The adrenaline took over and I felt clearer now. What was I doing? What was happening to me? Why did I let him touch me? I just wanted to get home and forget about it. The cabbie dropped me off in front of my building. It was over twenty dollars, but he didn't care. I got out. It was the first time I was coming home alone at night. The usual group of guys were outside the door. I looked straight ahead. I could feel them staring.

"Why are you all alone, snowflake?" one of them asked as I unlocked the door and slipped inside, closing it hard behind me.

I walked upstairs, rushed inside, and laid on my bed, crying. I howled like I used to when I was younger after my father and I had had a fight. It felt good to let it out. I wanted these horrible feelings to disappear and leave me. I got up and went into the bathroom to shower. I made the water scalding hot so that my skin turned red. The stinging pain was comforting. My sinuses opened up and my nose began pouring snot. I scrubbed my arms, legs, and stomach with my pear-scented shower gel. I wanted to be sucked into the drain with the suds. I wrapped myself in a towel. I could hear the phone ringing. I went to the living room and picked it up.

"Hello?"

"Babe, what the fuck? We've been looking for you. What happened?"

"I'm fine. I felt really sick. I threw up and I just needed to get home."

"You should have told me, looked for me," he said.

"I know. I'm sorry. I couldn't wait. I needed to get home. I'm sorry."

"Oh, babe . . ."

"I feel better already. I just took a shower. I'm fine, don't worry."

"I'm gonna hop in a cab now so I'll be home."

"You don't have to leave, I'm fine. Please stay, have a good time. I'll be here when you get home," I said.

"You sure?"

"I'm sure," I said.

"Okay. I love you, if you need anything call me on my cell."

"Okay. I love you. 'Bye."

"'Bye, sweetie," he said.

I hung up the phone and went into my room. I put on some Massive Attack and slid into my green scrubs and Mason's wife beater. I fell heavily onto my bed. So much was flying around in my head. I began to think about my family. That guy's lips on mine. School, Lucy, Brian, my old roommates. I couldn't clear my mind. It was overflowing with the past, my mistakes, my regrets. I felt a void deep inside of me, a blackness that needed to be filled, now. I got up and went to the dresser and opened Mason's sock drawer. There was a bag full of pills. I reached my hand in and got two. I went into the bathroom and turned on the cold water in the sink and washed them down. I looked in the mirror. My pupils were still wide from the first two that I had swallowed earlier. I splashed water on my face. The shadows under my eyes made me look old and my cheeks were becoming gaunt. This life was eating the flesh from my body. I didn't like what I saw. I hated how I felt, but I didn't know how to change it, how to get off this ride.

I went back into my bedroom and closed the door. I turned off the overhead light and put the little lamp on next to my bed. I started straightening up my room, folding clothes, organizing my closet. I felt the drug rushing through my veins. It was taking over, taking me away. Detaching me from myself. From my mind. I turned the volume up as loud as it could go. The noise still couldn't drown out my racing thoughts. I began to move around, spinning in circles like a coin, running my hands through my wet hair, swaying from one side of the room to the other. Tears started to stream down my face like a flood that I had no control over. I didn't stop dancing, I couldn't.

Just Say Yes

Pink? Green? Yellow?
Or maybe even white?
The choice is all yours,
depending upon your appetite.
I grin at you,
begging to be consumed,
most people crave me,
when I enter a room.
I am your ticket,
an all-access pass,
music, dancing, loving,
hurry, this deal ain't gonna last.
I will give you the family
that you've never had.
They will all love you,
even your dad.
You won't have to snort me,
or stick a needle in your arm,
all you have to do is swallow,
who can resist my charm?
Chills surge through your core
everything feels like a dream,
You can always get more.

No, no, no, trust me . . . I am your friend
once you swallow,
together till the end.
While under my spell,
your problems are resolved,
I'll take you to heaven
no work involved.
Keep me in your pocket
I am so easy to hide,
go ahead choose the one you want
in me you can confide.
Take me in your hand
give me a try,
look at my face
do I look like I lie??
Your life will be better
as soon as I dissolve,
prettier, kinder,
even more evolved.
Come on, just do it,
what's the big deal?
The other shit is deadly
but I am for real.

Gulp . . .
Here I go into your stomach
just give me a few.
Now everything I said
just might come true.
Twenty minutes go by
I rush through your veins,
up into your head
I am tickling your brain.

Your limbs are light,
your heart open wide,
each person you see,
is a member of your tribe.
I make you excited
butterflies dance,
you stand up from the couch
you are now in a trance.
This room is your stage
live here forever,
the whole world is your age
Floating in the air.
The music takes hold
the bass feels like sex,
now you are sold
hours go by.
You're still flying high
skin glistening,
let out a big sigh,
it is now morning,
but only outside.
These clubs stay black
somewhere to hide,
I am fading away.
But you'll never forget
I've marked your spirit
our relationship set.
Your chemistry changed
working better rearranged,
you will return to me.
I have taken control,
remember eight hours ago . . .
you gave me your soul?

Kids are so stupid,
so gullible,
naïve.
They question nothing
and always believe.
My job is so easy,
my packaging cute
who can resist me
even a man in a suit
swallowed me last night,
his life altered too.
He came for escape
his work was too tense
so I gave him a taste of freedom
outside of the fence.
Tell all your friends
send them to me,
Happy
Harmless
Mysterious
Carefree.
Tell them the lies
don't be afraid,
all for one
one for all,
we now have it made.
People who don't
just can't understand,
they question too much
always raising their hand.
Lame and uncool
listening to everything
that they learn in school . . .
Like the facts and the truth

I will damage
or kill,
eat away at your brain
take your life and last breath
or perhaps make you insane?
The first time you swallow
could be your turn,
and after that
it's just too late to learn
the truth about me . . .

part 4

*

thE crash

You're Next

The phone was ringing, it was late, and my bedroom was dark. I stumbled around, grabbing at the air until I found the receiver.

"Hello?"

"Lynn, Lynn . . ." her voice shattering like glass.

"Steph? Is that you? You sound so far away."

"Lynn, help me. Please God, help me. It's bad, something bad has happened."

"What? Steph, calm down and tell me."

"Stacey and Mom are dead . . ." The words stabbed me in the chest.

"Steph . . ."

"It's Dad. He's killed them and he's after me. No. . . . no . . . please don't!" She began screaming like that baby downstairs.

Then I heard gunshots. They sounded like they were coming through the phone. "Steph? Steph? Run. Run out of the house. Get out. God, no, please. I'm calling the police. Leave. Do you hear me? Leave! Steph?" Silence. Dead Silence. Until I heard his voice.

"Hi, Lynnie . . . you're next . . ." Dial tone.

I shot up out of bed and onto my feet. I was gasping for air. "Fuck, fuck . . ." I looked around. I pulled on Mason's arm. "Mason, wake up. Wake up."

"Huh? What . . . what? Are you okay?" he asked.

"No, no, I am not okay. Oh my God, I just had the most awful dream . . . it didn't feel like a dream . . . it felt real. My father, my father . . . I can still hear the shots and his voice," I said, covering my ears.

"You're all right. Calm down," he said, wiping the tears off my face.

I laid back on my bed, staring at the ceiling. "He killed them. My mom and my sisters. He shot them."

"Who?" he asked.

"My father. My father shot everyone. Steph called me . . . it was so real. I heard the shots . . . and then he picked up the phone and said . . ."

"What?"

"He said I was next."

"It was just a dream. Your family is fine . . ." he said.

"You don't know my family."

"You know what I mean."

"Mason, something is wrong. It's not right. My sleep . . . these dreams. They are restless and spooky . . . it's fucked-up . . . it's too real. It scares me to close my eyes. I don't know . . . I don't know anymore," I said.

"Babe, you need some rest. Your body needs sleep. We've gone out a lot this week and—"

"What's new? We've gone out a lot for the past four months. Since the first day I met you we've been going out . . ."

"I know. I know. Maybe we should take a break. Take some time off from the scene. Okay?" he said, rubbing my arm.

"My brain hurts, my body hurts . . ." I said, turning on my side so we were face-to-face.

"I know, sweetie."

"Mason?"

"Yes? What is it?"

"We are better than this. Better than what we are doing. You are . . . I am . . . Mason?"

"I know. Let's try to get some sleep," he said as he rolled his body the other way.

I laid there, staring at the shadows on the ceiling. I thought about my dream. I knew my dad would never hurt any of us. Physically, anyway. I thought about my mom, at home sleeping in her separate bedroom. My old room downstairs. Last time I was home she showed me how she'd redecorated it, making it her own with new paint, cucumber-scented candles, and a new bed. It made me sick. Her in the basement, in my old room, while my father slept upstairs. Their lives separated by floors, walls, beer, silence. What was she thinking? That she could just go on hiding in the basement, ironing his clothes, watching him stumble in every night as she sat home alone or with my younger sister playing cards? And what about Stephanie? She was only sixteen. Living in that mess. Listening to the fights, living in that tension day in and day out. Seeing my father get hammered and comforting my mom.

I wanted to rip my hair out, strand by strand. I felt a heat rushing through my chest and into my face. I realized how much I missed my mother and sisters. How sad it made me to think about my family. I wanted everyone out of that house. Far away from my father. I sensed my mom's pain as I lay in my shitty apartment building three hundred miles away from her. I knew she was slowly dying in that house. In that life. How could I stop it? I wondered if she knew how parallel our lives had become. I once said that I would never be like her, never be like my father. And here I was, trapped in my own life. Could she feel my pain? Did she know I was killing myself in this apartment, one pill at a time? Digging my grave right next to hers? I put my hand on Mason's back. I could feel his slow and steady breath. I wanted to crawl inside of him and hide. Curl myself up into a ball next to his heart and let it rock me to sleep. But that was impossible. Everything seemed hopeless. So I pressed my ear against his back and closed my eyes.

The Breakthrough

I crawled out of bed and felt a black cloud surrounding me. A sense of dread lived inside me, it never slept, and it didn't want me to, either. I staggered to the bathroom to wash off the previous night's grime. Everyone else was asleep. It was three in the afternoon and the apartment was completely silent. The natural rhythm of life had long been destroyed. I hated the sound of nothingness, of silence. I didn't know what to do with it. I continued getting ready for work, digging around my room for something clean to wear. My laundry had been piling up since we moved into this place, forming little hills on the floor. I began slamming the dresser drawers and stomping around the bed, full of rage, cursing myself, cursing the world for my misery. Mason sat up in bed.

"Hey, babe, what's going on?" he said, rubbing his eyes.

"Nothing. Nothing. Go back to sleep, you're good at that," I said, tearing my closet apart. "I'm trying to find a clean pair of pants, but I know that's too much to fucking ask . . . I don't want to go sling drinks right now . . . I hate Pisces, I feel like shit . . ."

"Babe . . ."

"Stop, Mason . . . shut up. Don't look at me like that. Go back to sleep!" I screamed.

I continued spewing negativity, vomiting my inner turmoil all over Mason. The words kept flying out. I felt like I had no control, like I had Tourette's syndrome. I went from crying to screaming back to crying again. If someone didn't know any better they might have thought I was rehearsing a Greek tragedy. I was sitting on the floor wearing only a bra and pair of unmatched socks. I stared into the dresser drawer on my lap, the one that I had ripped out during my rage. Mason tried to move closer to me, like a lion tamer reading the animal that he was trapped in a cage with. I wouldn't let him comfort me. I pulled myself up and pieced something together. I looked at my watch. It was too late to take the train, I was going to have to call a car service. Mason stopped following me around the apartment and disappeared into the bathroom. I heard the shower running. I tried turning the knob, but he had locked it. He never locked it.

The two days a week that I had to work were becoming such a pain in my ass. It was harder and harder each time. It seemed unreasonable to me that I should have to do anything. It was slave labor. My cell rang and a man's voice told me he was waiting downstairs. I grabbed my bag. My hair was still wet and I had no makeup on. I ran out the door. Not saying good-bye to Mason made me feel even worse. I knew that I had changed. I didn't want to be a sad, scared, angry human being, but I felt defeated. His warmth and love was undeserved. I didn't want him to love me, but the thought of losing him was inconceivable. He was all I had in this dark world.

I got into the black Lincoln Towncar and told the driver, "Lower East Side, Sixth Street and Avenue A please. Oh, and take the Brooklyn Bridge, not the Manhattan. Thanks."

The sun was beating down on my face. Summer was right around the corner, I could smell the city ripening. "Could you turn on the air?"

"No work. Sorry," said the driver.

"Great," I said, rolling down the window.

I tried to relax my mind. I was consumed by everything. Nothing felt right, nothing felt good. The sun was too hot, my hair was too short, my pants were too dirty, my shift was too long. The pressure cooker inside of me was overheating and I was about to boil the fuck over. My feet began to sweat. I rubbed my wet hands on my dirty black pants. I looked up at the rearview mirror and saw his dark eyes on me. I was sick. The car was shrinking, getting smaller by the second until I was suffocating inside a tiny box. I looked outside. *Is this the right way? Where is he taking me?* As we drove across the bridge I considered opening my door and jumping out. Far out into the water, it was safer out there. *Lynn, calm down.* I began talking myself down from the ledge that I was on. I didn't know it at the time, but I was having my first panic attack and it wouldn't be the last.

The driver turned on the radio. It was some kind of Indian chanting and singing. All the voices, the clanking of cymbals, the racket, calmed me. He made a right on Essex which turned into Avenue A. People were out crowding the sidewalks, shopping and buying fresh produce. The minute the city warmed up, you could see skin everywhere. Girls in little shorts and crop tops. Shirtless guys showing off their bodies and tattoos. I sat in that car, watching everyone come and go. I was observing an alien species. How did they do that? Smile, laugh, walk around in the daylight buying fruits and vegetables. What was it like to buy a head of broccoli and take it home and cook it for dinner? What was it like to be among the living?

"Miss? Hello? Hello? Left or right?" asked the driver.

"Right side, please, far corner," I said, reaching into my bag and unwadding some bills to pay for the fare.

I walked into Pisces and went directly upstairs toward the bathroom. I passed the fish tank. It was dirty, and cloudy with a green slime coating. It looked like it hadn't been cleaned in months. Artie, my manager, rose from behind it.

"Hey, hon," he said, putting strands of his long brown hair behind his ear.

"What happened here?" I asked.

"Looks like some kind of bacteria got in there over the weekend. The tank is contaminated. All the fish look pretty sick. It's a shame," he said, crouching down and tapping on the glass.

"I know how they feel," I mumbled to myself.

"Are you okay? Is something up? You don't seem like yourself lately. Is everything okay with Mason?" he asked.

"Yes, everything is fine. I'm fine. My allergies have been acting up . . . changing of the seasons, you know? Well, I have to use the restroom and get downstairs to set up the bar."

"See you down there," he said taking the top off of the tank.

I got into the bathroom, locked the door, and took a few deep breaths. I sat down on the toilet. There was a small spot of blood on my underwear. I hadn't gotten my period for the last three months and I was getting it now? The first month I'd missed it I thought I was pregnant because I was always so regular. I took a test and it was negative. It just never came back. I never gave it much thought. It didn't seem like such a bad thing. I finished peeing and wiped, there was no more blood. Who fucking knows.

I zipped up and went over to the sink. I moved my face closer to the mirror. Those tiny invisible bumps that I first felt a week or two ago were now red. Small round spots were on my chin and more were forming around my mouth. I was just now seeing them for the first time. How long had they been there? Did I just get them in the taxi? I started to panic, my face heated up, and I pictured more bumps sprouting out like weeds. Now I knew that something was wrong. I could rationalize the nightmares, the mood swings, the missed periods, the weight loss, the panic attacks, but these zits I couldn't explain. Ahh, the vanity! The outside of me finally matched the inside. I was ugly and I hated myself.

Better Off Alone

We had been in our new place for over a month and had been having people over all the time, but we decided it was necessary to have an official housewarming party. All of those other gatherings really didn't count. It was a Saturday night. People started pouring in around nine. This wasn't the type of get-together where friends brought candles and dishware as gifts. The only thing we burned were joints and the only plates we passed around had coke on them. It was BYOD. Bring your own drugs. It all depended on your appetite.

There was a little of everything. A buffet-style, all-you-can-eat, serve-yourself event. Jake and his girlfriend, Sandra, brought coke, Mason had plenty of rolls, a group of strange guys that no one seemed to know had tequila, and a few people from Pisces showed up with enough weed to stone a small army. Before the clock struck twelve, everybody was fucked-up on their drug of choice. Mason and I swallowed a couple pills before the first knock at the door. Music was pounding. Vinnie was our resident DJ. He had his table out and was spinning a mix of everything to shake up the crowd.

I mingled, walking around the room, smiling and talking. Pretending that I cared, pretending this was fun. I talked with friends and strangers. It was the same conversation. The same vibe, the same drug talk.

"What are you on?"

"Cool, what are you on?"

"I am so fucked-up . . ."

"I am so fucked-up . . ."

"I love this beat."

"This break is off the hook."

I went into the bathroom for a breather. I think I swallowed two more pills. I can't remember. I couldn't feel it anymore. I couldn't feel a thing. I wet my hands and ran them through my hair. With all of the body heat steaming up the apartment, my hair was turning into a Chia Head. My stomach began to make the strangest sounds. Churning and growling like a rabid animal. Did I eat today? I forgot what hungry felt like.

I went back out into the party. I stared at the thick clouds of smoke floating around the darkened room. All of the pale faces, the hard, spastic music. If I didn't know any better I would have thought this was a Halloween party and everyone came dressed as a skeleton. Mason's smile broke my train of thought. He was sitting on the couch with a girl with orange hair and a guy with a sparkly nose ring. I'd never seen them before or maybe I had and didn't remember. Everyone was starting to look the same. You hear of people looking like their dogs. All of us, the gang, the crew, were beginning to look alike. Hanging out, spending so much time partying together, doing the same shit. Pale faces, dark circles under our clouded eyes. We were cookie cutter images of one another. The hair color was the only thing that differentiated us. I looked around the room. *Who are all of these people and why are they in my apartment? Who the fuck am I? How well do I know anyone here?* I wanted to believe that I had a tight group of amazing friends, but the only thing we had in common were the drugs. I stood against the wall in my crowded living room, filled with people, music, laughter, and I had never been so alone.

I walked into my kitchen. I wasn't looking for anything, but I saw this kid snorting white powder from one of my plates. He looked up and nodded, handing me the plate.

"Here you go," he said, wiping his nose and inhaling deeply.

I took the straw and snorted the little mound that was left. I was expecting the taste of coke, but this was different. It was unfamiliar to me. "This isn't coke," I said to him.

"Nobody said it was, sweetheart," he said, patting me on the back.

"What is it?" I asked.

"K . . . special K . . . it's special, like you."

I handed him the plate and went back into the living room. I wasn't interested in much after I reunited with ecstasy. I'd heard of K, but had never tried it. Something about snorting a cat tranquilizer and feeling physically detached from my body never excited me. I was more of an "uptown" girl—anything that sped things up, kept me going. But at that point as long as I was moving around and filling myself with something . . . anything . . . that was enough. I sat on a stool in the living room. It became quiet, everything was silent in my mind. I didn't want to be here, in this smoke-filled den around this bullshit. I got up and started to walk down the hallway toward my room. There was a loud knocking at the front door. I opened it. A curly-haired blonde girl and a tall transvestite-looking fellow, gal, whatever, stood there smiling. Their pupils were as big as fifty-cent pieces.

"This is where the party's at, right?" she asked. "We're friends of Lisa . . . I mean Lynn, we're friends of Lynn."

I nodded, pointing behind me. "She's in there, have fun." They pushed passed me. I had no idea who they were. They could have had bombs, grenades, knifes, and I just let them right in. No questions asked.

I walked into my room, shutting and locking the door behind me. There was a mountain of coats and bags in the middle of the bed. I untied my pink Converse sneakers, threw them to the side, and turned off the light. I laid down across the top of my bed. That was the only place I could fit. I was numb. I listened to the movement. I felt the shaking apartment. Everyone's laughter, dancing, and conversation merged together, becoming a long, steady moan. I've never experienced a tornado, but I've heard the survivors say that their houses moaned right before they imploded and collapsed. That was the same sound that I heard as I laid there. I could hear a few words of the song that was playing. *Do you think you're better off alone?* I did think I was better off alone. I no longer wanted to be in the center, the focal point. I didn't want a stage.

My heart began to race. I could feel the chemicals sloshing around inside me. More them than me. They had taken up residence in my body, in my soul. This all started as a choice, my choice, but now I was a slave to it. Every time I swallowed a pill I was tricking myself into seeing and feeling what was not there. What was not mine. But I could only trick myself for so long. I wanted to pretend that I loved my life, my friends, my new apartment, but I didn't. Nothing felt right. The ecstasy stopped doing what I wanted it to do. The party ended a while ago. I no longer swallowed it, it swallowed me. I was in a fog, a thick haze surrounded me. I felt light and detached. Seeing myself from a distance. I thought about death. My death. I knew it was waiting for me, that it was close. I closed my eyes and silently welcomed it in. *Please, come get me. Make me disappear. Erase me from this earth.*

It's Not Christmas

I don't remember much about the first few days in the ward. I vaguely recall my mom picking me up. I remember being in a small room. I wore a blue hospital gown that was too big for me. I was cold and there was a woman with dark hair sitting in front of me. Her mouth was moving, but I couldn't hear words. My head was full of noise. I looked behind and all around me. *How long have I been here?* The woman stood up and came around her desk, moving my body in front of a chair, she pressed down on my shoulders until I was sitting. She stared directly into my eyes. I didn't trust her. She began talking again, I could hear a few words. *Psychotic . . . drugs . . . addiction . . . recovery . . .* everything she said became more noise bouncing around in my head. My ears hurt. I was so confused. I got up and ran out the door into a larger room. There were several tables and chairs and a small kitchen area with a sink. I needed darkness. There was a constant flashing in my eyes, as if someone was pointing a camera at my face and snapping pictures one after the other. Images were blurred and moving all around me. *Where am I? Am I still in my apartment?* A black man grabbed my arm.

"Lynn, my name is Dan. I am one of the nurses on the ward. I want to show you your room."

"Is my mom coming?"

"Lynn, your family is fine. They are at home. They brought you here so you could get better. Do you remember?"

"Yes, no." *What is happening?* It was hard to talk. I couldn't seem to form any sentences. All that came out were moans and sighs. He guided me down a hallway. It smelled like urine, gravy, and bleach. I began to gag. He opened a door and led me into a small room. There were two single beds and a large window that faced out the front of the hospital. He pointed to the bed closest to the window.

"This one will be yours while you stay here."

"I want to go home."

He ignored me. "This is a bag your mother put together. Your clothes and personal belongings are in here. I have to lock them in this closet until you show improvement. You will have to remain in that hospital gown and slippers until then."

"What? What? I don't understand. Is my mom coming? Can she stay here with me?"

"I'm afraid not, Lynn. There is a group meeting in the living area in a few minutes that you will have to attend. Just try to relax," he said as he walked out of the room.

I ran over to the window. It was too high off the ground to jump out, plus there were bars over them. I guess somebody else already had that idea. It was so familiar. *Am I in Pennsylvania?* The green hills and trees. I could practically see Bloom Street, my street, my family must be right out there. If I could just get out of here and run down that hill, I could make it home. I paced around the room, then sat on the bed. It was as hard as a rock. My head was throbbing. I hadn't slept in days. I knew it was afternoon by looking outside, but time had collapsed and I felt trapped inside this horrid and awful abyss. I couldn't sit still. A knock came at the door.

"Hi, Lynn. I'm Helen. My room is right across from yours. They told me to come get you for group."

She was older with long, frizzy, bleached blonde hair. She wore glasses that covered half her face. I looked at her shirt. There was a beautiful angel with its wings spread on the front. MERRY CHRISTMAS was written across the bottom in red. "It's not Christmas," I snapped at her.

"Oh, I know, sweetie, my oldest daughter, Sheryl, gave this to me last year. I like wearing it."

"Are you my angel?" I was desperately looking for a sign that I was safe and in good hands.

"No, I don't think I am. Come on, we have to go. It's started already."

I followed her down the hall. The smell of this place was over-powering. I watched Helen take a seat at one of the tables in the dining area. There were several people already sitting down. I felt them staring at me. I sat at one of the empty tables. Dan was standing up in front.

"Today we are going to do a word scramble. Each word is an emotion. I am going to pass around the sheets and pencils. After everyone is done we will discuss each emotion and relate it to your own life and how you're feeling today."

Where the fuck am I? I must have traveled back in time. Am I back in elementary school? My legs began to shake underneath the table. A younger boy with bandages on his wrists came over and handed me a sheet and pencil. He smiled.

"Hi, I'm Bryan. This is bullshit, but you got to do it."

I nodded and looked down. All the mixed-up letters made me want to vomit. My brain was already scrambled. How the hell was I supposed to figure this out? I could only look at the paper for a second, everything was blurry. I felt like I was in some kind of sick and twisted parallel universe. I looked up and Dan was standing over me.

"Lynn, you haven't started. Is there a problem?"

"I can't do this. My head . . . what is this? A riddle?" If this was my way out, I was screwed.

He started to laugh. It sent chills down my spine.

"Why are you laughing? Do you know something? I can't stay here."

"Well, you are here and you will be staying here for a while. Cooperate and it will be a lot easier."

Cooperate? What was he talking about? I couldn't keep my mind focused. My antennae were tuned into every radio station at once. I heard the others talking and tapping their pencils. "No, no, no. I can't do this," I said, getting up from the chair. "You're evil. I have to leave. I won't play your stupid game."

I ran down the hallway, feeling trapped inside a carnival funhouse. I heard laughter as I entered my room. I was panting. My body was like lead. I went into the tiny bathroom and knelt down on the floor, crying. I lifted the seat and began to gag and spit into the water. I wanted to purge myself. I was contaminated. Nothing came out because there was nothing inside. I was empty. I began wiping my face with my gown. Snot streamed out of my nose. I stood up and went into the room. I could feel the cold floor through my thin blue booties. *What am I going to do?* I couldn't stay here. I didn't want to be around all of these strange people. I couldn't trust anyone. I frantically paced around my room and tried to open the locked closet. I wanted my clothes, NOW. I needed to see and feel something familiar. It was getting darker outside. It frightened me to think about staying here overnight. I went from sitting on my bed to sitting on the floor to sitting by the window, musical chairs without music. I don't know how long I was doing that, but a knock came at the door and it was my angel, Helen.

"Hi, are you here to take me home?"

"No, hon. It's dinnertime and you have to eat. Listen, they watch your every move here and if you want to leave, you have to start doing what they tell you to."

"Why? I don't trust them. Help me, please."

"I wish I could. I can't even help myself. I'm in here for the same reason you are. I'm sick and unhappy."

"Why are you unhappy?"

"I don't know. That's what I've been trying to figure out my whole life. I have taken every medication, electric shock therapy, and just when I think I'm getting better, I end up back in here. Come on, let's get some food."

"I can't eat."

"Yes, you can. You have to, if you want to get better."

She made me feel slightly calmer, which wasn't saying much. I walked back out into the dining area. I forced myself to sit. Two women rolled carts in, carrying trays of food. The smell made me nauseous. A heavy-set nurse, named Maggie, called my name. She came over and placed the tray in front of me.

"Here you go, princess. You need to start eating." Her piercing blue eyes were staring at me from behind her black cat-eye glasses.

I looked down at the lumps of hot food on my plate. There were mashed potatoes that had been dished out with an ice-cream scoop, and covered in thick brown gravy. A piece of round, pink meat, maybe it was ham, I couldn't tell. There was a little bowl of Jell-O with an orange slice trapped inside. Everything smelled the same. One putrid aroma filled my head. If I had anything in my stomach, it would have been joining the other lumps on this tray. I looked around and everyone seemed to be gobbling it up.

"You better eat something. They will write it down in your chart if you don't," said Helen.

"I don't care. I can't eat this. I'm going to be sick."

"Can I have your Jell-O?"

I nodded. I watched the green square jiggle in its bowl as she moved it over to her space. I knew how that orange felt, trapped inside that green slime. I was trapped inside this place, inside myself, wanting to find a way out. I began to cry.

"Oh, sweetie, did you want your Jell-O? I'm sorry. I really am. I'm always fucking things up," said Helen.

"I'm just so confused. Nothing makes sense. Nothing seems real." I got up from the table and there he was, standing in front of me.

"Hi, dollface," he said as a tiny string of drool crawled down the right side of his mouth. His teeth were yellow and what little hair he did have was white. He was shorter than me, and had to be at least sixty-five, maybe more.

"Hi." I was comforted by him. It had nothing to do with the way he looked. But there was something soothing behind his pale green eyes.

He walked over toward the couches and sat down. My face was wet. I guess I was still crying. I sat down on the floor and put my head in my hands.

"I took you out of that crazy city . . ."

I looked up, stunned at what he had just said.

He moved his eyes around the room as he talked. "Those dreams, those wild dreams of yours, you're safe now."

"What? How do you know . . . ?"

"I know everything," he said, laughing. "I'm Sam."

I was terrified and comforted at the same time. He got up from the couch, scratching his ass, and began to walk away. He was wearing hospital garb, too. Oversize pants and a loose top that tied in the back. I could hear him mumbling as he went back to his seat and continued eating what was on his plate.

Maggie, the nurse from earlier, brought a tiny cup of water. "Here, these are for you," she said, holding out her hand with two different-shaped pills on it.

"No, I can't take those. No . . ."

"These are your meds. You have to take them if you want to get some rest and get better."

"I won't swallow them. Please, no. No more pills. No more pills,"

"These are prescribed by a doctor, Lynn. These will *help* you. They aren't like the street drugs you were swallowing in New York."

"How do you know about New York?"

"It's all in your chart, Lynn. Remember, you came to the emergency room to get help? You told the doctor about your drug problem?"

"I can't. No, I won't. Please, leave me alone," I said, as I got up and ran down the hall toward my room.

This had to be some kind of sick joke. I was in a movie or a nightmare, this couldn't be real. I was stuck somewhere between reality and hell. They said I needed to rest to get better, yet they put me in a smelly old hospital gown, stuck me in a room with a spring-less bed and overhead fluorescent lights. The room was too bright. Why did it all have to be so bright? Nothing made sense. *I have to leave. I have to leave. I have to leave.* I turned around and walked slowly down the hall. The mantra repeated over and over inside my swollen brain.

People were watching TV and playing cards. We had all been thrown in here together. Strangers, each in their own fucked-up world. I looked through the glass into the nurses' station. I saw Maggie typing away at the computer. The brown-haired woman from earlier was chatting with a male nurse. I turned and looked through the double doors. There was an elevator out there. I felt like James Bond planning his mission. If I could just make it through the doors, jump into the elevator, go down to the lobby, run out-side, I could get home to my mom. I didn't care, what did I have to lose? *And she's off.*

I rushed to the first door as if I had just hit one into left field. I pushed it open, got to the next one, and pushed my way through again. I was out. I pressed the down button. I didn't think to keep running. Not really Bond-like. I thought waiting for the elevator was the best plan. Just then, two male security guards came from around the corner. Each one grabbed me by an arm and carried me back inside. I guess I caused a lot of excitement because all the other patients were crowded around me.

"Fuck you! Stop it, stop it . . . let me go," I screamed.

Maggie rushed over and began ordering the guards to move down to the other hall. I had never been back there. I was kicking my feet, which weren't touching the floor. I wanted to explode, break free, run, and never stop. I could hear my screams echoing off the bare walls. The guards held on tight as Maggie asserted that I was a danger to myself and others, and that I would have to spend the night in this cold, dark room.

"You are the only fucking danger." I stared into the gold angel pin on the pocket of her uniform. "You are no angel."

"I've been called a lot worse, honey."

The sound of the door shutting and locking vibrated inside my head. I was a caged animal. I began pounding on the door.

"Let me out. . . . Please, let me out . . . help me . . . help me . . ." I screamed and pounded until my hands and throat were raw. No one was coming back for me. Only silence. I fell to the ground like a wounded animal. I looked around the darkened room. It was empty. No window, no way out. There was a small bed that was a few inches off the ground, I guess to prevent me from plunging to my death. There were no sheets or blankets, just an old dingy mattress. I was delirious. I collapsed on the bed. I knew I was dead, a ghost, but where was my body? Maybe I was on another floor, in intensive care or something, on a respirator, and I was stuck in this box until my body decided to expire.

God, please help me.

The Marlboro Man

"Time to get up. It's seven-thirty. Lynn, let's get ready for the day." The sharp voice cut through my daze.

I opened my eyes. The room was light. *Did I sleep? Where am I?* I sprang to my feet, feeling the blood rush to my head. Even though I hadn't eaten in days my body weighed a thousand pounds. I stared at the woman and man standing in front of me. I guess they were nurses, my handlers. The woman was familiar, she had brown hair. CINDY was written on her badge. Yes, she was the first person I remember seeing in this place. I had no recollection of the man, but his beady little eyes made my stomach drop.

"It's time to get in the shower, come with us."

I did what I was told and followed them out the door and down the hall. The noise outside that cell was overwhelming. After having been in a vacuum, it felt like I had just turned the volume the wrong way on my headphones and my eardrums were about to explode. The rooms that I walked by were all empty. The smell of rotten farts filled my nostrils. Someone either shat on the floor or they were serving eggs for breakfast. Neither thought was comforting. Cindy opened the door and I saw a large room filled with four shower stalls. There were no doors or curtains. I went in after her. The strange man stood behind me. I heard him close the door. I began to panic.

"You have to shower."

"I don't want to get in there. There's no curtain."

"Lynn, there is no curtain so you won't hang yourself with it. You are in a psychiatric ward, not a hotel."

Two sets of eyes were burning right through me. This nightmare was getting worse. I was cornered in a bathroom with two uniformed strangers who wanted me to strip down and shower like this was a normal activity. "I will not get in there . . . with the both of you here . . . please, no, I can't do this." I started to cry. The salty tears burned as I looked at my wrist. A plastic bracelet with my name, Smith, Lynn M., written on it. Above it were a set of numbers, 00616764. I was tagged like a cow ready for slaughter.

"If you don't get in, I will tell him to take your clothes off and touch you," she said.

My gag reflex kicked in. "What . . . ?" I looked over at the male nurse as he stood expressionless.

"You heard me," she said. I could hear her dry tongue stick to the words.

I disappeared further into myself, trying to find a safe place, far away from this ugly green bathroom. I blacked out. I remember doing that when I drank too many cocktails. I would have no memory of the previous night's activities. Now it was fear, not Ketel One, that poisoned me. My body operated without my permission, taking my clothes off as I hid deep inside, completely unaware. I don't remember the temperature of the water. I was numb. When I found my way back into my body I looked out, expecting a captive audience, but the room was empty. Maybe that was their idea of fun. I didn't care. I was relieved. I wasn't given any soap or shampoo. I patted myself off quickly and slipped back into the blue gown and pants that were lying folded on the floor. I felt dirtier than before.

The door was slightly open. I walked through and down the hall toward the dining room. People were sitting and eating at the tables. Maggie came to greet me.

"Hi, princess. You had a rough night. Let's eat some food and try to have a better day than yesterday."

I nodded and followed her to a table. She uncovered a tray and the steam rose up, slamming me in the face.

"Yuck."

"Yuck, shmuck. You will eat today."

She pulled the chair out for me and I sat. She walked around the table, taking the seat across from me. "Listen, if you want to get better and get out of this place, you will take some bites of this breakfast," she said. "I don't think you want a needle in your arm or tubes up your nose to get fed, so let's do this."

I looked down at my plate. I've never been a big fan of eggs. I was a French toast and pancake kind of girl. Even the gourmet omelets that I had tried to eat in New York City cafés made my stomach turn. These were bright yellow scrambled eggs that were still soft and runny in places. The smell alone was enough to make me hurl. On a smaller dish sat three sausage links. The clear film coating shined under the fluorescent lights. Even on a good day, even if I was famished, I would run the other way from a meal like this.

"It's going to get cold, it won't taste too good then."

"I don't think it will taste too good hot . . ."

I saw the corners of her lips begin to turn up as if she was fighting a smile. "Well, I will sit here all day with you if I have to. I've heard some of the other nurses call you stubborn. You have no idea what stubborn is, sweetheart."

I wanted to get out of this place and if that meant eating runny eggs, I would give it the old college try. I picked up the fork and took a stab at a piece of egg. I placed it on my tongue and swallowed it without chewing. I took a swig of orange juice, the acids stung my throat. I swallowed a few more pieces without chewing. I was nauseous and my shrinking stomach was full.

"You are doing good. Now, have a bite of sausage," she said.

I felt like a five year old in front of a plate of lima beans. I picked up one of the slimy links with my hand. I bit off the top. It was a step up from the eggs. "Done. I can't eat anymore."

"I know that was hard for you, but you need your strength. That will help you. Good job, kid," she said as she got up from the table. "Morning group meeting will be right over there."

Great, I thought to myself. *First scrambled eggs, now scrambled words.* What was up with this place? And if I was able to unscramble eggs and words, would I be that much closer to cracking my own case? I made my way over to one of the chairs in the living area. I saw Sam sitting across from me. He winked. I felt connected to this little old man. I knew that he was looking out for me. A nurse I had never seen before stood in the middle of the room. Her smile was way too big for this place.

"Hi, my name is Jane for those of you who are new here," she said, glancing my way.

Like it wasn't obvious. I was the only loon still in hospital garb.

She held up a piece of paper in her right hand. "Today we are going to talk about daily affirmations. Does anybody know what an affirmation is?" Nobody raised a hand.

I wanted to scream at the top of my lungs, "I will get the fuck out of this place! I will get the fuck out of this place!" I knew that was an affirmation, but I decided to keep quiet.

"An affirmation is something we can tell ourselves each and every day to make us feel better about life and who we are as human beings."

I looked around the room. One woman in the corner was catatonic, staring through the walls. Helen was biting her nails and tapping her foot on the ground as if she was listening to a good tune. A man with coke-bottle glasses and a trucker hat was writing fast in a tiny notebook. Sam was drooling. Bryan was peeling away the tape from around his wrists.

Jane continued. "In this space and in this time, I am an essential person to the world."

I thought I was going to lose my eggs. I began to get antsy. It all seemed so unreal.

"I have ample leisure time without feeling guilty."

Who did she think she was talking to? A bunch of Wall Streeters on vacation? Leisure time . . . what?

"Just for today, I will respect my own and other's boundaries."

Boundaries? What did they know about respecting boundaries? I wanted to be with my mom at home. Jane went on and on. No one was listening.

"Just for today, I will act in a way that I would admire in someone else. Just for today, I will make decisions today that will feel good tomorrow," she said, taking a deep sigh in as if she was really proud of herself, really moved by what she had just read to us. "Okay, visiting hours are from twelve until two this afternoon. You are free until lunch."

Everyone scurried away like roaches when a light was turned on. I got up and walked behind Helen. "Hi, I'm going out for a smoke, come join me."

"NO," I said as if she just asked me to commit murder.

"Calm down, honey, I'm not forcin' ya to do anything. Just get some air."

I didn't even know we could go outside. I followed her through a room with a pool table. Where was I? My mind began to spin backward. Was I in a bar? She opened a door that led to a small cement courtyard. There was a basketball hoop with no net. She sat down at one of the round wooden tables. There was an ashtray overflowing with butts. I heard the door open. It was Sam.

"Oh, hi, Sam," Helen said, as if she was talking to a little boy.

"Hi, dollface," he said as he took the seat next to mine.

Helen laughed. "I'm going to stretch my legs," she said walking around the perimeter.

"Hi, Sam," I said.

"I can't believe you tried to leave," he said, shaking his head. "You have to start taking your medicine. Start helping yourself."

"How do you know about me?" I asked.

He started to laugh. "Ahhh . . . I know everything. I'm always watching."

"Are you my guardian angel?" I asked.

He laughed even harder. "I work up there," he said, pointing to the sky. "I have so much work to do. You should see my desk, everything is piling up." He pulled a cigarette from his shirt pocket and reached back in for the lighter. He began puffing away.

I believed and still believe he was sent for me. I stared at this little old man with yellow teeth, green eyes, and knew that he was from heaven. I was sure of it. Granted, I never imagined God, or angels, to have a Marlboro hanging out of their mouths, but this was *my* higher power we were talking about. I guess they came in all shapes and sizes.

"You shouldn't smoke. It's not good for you," I said, standing up from the table coughing.

"Don't tell me how to behave, dollface," he said as he smashed the cigarette into the ashtray.

I looked up at the clear sky. My head ached with chaos and my skin itched. I made eye contact with someone staring down from one of the windows above. I was a monkey in a zoo. I rushed back inside. Two men were playing pool. There was a radio on. I made my way around them out into the hall. I began to sob as I walked back to my room. I fell face first on the bed. I was desperate for comfort. I wanted my mom to hold me. I thought about Mason. Where was he when I needed him most? We were on two different planets. He was stuck in that dark world, but it felt even darker here. I didn't want to think about him. There was no room in my brain. I just wanted to wake from this nightmare.

Visiting Hours

A quick knock jolted me up from the bed. The slightest noise was a shock to my system.

"Lunchtime and visiting hours . . ." the voice echoed down the hallway to all of the other rooms.

More food? It couldn't be that time again.

I was thankful I would be seeing my family, though—I needed them. I made my way down the hall. The smell of hot food hung in the air. My body was exhausted. I felt like I was walking through thick pea soup. Every step took colossal effort. I turned the corner and saw my family sitting at one of the tables, even my father was there. My mother jumped up and ran over to me, holding my body so tight that my breath shortened.

"You're okay," she said, continuing to rub my back.

"No, I'm not," I said, pulling away from her. "I need to get out of here. You have to get me out of here . . . they locked me in a room . . . they made me eat runny eggs . . . they're trying to force me to swallow pills . . ."

"Calm down," she said, looking around the room. I guess I was screaming. I didn't care. "Lynn, come over and sit with us while you eat."

"I'm not hungry. I can't eat this stuff."

My mom guided me to the chair. Stephanie sat next to me with her eyes fixed down at the table. Stacey was sitting across from her. She smiled.

"Hey, how are you feeling?" Her eyes darted over me. I could tell by the expression on her face that I must have looked scary. My dirty hair was matted to my head and I couldn't remember the last time I had brushed my teeth.

"Not good," I said, looking down at my plate. A large square of crusty lasagna stared back at me. I could hear it laughing. I pushed the tray away. My father sat at the far end of the table. He wouldn't look at me. The smell of beer was leaking from his pores. He began shifting in his chair, looking around the room. My mom sat on the other end, next to me.

"Maggie told me about last night. You tried to leave. Why would you do that?"

"Because this place is killing me. Look at what I am wearing. They won't let me have my clothes . . ." I wanted to tell her about the nurse this morning in the bathroom, but I didn't think anyone would believe me. I didn't have much credibility at this point.

"Listen to me," she said, holding my hand. "If you want to get better and get out of here, you have to start doing what they tell you. I know it's hard, Lynn, but the longer you fight this, the longer you will be in here."

I laid my head down on the table and began sobbing. I felt a hand on my back.

"Hey, dollface . . . what's wrong?"

I looked up to see Sam standing by my side.

"She's a good girl," he said to them as he put his hand on top of my head.

I could see the discomfort on my mother's face. Everyone was silent. My mom spoke up.

"She is . . . you're right," my mom said, looking at me.

He walked away into the living area, and I watched him turn the television on, sitting down on the couch. He was the only one here without visitors.

"That's Sam. He is watching over me. He told me that he knows everything about me. I think he is Jesus or my guardian angel. I'm not sure, but I know that he's from heaven." I looked around the table. No one knew what to say. Stephanie glanced at Stacey. Stacey looked at my mom, and my dad was staring over his shoulder at the television.

"You need to start taking your medication, Lynn. It will help clear all of these thoughts. You need to rest . . . that's what those pills are for."

Maggie approached my chair with the official cup of water. What timing. "Here you are, princess. Let's do this. Your family is here. We don't want to spend another night in that room, do we?" she said, signaling toward the jail cell.

Everything in here was "let's" and "we." I didn't see the nurses swallowing these pills with me, I didn't see Maggie lying next to me in solitary confinement last night. *So let's cut the "we" bullshit.*

"Please, I can't swallow those pills." I could sense my mom tensing up.

"Lynn, these aren't bad pills. This isn't ecstasy. Look at me," my mom said, lifting up my chin. "These will help you get better."

I wanted to believe her, but my fear wouldn't let me. I kept hearing my inner voice tell me, " No . . . no more, Lynn. These aren't good. Don't trust them, they're trying to trick you."

Maggie stared at me. She was tough, but she didn't scare me. I stood up and darted into the small conference room. It felt like I had been in this place for years already. I sat down on a chair against the wall. The door opened and my mom and Maggie entered. Maggie was frustrated. My mom's eyes were red and swollen.

"Listen, I never do this, but I am going to give your mother your medicine. You can sit in here with her, but you have to take them. This is your last chance, Lynn. I mean it," she said as she handed two pills to my mother. "I'll be back to check on you."

The door closed and my mom took a seat next to me. She held out the pills and dropped them into my palm. Touching them made me want to scream.

"Lynn . . . I am your mother. I love you. I want you to get better. I don't want you to be tormented."

I stared into her brown eyes, I wanted to do this for her. I looked at the pills again. Shivers went up and down my spine. "Mom, don't make me do this. Please, I am scared. What if these don't help me? What if they make me worse . . . ?"

She took my left hand in hers. "Have I ever lied to you? Have I? Lynn, listen to me." Tears began to cover her blotchy face. "I love you more than anything in this world . . . you know that. I would never try to hurt you . . ."

Her words slowed my racing heart. I loved her and didn't want her to be in pain, but I felt like she was asking me to swallow poison.

The door swung open. It was Sam. He walked over and stood in the center of the room.

"Please, not now, Sam," pleaded my mother.

He had a blue book in his hand. When he held it up I saw that it was the Bible.

"Obey your father and mother," he said, staring directly into my eyes. He then gracefully put his arms down and left the room. Just like that.

A complete calm washed over me and I was no longer afraid. I placed the pills on my tongue and down they went. I couldn't go against a divine ordinance. My mother sat in her chair, speechless. I think she was starting to believe that my smelly old friend with yellow teeth could be from heaven.

Maggie entered the room. "So?"

"She took them . . . she swallowed the pills . . ." I could sense the relief in my mother's voice.

"Good girl, I knew you could do it," she said, waving us out of the room. "Now you need to eat some food."

My mom led the way back to the table. I sat down.

"Lynn took her medicine," she announced as if I had just won an Olympic Gold.

Stacey smiled. Stephanie let out a small "good," and my father remained jittery and silent.

The pills hadn't kicked in yet, but somehow I knew that I had fucked up, that I was a sick girl. Sitting in the center of this silent family circle, I knew that I wasn't the only one with problems. I stared at my father, the elephant at the end of the table that everyone ignored.

"Dad, you're an alcoholic." The words bolted straight out of my mouth.

For a split second there was dead silence, like two cars had just collided, crashed, and burst into flames.

Stacey and Stephanie simultaneously shot up out of their chairs and walked straight out of the ward. Five was now three. I stayed in the center chair with my mother and father at each end.

"Lynn," my mom touched my hand. "I don't think . . ."

"Mom, I'm talking to Dad . . . please," I said, moving my hand away.

"I . . . I . . . don't know what you're talking about," stuttered my father.

"Dad, you drink so much, I can smell the beer on your breath from over here . . . I don't want to live like this anymore," my voice began to break. "I want us to be a family, but it can't be like this, you and Mom don't spend time together . . . she sleeps in the basement . . . none of us ever talk about this." It was a full-blown cry now.

"Lynn . . . you need to think about getting better . . ." my mom said, moving her chair closer to mine. "Don't worry about us. . . ."

"What do you mean? It's not like it's just between the two of you. We are all in this, all of us, and if I am going to get better, this is a part of it . . . I need my family . . . I want a real family . . ."

"You need to get some rest," my father said.

Everything was pouring out of me. Twenty-two years of pent-up sadness, confusion, and frustration. I wanted the truth to be told. There was nothing left. I had nothing. Sitting here in this psychiatric ward with my parents, I let down my guard. There was nothing for me to hide anymore. "Please . . . look at us . . . look at this," I said, looking back and forth at each of them. "I am coming clean with my life . . . I know it's not gonna be easy, but we all have to do this . . . together. Dad, you need help."

On that note, he got up from his chair and left. And then there were two. Tears streamed down my mom's face.

"I'm sorry, Mom . . . I'm so sorry. I just can't live a lie anymore. My whole life has been a lie . . . I can't do it anymore. I am sick of hiding. I can't run anymore. I've been running since I left Danville and look where I'm at . . . right back here. Face-to-face with what I was running from . . ."

"I love you . . . don't be sorry . . . you're right. Everything you said is the truth. I am proud of you . . ."

"Visiting hours are now over," the voice echoed over the intercom.

"I don't want you to worry about all of this right now. You need to eat, sleep, take your medicine, and concentrate on getting better. You are going to be okay," she said, hugging me. "We are all going to be fine . . . I promise you that. I love you."

I watched all the other families filter through the door. I didn't want my mom to leave. I wanted her to make me tea and lay next to me on my bed until I fell asleep. I was a baby again, vulnerable and defenseless. I walked with her to the door. I felt the nurses' eyes all over me. I'm sure they were all thinking I was going to pull a James Bond move and try to escape again. I hugged my mom one last time and stared through the glass until she got on the elevator. She blew me a kiss.

I shuffled back to my room and sat on my bed. The medicine was starting to take hold. My eyelids were being pulled down by an invisible force. My head was a lump of lead and my thoughts were turning into mush. I put my head on the pillow, feeling like I was immersed in warm liquid. Every muscle released. I stared at the white ceiling until it was black. All black.

Believing in Tyler Durden

I woke up to Helen shaking me. "Lynn, time to get up . . . Lynn, it's breakfast time . . ."

I opened my eyes. I must have been in a coma. How long had I been asleep?

"Come on, sweetie, get up and get ready. I'll save you a seat next to me."

"Okay," my voice cracked. My throat was the Sahara.

I heard the door shut. It took all my energy to sit up in bed. The morning sun blanketed the room and I looked around as if I was just seeing it for the first time. There was a duffel bag lying on the floor next to the bed. I picked it up and sat it next to me. I opened it and a small white bear with a pink ribbon tied around its neck greeted me. I pulled it out and unfolded the piece of paper that came with it. *We all love you. Everyone is praying for you to get better and come home to us. Love, Mom, Dad, Stacey and Steph.*

It was all becoming clearer now. This wasn't a nightmare, this was my life. Reality was creeping in. I emptied out the bag. A pair of Stacey's gray, cozy drawstring pants, a couple of Stephanie's T-shirts, a package of Hanes Her Way underwear, a roll of quarters, socks, flip-flops, a towel, toothbrush, toothpaste, deodorant, comb, shower gel, and a journal. I had just won the lottery. I guess this was my prize for taking my meds yesterday. I suddenly had a surge of energy and rose off the bed, taking some of my prizes into the bathroom. I tore my hospital gown and pants off. I turned the shower on and stood under the warm water. I was present inside my body again, it was surreal. I lathered myself with the lavender-scented shower gel. It reminded me of flowers, spring, trees, and the outside world. I began to cry. I was paralyzed with a sense of joy, sadness, anxiety, relief, and love all in the same moment. All of my mixed emotions blended together until I couldn't separate one from the other.

I stepped out of the shower and wrapped myself in my very own towel. I opened my new underwear. There were three pair, yellow, pink, and white. I chose the yellow ones. I pulled them on under the towel. They were loose. I'd lost even more weight since I'd been in the hospital. My muscle tone was gone. I was skinny and soft. There was no bra in the bag, so I slid into the red T-shirt without one. I towel-dried my hair and climbed into the soft pants. I was a new woman. Having these things from home granted me a sense of peace. I went into the bathroom and brushed my teeth, I never re-membered brushing feeling this good. Ahh, the little things. I looked into the mirror, it was the first time I'd seen myself in days. Fuck . . . I looked rough. Pale face, glazed-over eyes, dark circles, and my chin was still covered with tiny red bumps. Zits. I needed new highlights, my roots were showing. I doubted they had a salon in this place, but a makeover would certainly help the recovery process. I put my feet into the blue flip-flops; they were too big. I had the smallest shoe size in my family and I was a nine. Sasquatch women, all of us.

I walked down the hallway. I felt clearer. I sat down next to Helen and Maggie approached the table.

"Well, hello, Sleeping Beauty . . . how do you feel?"

"Like I've been hit by a train, but it's an improvement."

"That's to be expected. Last night was probably the first good night's sleep you've had in months. I see you have your clothes on . . . I told you things get easier when you cooperate," she said, setting a tray in front of me.

Pancakes . . . things were looking up. *Thank God,* I said to myself as Maggie walked away. I gobbled them up in minutes. I washed them down with apple juice. Helen stared at me.

"Well, I guess you are feelin' better . . . do you want this one? I can't eat too many of these . . ?" she said. "I'm too nervous to eat."

"No thanks. My stomach is bursting at the seams already." It was so strange to be full. "Why are you nervous?" I asked.

"Today I start electric shock therapy again . . . giving it another try. I miss my girls . . . I miss my husband. I can't do this to them anymore. I just want to be fixed . . . living like this is no life," she said, getting up and walking away from the table.

It hit me in that moment. I wasn't at summer camp. This was no vacation. As good as it felt to have comfy clothes on and pancakes in my belly, I had to face the fact that I was in a psychiatric ward, surrounded by sick, depressed, and wounded souls. I looked around. There were people playing with their food, staring off into space, talking to themselves. Sadness everywhere. All of us had different stories, different sicknesses, but we were all put here together. A common thread united us. As much as I wanted to believe that I didn't belong here, I knew that I did. It was probably the first time that I truly fit in with any group. This brutal realization made my undigested pancakes sneak back up my throat. My moods were all over the place. I went from serenity to dread within minutes. I got up from the table.

"Not so fast, sweetheart, you need to come over to the nurses' station and take your morning meds . . ." said Maggie.

She was growing on me. Tough love, but I knew she cared. "What am I taking? Could you tell me what these pills do?"

"Let me double-check your chart before I tell you for sure."

I followed her over to the nurses' station. On the outside of the door was a white wipe-off board with patients' names written in different colors. Next to each name was the word "goal" and then a sentence stating what each one was. I found my name. *00616764 Smith, Lynn—Goal 1) Patient will verbalize in a normal rate and flow of speech, thinking processes that are reality based and goal directed.* Wow, some goal. It wasn't exactly a role opposite Johnny Depp, but I wasn't exactly in leading lady condition. So now I had to focus on slower speech and reality-based thinking. I was up for the challenge. Maggie came out and saw me reading the board.

"That changes on a daily basis . . . since you're already showing improvement, yours will change today. You came in as a level D. That's the lowest level. No clothes, no phone calls, no privileges. Since you are better today you are a C. That's why you are wearing those clothes. You can also use the pay phones over there against the wall. Now let me tell you what your meds are," she said, handing me two pills. The darker one is called Resperidol. It is an antipsychotic . . ."

Those words stung me. "Antipsychotic . . . so that means I'm psychotic, great . . . wonderful . . ."

"Listen, Lynn, I know this must be scary for you to hear, but the way you came in here . . . you were completely psychotic. All of those drugs you were taking in the city did some damage to your brain. These medications are going to help you . . . bring you back down to planet Earth. Now the white pill is called Clonapin, it's an antianxiety medication that will relax you and help you get some rest. You will take both of these twice a day unless Dr. P. changes something."

I tried to take in all of this information. It was overwhelming for me to think that I needed to take more pills in order to get better. "Will I have to take these forever?"

"Let's take it one day at a time, okay? Now swallow those," she said, handing me the Dixie cup.

I washed them down.

"Good, lift up your tongue," she said.

"Ahhhh . . ." I wagged it all around. "Do you have to do a cavity search also?"

"You're a funny one," she said, walking away.

Here I was on a psychiatric ward, a level C, name tag on my

wrist, taking more pills, unable to go anywhere. No boyfriend, no friends, no apartment, nothing. I walked over to the couch and sat down. I was heavy with thought. I couldn't believe this was my life. A man in a ripped flannel shirt, jeans, and a baseball cap covering his face was snoring on the couch across from me. It became the background music for my scattered thoughts. I looked over at the pay phones. I hadn't noticed them before and remembered the quarters in my room.

I retrieved the roll of coins and headed toward the phone. One of them was ringing. No one was around, so I picked it up.

"Hello?"

"Yes, could I speak to Charlie?" the man's voice asked.

"Umm . . . I don't know a Charlie . . . maybe he's outside or in his room, I'm not sure . . ."

"Well, I guess I'll try back later . . . thank you."

"'Bye," I said, hanging up the phone.

"Who was that for?"

I turned around. It was the man from the couch. "It was for someone named Charlie . . ." The look in his eyes told me that he wanted to strangle me.

"I AM CHARLIE . . . you should always look for the person or take a message. The rules are written right there by the phone . . . you really fucked up. . . . fuck, fuck, fuck."

"I'm sorry. I didn't know. I am new here and I didn't see the rules . . ."

"Did they leave a name?"

"No."

"Great . . . great . . . great," he said, stomping his boots on the floor.

"Listen, I have quarters if you want to try to call the person back . . ."

"I don't want your money," he said, running away down the hall.

Oh my God. This wasn't good. My heart was racing and my

palms were wet. What if he tried to suffocate me in my sleep or something? I took some deep breaths, placed a few quarters in the slot, and dialed the number.

It was ringing.

"Hello?" hearing his voice took my breath away. "Hello . . . ?"

"Mason . . ." I said.

"Lynn . . . oh my God . . . hi . . . How are you?"

"I've been better. . . . Mason—"

"I've called your house so many times. Your mother picked up once and told me you were in the hospital. She sounded pissed at me . . . I don't blame her. How are you?"

"Tired . . . they've been pushing pills down my throat. My body aches. I had to be in solitary confinement my first night because I tried to escape. Everyone here is sad, sick, and crazy . . . like me."

"Babe, you're not crazy . . ."

"I'm in a fucking psychiatric ward, Mason, I'm wearing a fucking wristband with my name on it, and I'm taking antipsychotics . . . so you do the math."

"I'm so sorry." He was crying. "I feel like this is all my fault, if you wouldn't have met me you wouldn't be in this mess . . . I love you and I hate myself for letting this happen . . ."

"This isn't your fault. You never forced me to do anything. What we did, we did together. This is my doing . . . this was my choice . . . and I have to live with it. I just can't believe I'm back in Danville locked in a hospital . . ."

"You are the strongest person I know. You'll get through this . . . we'll get through this, I promise you . . ."

"Will we? You're in New York City, and I'm in Pennsylvania. I don't know what's gonna happen once I get out of here, if I ever get out of here . . ."

"You will, don't talk like that. I love you . . . you know that, right?"

"I do, but I have to tell you this, Mason . . . I love you, I know that . . . you are my best friend. You are all that I have, but . . . I can't live like we were living. I can't go back to that life . . . the drugs . . . the clubs . . . no more . . ."

"Please deposit another fifty cents for the next three minutes . . ." the voice interrupted.

"Fuck." I shoved two more quarters in. "Sorry . . . I just want you to know, as much as I love you, as much as I want to spend the rest of my life with you . . ." speaking those words made my heart sink and my eyes well up. "You have to choose . . . it's either me or the pills, me or that world. I don't want to die or go insane . . . again. I want a fucking life, a real life . . . a job, a house, babies, something more than this shit. I know it's going to be hard, but I am going to fight and if that means losing you, then I guess—"

"Stop . . . I love you . . . and I'm going to fight alongside of you. For both of us. I want a better life, too, I know that . . . I want you in my life. I choose you. I will always choose you. Please believe me."

We both began to sob. I loved Mason, I was sure of that. I knew that our relationship centered around drugs, but I thought that we had something real, something that transcended our dark lives. I needed to give it a chance.

"Babe, we are going to get through this, stay strong . . ."

"I wish I could see you, I need a hug."

"I wish I was there." His words wrapped around me like a warm blanket. "When you get out, I will take a bus to see you. I promise."

"I will talk to you again soon. The number that came up on your caller ID is the pay phone here. You can call me, too. Be good. I love you, Mason."

"I love you, too. 'Bye, Lynn."

"'Bye . . ." I held the phone close. "I don't want to hang up."

"Neither do I, but we have to . . . 'Bye. I love you."

"'Bye."

I sat in the chair, thinking about Mason. *Do I have any idea what loving someone truly means? Have I ever loved myself? What's going to*

happen to us? How are we going to make this work? What's going to hap-
pen to me? I didn't want to think about him in that city. I didn't
want to think about any of it. There were an endless amount of
questions and I didn't have an answer to any of them. The only
thing that I was sure of was that I was at the bottom of a black
hole that I had dug for myself. There was nowhere else for me to
run. One of my favorite movies is *Fight Club.* Tyler Durden says to
Ed Norton's character, "Not until we lose everything do we have
complete freedom." I prayed that there was truth to that line.

Walking on Sunshine

Days went by. I followed the rules, took my meds, finished every puzzle and word scramble they threw my way. I became an expert at explaining how a certain color represented me as a person. "I am blue, I am sad and introspective . . . I am red, I am angry and frustrated with life." I chatted with other patients, cracked jokes with the nurses, and did my daily chores—whether it was cleaning the kitchen or being the "tail wagger," which meant I had to wake everyone at 7:30 in the morning. It all seemed so juvenile, but I played the game. Some might even say that I was moving to the head of the class. I was no longer a level C. I was officially crowned a level B. Maggie told me after lunch one day, "You are now a B, kiddo. You can go for a walk outside today, if you want."

"Are you kidding?"

"No. Everyone is impressed by your rapid improvement," she said, handing me a square piece of paper that read "B—hospital pass."

I felt like I was in high school again and this was my hall pass. Who was I going to have to show this to anyway? The guy mowing the lawn outside? Pedestrians? I could just picture it. "Hi, my name is Lynn, don't worry, I can be out here, I'm a B," I would say, flashing my official slip of paper. Whatever worked.

"Thanks, Maggie. When can I go?"

"Now, if you want. Take a half hour. You can't leave the hospital grounds and you must always sign in and out."

"Great. I guess I'm ready then . . ." I walked over to the nurses' station and signed the sheet with my name and the time.

"Be careful and have a nice time. Remember, only half an hour."

"Okay, Mommy," I said, pushing through the doors.

I couldn't believe this was happening. I was going to make it to the elevators without being snatched up by guards. I pushed the down arrow. It felt weird being free. A nervous energy made my stomach twitch. As much as I wanted to get out of this place and go home, there was a sense of safety that came with being locked on that floor. Nothing or no one could get me. There were no bills or jobs. My schedule was planned, my meals were placed in front of me, and I didn't have to think about the day ahead.

I entered the elevator and my heart started beating faster and my underarms began to sweat. When I exited I was stunned. People walking, talking, and going about their routine. For a moment I was one of them. A "normie." I walked toward a set of automatic doors. I felt dangerous, like I was doing something highly illegal. The doors slid open and the fresh spring air kissed my face. It had been over a week since I'd been outside. I glided down the stairs onto the sidewalk and began to move forward. The smell of fresh-cut grass filled my head. The sound of passing cars and the sun hitting my face were enough to turn me into a puddle. I followed the white cement around the hospital. It was my very own yellow brick road. When I got to the back of the hospital everything became quiet, like I was the only one on earth. I looked up at the trees flowing in the wind. Warm tears started to roll down my face. The sky was bending down toward me and whispering in my ear . . . *Welcome back, I've missed you.* I listened to my feet touching the ground and with each step I felt stronger, present in every moment. It was the happiest half hour of my life. Each second was precious and powerful. *I'm alive. I'm alive. I'm alive.* I continued my journey around the hospital until I was back where I started. I sat down on the step. I was filled with pride like I had just run a marathon and finished in first place. I closed my eyes and held onto the moment. I had never been here before. This was true happiness. It was authentic and it didn't come from a pill. With ecstasy, my happiness was not earned, not truthful, it was never mine, but this came from inside of me and it was all mine. I earned it and I owned it. This was only the beginning of my new journey, but this short walk gave me a glimpse into possibility. The possibility that my life could be peaceful, beautiful, and honest. This day would be the little ray of sunshine that I would pull out of my mind when I needed it. And boy, would I need it.

When I got back inside, my heart sank. What goes up must come down. I knew that by now. I rode the elevator back up to BP2, the floor that most people talked about and stayed away from. I prayed I would see the outside again very soon. After being buzzed through the double doors, I signed my name on the sheet in the nurses' station. I walked back to my room. I sat on the chair by my window and propped my feet up against the wall. Ever since my racing thoughts slowed down, so did the passing of time. Everything moved slower. The minutes crawled by as I waited for visiting hours. My mom and sisters would be coming. My father never returned after that first visit. I had exposed him. I don't know what I thought would happen as a result, I guess I wanted him to come back the next day, give me a hug, and tell me that we would be fine. But he was not willing to look at his life and I was not willing to pretend anymore.

Visiting hours went as usual. My mom and sisters put on a happy face, telling me that I looked good and was getting better. I told them I wanted to get out. I was over pill popping and word games. It wasn't therapy. I never talked to anyone in there about my drug problem, about my addiction. I had to make this my own crash course of rehab. It was all that I had. Maggie came over to us with my chart.

"Ms. Lynn, you have an appointment in Radiology tomorrow morning at eight. The doctor has ordered a neuro-spec scan to be done."

"What's that?"

"A machine that takes pictures of your brain, so we can see what is going on in there."

Fear took over. "I don't want one . . ." I said.

"Well, it's the last piece of the puzzle before you get out of here and I have a feeling you're ready to leave . . ." she said. "Listen, we can talk about this later. Enjoy the last few minutes of your visit," she said, walking away.

I looked at my mom. "I don't want to have one of those scans. Is it like an MRI? Does it hurt?"

"I'm not sure, Lynn. I'll be with you. Everything is going to be fine. Like Maggie said, the sooner you do this, the sooner you leave," she said, rubbing my back.

I hoped so. I'd been in here for almost two weeks. I was ready to go.

"Visiting hours are now over . . ." echoed the annoying voice on the intercom.

"'Bye, see you soon," Steph said, giving me a quick hug. She was like my father when it came to showing affection. She could only handle a few seconds of human contact.

"I love you," Stacey said. "Maybe tomorrow I'll bring my makeup and give you a makeover."

"Why? I really like this crazed, tired, lunatic look. It's so new millennium."

I watched them leave. Staring out from behind the glass, I waved one last time before heading back to my room.

"Hello?"

"Come in," I said.

Maggie entered. She was a large woman, but carried herself with such grace. Hard to believe those compassionate blue eyes once scared me. She sat down on the other bed and crossed her feet at the ankles. "Do you want to talk about tomorrow?"

"Yeah. I just want to know what that scan is all about. What will happen?"

"First you will be injected with a blue dye. It's painless. It enables the cameras to take pictures of what's inside you. In your case, your brain. Then you lie flat and your head goes inside the machine. Cameras circle you and take several pictures. The whole thing takes about a half hour."

"My whole body isn't closed in?"

"No, just from your shoulders up. You are gonna be fine."

"I don't know why this is scaring me so much. I feel like I've already been through hell . . . I just don't know," I said, laying my head down on the bed.

"Lynn, this is scary. It's unsettling not to feel like you have control over any of it. You have been through a lot, but this isn't the end. You are going to have other obstacles on the way. We all do," she said.

Maggie was the humanity of this place. She wasn't a medical robot that spit out orders. I felt she truly cared about me. "You're so strong and confident in yourself. I want to be like that," I said to her. "I am so unsure of what is going to happen to me after I leave here."

"We all are. It's taken me years of practice to get to this point. You're stronger than you think, believe me. I don't talk to many people about this, but I want to tell you something."

I sat up in my bed, putting my journal to the side. "What is it?"

"I was recently diagnosed with breast cancer . . ."

"I'm so sorry."

"Don't be sorry. I'm not telling you this for pity. I'm telling you this because life is uncertain. You never know what's around the next bend. Just because you're in here doesn't mean everyone out there," she pointed to the window, "has it together. I don't know what's going to happen to me, none of us do. All we can do is live our lives the best way we know how. You are going to have a lot of guilt and shame once you're out of here. Don't dwell on it. Do something with it. We all make mistakes, but it's our job to learn from them. You're a smart kid. You'll figure this mess out." She stood up from the bed, gave me a wink, and began to walk toward the door. "Try to get a good night's sleep. My shift is over. I'll see you in the morning, kiddo."

"Maggie?"

"What?"

"Thanks for everything. You've helped me more than you know."

I listened to her footsteps walking down the hall, until they disappeared. She was an amazing woman. I laid down on my bed, bringing my knees to my chest. I thought about the brain scan. The wheels were turning. *What kind of damage have I done? What if it's really bad? What if there's permanent damage? What if I have to be medicated for the rest of my life?* I felt like someone who had lots of unprotected sex and tomorrow was the HIV test. There was no turning back now.

Gram Witmer

There was an IV in my right arm, pumping dye into my body. I laid on the freezing table with my mom holding my hand. Hospitals were too cold and too bright. For a place we're supposed to go when we're sick and need warmth, it didn't make any sense to me. I watched the liquid in the bag sink until there was nothing left. A bleached blonde nurse named Sherry came over and took the needle out. She was gentle.

"Okay, sweetheart. Now we are going to move over there," she said, pointing to the large machine in the corner.

I sat up and my mom helped me down to the floor.

"You're doing good. It's almost over," she said with her arm around me as we walked.

There was a long table. Around it was a circular mechanism with square objects hanging from it.

"Lie down here with your head at that end," she said, pointing toward the machine.

I followed her instructions. The table wasn't very wide. What did they do with overweight people? Maybe this was made specifically for skinny drug addicts.

"Now I'm going to push a button to move the table toward the cameras."

The sound reminded me of a video game. The table stopped when my shoulders were in and my head was completely surrounded. I felt like I was about to do a quantum leap into a different time period. I wished that were possible. Then maybe I could go back and make a few changes. Then maybe I wouldn't be stuck inside this fucking machine. *Stop, pull it together.* It was pointless to be thinking like that.

"Are you okay, Lynn?" the voice echoed outside.

"Yes," my response bounced around the tiny space.

"Now when I start the machine, cameras are going to move all around your head. They will stop in certain places to take pictures and then keep moving. You have to lie completely still and try not to move your head. It will take about a half hour," she said. "Are you ready?"

"Yes," I said, trying hard to mean it. I could do this. I had to.

I heard her hit a button and the machine above me started moving. It sounded like tiny robots were all around me. They stopped and then I heard clicking sounds. I guess it was taking my picture. This gave a whole new meaning to the word "headshot." I always dreamed of being a star. Being interviewed by *Entertainment Tonight*, and having my picture taken by paparazzi. I never thought it would be like this.

Each second was an hour. Lying still was a lot harder than it sounded. I've always been a high-octane individual. I rarely stayed in one place for long. My foot began to itch. It felt like there was a tiny bug moving around inside my shoe. I wanted to scream. After that, it all went south. Everything itched, from my hair down to my toes. I was stuck inside this heap of plastic with cameras circling me. I was abducted by aliens. The space seemed to be shrinking. I wanted to bang my feet against the table and say, "Get me the fuck out of this thing!" I didn't. Instead I closed my eyes and tried to let the constant noise serenade me. I took a few deep breaths. Tears snuck out from behind my closed eyes and moved down the side of my face. I disappeared inside of myself until there was quiet. I heard a familiar voice.

"Oh, hon . . . I love you . . . you're safe . . . I'm right here," she said. And then I heard singing. "Dutsie, dutsie, dustsie, doo, dutsie, dutsie, doo, doo . . ."

It was my great-grandmother. My Gram Witmer, my mother's grandma. I could place that voice anywhere. I was only seven when she died, but she used to baby-sit me and my sisters. She would cross her legs and I would sit on her foot. She bounced me up and down while she sang that song. I adored her. The song continued playing in my head. It soothed me.

"Lynn . . . Lynn," she said, squeezing my hand.

I opened my eyes and saw my mother standing over me. "What? Oh, I didn't know it was over . . ."

"Did you fall asleep in there?" she asked.

"No . . . maybe . . . I don't know," I said sitting up. "Gram Witmer sang to me . . ."

My mothers eyes stared into mine. She always talked about how much she loved her grandmother. She was closer to her than she was to her own mother. "I prayed to Gram this morning . . . I pray to her every morning, but today I asked her to be with you," she said as a single tear danced down her face.

We hugged each other. First Sam, now my Gram . . . my faith in a higher power was strengthening by the minute.

"We won't have the results for a week or two. I'm sure your doctor will set up an appointment with you when it's ready. Take care of yourself," said Sherry.

"Thanks a lot," I said, getting off the table.

My mom and I walked out of Radiology and made our way back to BP2.

"Look at that smile. Who told you?" Maggie asked as we entered the ward.

"Told me what? What are you talking about?"

"Oh, I thought someone told you that you were going home . . ."

"What? Shut up . . . no way. Are you serious?"

"You've been in here two weeks . . . have I joked with you once?"

I ran over to her and gave her a hug. "Thank you. Thank you so much," I screeched.

You would have thought that I had just won an Oscar. This was better. I was sure of it.

"She can be discharged first thing in the morning. You can pick her up anytime. Boy, are we going to miss her in here," Maggie said as she walked back into the nurses' station.

I looked in and saw Cindy. I flashed back to that morning in the shower. She avoided making eye contact with me. I wondered how she treated the other patients. I was beginning to understand karma and I was sure she was going to get hers.

"Well, I have to get back to work. I'll see you again tonight at visiting hours," said my mom. "And then tomorrow you'll be home."

"Thank God," I said, walking her to the door.

I waved as she made her exit.

I turned around and saw Sam sitting on the couch with a bag next to him. I walked over and sat down next to him.

"Where do you think you're going," I asked.

"I thought I was going home today, but it looks like it'll be tomorrow," he said.

"That's when I'm leaving. I'm going home tomorrow, too . . ." I said, putting my hand up to give him a high-five.

His little hand met mine. "Oh, dollface . . . we came in the same day and we leave the same day . . . I should have known," he said, slapping his head. "My job here is done."

"Oh, really? And what job is that?" I asked.

"Ahhhhhh . . . come on. You were my job," he said, getting up from the couch, carrying his bag with one hand and waving the other in the air. "You're a slow learner . . . a slow learner."

I watched him shuffle down the hall. What a man. I wasn't going to leave here and tell everyone on the street that my guardian angel was in the psych ward with me. That might send me right back in. It was just for me.

I walked back to my room. The thought of leaving made each step lighter. Tomorrow I was going home . . . home . . . home. I sat down on my bed. I didn't mind the hardness of it anymore. I kicked off my flip-flops. One more night. Then what? I hadn't lived in that house since high school. How was this going to work? What about my father? I knew there would be no family hug waiting for me when I walked in the front door. What would be waiting? I would soon find out.

The Homecoming

I didn't sleep at all that last night on the ward. When it was finally time to get up I showered, dressed, and packed my duffel bag. This long sleepover was coming to an end. I walked down the hallway one last time. Maggie headed toward me with a young girl in a hospital gown. The girl looked at me and I smiled. She didn't smile back. I knew she was scared. I heard Maggie explaining some of the rules. "No razors . . . no male patients allowed in your room . . . you can have your personal items when you show improvement . . ." her voice trailed off as I entered the dining room. I filled a cup with cold water and sat down at one of the tables.

Smiley Jane came over to me with a folder and sat down.

"So we're leaving today," she said as if I were two years old.

"Yeah, I guess we are leaving today."

"You need to sign a few papers first. Basically you are signing yourself out," she said, sliding two forms my way.

I pretended I was reading down each one. They could have said, "I hereby declare that I, Lynn Smith, will eat dirt for breakfast, lunch, and dinner for the rest of my days . . ." I didn't care. As long as scribbling my signature meant that I was leaving, it was all good.

"Very well. Here are the prescriptions for your medications. You can get them filled at the pharmacy downstairs," she said, putting the signed documents back into the manila folder. She got up from the chair. "Good luck, sweetie." I swear, one of her pearly whites twinkled.

"Thank you," I said as she walked away.

Good luck? I felt like I was in soccer uniform about to take the field. That was it? Simple as that. I signed my name and it was done. Game over. Wasn't there some kind of road map? No parting words to point me in the right direction? Just a couple prescriptions and a "good luck"? The ground was starting to shake. My head was sweating. I saw my mother enter the double doors. She was beaming.

"Hi there. Are you all ready to go?"

"I guess so. I just signed some papers and they gave me these prescriptions," I said, holding up the small squares of paper.

"Oh . . . they didn't talk to you about treatment or anything?"

"I take it it's all up to me now."

I stood up, picked my bag up off the floor, and walked toward my mom.

"Not so fast. Give me a hug," Maggie said, emerging from the hallway.

"Thanks for all your help, Maggie. You're the best," I said, as her soft arms wrapped around me.

"You stay strong. You're going to do great things, Lynn . . . I know it."

She walked with my mother and me toward the door.

I saw Sam barreling down the other hallway. "Hey, dollface . . . wait . . . I have something for you," he said, waving a book in the air. He was out of breath by the time he got to me. "Why do you always make me work so hard?"

"Sorry, Sam, I thought you were gone," I said.

"Not without giving you this," he said, handing me a blue Bible. "'Bye."

I leaned down and gave him a hug. I didn't realize how short he truly was until my arms were around him. "Thanks, Sam. You're the man," I said. "I'm going to miss you." I felt like Dorothy leaving Oz, saying good-bye to the Scarecrow.

"Go on and get out of here," Maggie said, smiling. "Don't be afraid to pop your head in and let me know what you're up to. I'll let you leave, don't worry."

"I definitely will," I said, praying that I would never have to walk through those doors again.

Standing in the descending elevator, I was free falling. Floating in space. There were no more locked doors, no more runny eggs, no more word puzzles, no more Sam and Maggie. No more. This was it. It was all up to me now and I wasn't sure if I was ready for that.

When my mom parked the car in the driveway, I was frozen in my seat.

"Lynn, come on, what are you waiting for?"

I entered the house, the smell of chocolate-chip cookies filled the room. I put my bag on the ground and followed the scent. There was a note written next to a plate of cookies: *Welcome home, Lynn! We've missed you. Love, Stacey and Steph. P.S. Don't think we made these from scratch.*

I bit into one. They were still warm. Nothing ever tasted so good. I walked around the living room, relishing my first taste of freedom. I knelt onto the couch, resting my arms on the back of it, and stared out the large bay window. I could hear the passing cars, but I couldn't see them through the giant oak tree.

"I have to go back to work, I'm sure Stace and Steph will be back soon. They must have just stepped out. Are you going to be okay by yourself for a little while?"

"Well, you never know . . . I might just jump right though this glass window instead of using the door," I said, laughing.

"I'm serious."

"Mom, I'll be fine. I promise."

"Okay. I'll get these prescriptions filled today. See you soon," she said, kissing me on the forehead.

I turned around and sat down on the couch. It was quiet. This was the first time I had been by myself in two weeks. No nurses to check up on me. No barred windows. I heard my mom's car backing out of the driveway. *Beep, beep.* I got up and walked down the hallway to the bedrooms and opened my father's door. The smell of stale beer. It lingered in my nose long after I closed the door. I wanted to vomit. I peeked into Stacey's room, it was as spotless as a showroom. Stephanie's, on the other hand, looked like a cyclone had hit it. Cigarette smoke hung in the air. Great, beer in one room, nicotine in the other, this should be fun. I went back into the kitchen and grabbed another cookie. I wanted to be out of the hospital, but did I want to be back here? The jury was still out.

I picked up the phone and called Mason to let him know I was finally "free." Talking took so much effort, my brain and body were hurting, so we said our "I love yous" and I promised that I would call him later.

The door swung open. Stacey and Stephanie ran inside, carrying flowers and balloons. "We didn't think you would be home this early," Stacey said.

"I just had to sign my name on a stinking sheet of paper . . . that's it. It was all very anticlimactic."

Stacey handed me the bouquet of flowers. There were pink and white roses surrounded by colorful carnations. Stephanie handed me balloons that said HAPPY GRADUATION!

"That's all we could find," snapped Stephanie.

"Calm down, killer," I said, giving her a hug. "Thanks so much, guys, thanks for the cookies, they're great."

"You need to eat that whole plate, you skinny beyotch," said Stacey.

"I will, don't fret," I said.

My morning meds were kicking in. My head and limbs were getting heavier. I put the flowers on the counter and tied the balloons to the dining room chair.

"I've got to sit down."

Stacey followed me in while Steph ran down the hallway.

"I'm going to bed, I'm tired . . ." she yelled before shutting her door.

I laid down on the love seat against the wall and Stacey took the couch against the window.

"I can't believe you're really home. Does it feel weird?"

"It's starting to sink in . . . it's definitely strange, I can say that."

"Well, it's business as usual here."

"What do you mean?"

"You know what I'm talking about. I just want to let you know nothing's changed around here, just in case you thought otherwise."

"Stacey, I'm not stupid, okay. I don't think anything . . . let's not talk about this right now. I just want to rest my head."

"Sure . . . fine . . . there's nothing to talk about anyway. Why don't you come back and lie in my bed. We can watch TV. I just washed the blankets."

I pulled the covers back and crawled in. This wasn't a bed, it was a fluffy cloud. She had a featherbed, on top of a foam bed, on top of the real bed. The down comforter felt like a warm marshmallow. I was asleep within seconds.

When I woke up, I was staring at the clock next to Stacey's bed. The red numbers told me that it was four o'clock. Had I slept through the whole day? These meds sure knocked me on my ass. Antipsychotic . . . antianxiety . . . so that was their trick. I guess when you're sedated you can't be too anxious or psychotic. I climbed out of bed. My body was still warm with sleep. I heard a lawnmower running outside. It'd been a while since I'd heard that sound. I was used to waking up to blaring sirens or homeless men arguing. I went into the kitchen, looked out the window, and there he was in his Mets hat on the riding lawnmower. The backyard was pristine. My father took such good care of it. He was obsessed with picking up every pebble and stick off the grass. Growing up, my sisters and I would have to do it as a Sunday chore. If the yard wasn't stickless, we'd hear about it all week. The breeze caressing my face was pleasant and the smell of fresh-cut grass was familiar. I heard the lawnmower stop and I walked out onto the screened-in porch as my father entered. I caught him by surprise.

"Oh, what . . . where did you come from?"

"Mom brought me home today. I fell asleep in Stacey's room . . . I just woke up . . ."

"How ya feelin'?" he asked, wiping his hand across his forehead. "I needed to mow the lawn . . . we've had a lot of rain . . . the grass was gettin' high. Are you hungry? Is your mother still at work?"

My father was good at asking questions, but he never stopped to listen for an answer. I was used to his nervous energy, but it still made me uncomfortable. Around him I always felt on edge, like I needed to be doing something or going somewhere.

"I wanted to ask you something," I said.

He began moving around, avoiding eye contact with me. I was between him and the door, I had him cornered.

"I wanted to let you know that I'm planning on going to AA, I want to start going to meetings at the church . . . and I wanted to ask you to go with me. We can do this together . . . get sober together. I know how you feel, Dad . . . I understand how scary addiction is, but we can do it together."

"Ahhh . . . I don't think so," he said, as if I had just asked him if he'd like an ice-cream cone.

He made more sounds. They weren't words, just some jumbled moans. *"Ahhh . . . ehhhhh . . . ohhhh . . ."* This was his normal language.

I think I was so stunned by his response that I didn't see him sneak past me. I stared out at the green lawn, it almost looked fake. At the end of the yard was a path to Odd Fellows Cemetery. It sat on the hill behind our house. How fitting a name for this moment. I turned around to see where he was and that's when I heard it. That sound. It stopped me in my tracks. The cracking open of a beer can. It was then followed by the sound of his shoes hitting the steps, then the side door opening and closing. He was gone.

I stood in the center of the basement, staring at the green refrigerator. It held cases of my father's beer, nothing else. Some kids were scared of monsters getting them when they slept. Growing up, I had nightmares about that refrigerator swallowing me up. My head started to spin. I wanted to run over and unplug it, kick it, roll it out onto the Astroturf and torch it. Sparks would fly into the air as I danced around it, waving my arms.

I couldn't live in this house with my father here, listening to those cracking cans and watching him get wasted. Not again. No more. There was no way I was going to survive and get sober under this roof. If I had to stay in a hotel, I would. I didn't have any money, but I would find a job. I didn't care. I ran up the stairs. *Where are my sisters? Why do I feel so fucking alone?* I heard a car pull into the garage. I looked out the kitchen door. My mom was smiling and waving at me. I just stood there.

"Wow, nice balloons," she said, looking up at the air behind me. "And what pretty flowers." She walked through the kitchen and sat down on a chair in the dining room. She looked exhausted. "So what's up?" she asked as she slid out of her shoes.

"I have to talk to you," I said, sitting down on another chair.

"What's going on? Do you feel okay?" she asked.

"It's Dad . . ."

"What did he do? Did he say anything to you?" Her face twisted up like it always did when she mentioned my father.

"I asked him to get sober with me. I told him I wanted to start going to AA meetings and asked if he would go with me. He just said no, blew me off, and then went to the fridge and cracked open a beer. A fucking can of beer! I ask him to get sober with me and he runs for a beer. I can't deal with this, Mom . . . I can't live like this anymore," I said, starting to cry. "I'd rather go back to the psychiatric ward than live here . . . it's safer there."

My mom's neck was breaking out in hives. I knew that I'd put her through hell, but I had to tell her what I was feeling. There was not a trace of sadness in her eyes. She looked at me with a clarity that I had never seen in her before.

"That's it, he's gone. I'm asking him to leave. He's got to leave," she said, standing up and walking back into the kitchen. "I'm going to change, I'll be right back."

What? Did she say what I thought she just said? What planet am I on? Am I hallucinating? I walked back to Stacey's room and let my body fall back onto the bed. It smelled like cucumber in there. I listened to the passing cars on Bloom Street, birds were chirping, and a warm breeze drifted in. Some might call this a beautiful day. Nothing was registering. Was my mom really going to do this? How? Stacey's entrance broke through my confusion.

When I filled both her and Stephanie in on the breaking news, we'd thought it would be best to head for the hills.

As we piled into Stacey's car, we saw my father walking toward the house.

"Go . . . go!" screamed Stephanie as if we'd just robbed a bank.

He was coming from the direction of East End. There was no doubt that he was good and tanked. Maybe that's a good thing. The three of us cruised around town like a few schoolgirls looking for something to do on a Friday night. We decided to stop at a sub shop on Mill Street. That was the main drag . . . and boy, was it a drag. The tiny restaurant reeked of BO. Stacey and Stephanie ordered cheese cosmos. The thought of eating anything, especially a greasy cheese sub, made my stomach turn.

We sat at a table staring at one another and laughing. We didn't know what to do with ourselves. Two weeks ago I was clubbing in New York City, then home to Danville to enter a psych ward, which I was released from a few hours earlier, then to find myself in a smelly little sub shop on Mill Street while my mother was kicking my alcoholic father out of the house. Did I get that right? Could this be true?

We all decided that enough time had passed and we should head home. We were silent as we pulled into the driveway. None of us had any idea what to expect. Stacey entered first, and we crept in behind. It was quiet.

"I'm out here," said my mother tapping, on the outside of the dining room window.

We all rushed outside to the deck. She was sitting in a chair with her leg crossed, moving her foot up and down.

"Where were you guys?" she asked.

"We got a bite to eat. Are you hungry?" asked Stacey.

"No, I'm fine. Listen I wanted to let you know something . . ."

Drum roll, please . . .

"I asked your father to move out. He agreed and he is going to look for a place tomorrow."

"Are you serious?" I asked.

"Yes. I told him it was over. It took about . . . five minutes. Let's just say he didn't put up a fight." She was so matter-of-fact about it.

"That's it . . . he's leaving?" asked Steph. "Great . . . what's next?" She got up from her chair and turned to walk away.

"Steph, wait. Wait up . . ." Stacey said, following her inside. She was such the older sister.

I sat on the porch next to my mother. I looked up at the pink sky. The clouds were moving so fast . . . and then she dropped another bomb . . .

"I called a realtor. I'm putting the house up for sale."

"House for Sale, Dad Gone..."

I walked into the church. There was a man with silver hair walking down a dark hallway and I followed him into a room. There were wooden chairs placed in a circle and people were crowded toward the front, filling their white Styrofoam cups with coffee. No one was my age. Everyone looked to be at least fifty or older, mostly men. I took a seat and played with the shiny zipper on my sweatshirt. What was I thinking? I didn't belong here. As I contemplated sneaking out the side door, a man began to speak.

"If everyone would please take a seat so we can start . . ."

A woman that smelled of Aquanet sat on one side of me and a man with a fluorescent orange hunting hat sat on the other side. There was no question that I was in Pennsylvania.

"Hi, my name is Robert and I'm an alcoholic," the man said, standing up inside the circle. He was holding a laminated sheet of paper.

"Hi, Robert," echoed the room.

Wow, these people sure get to the point. I guess we all knew why we were there.

"I want to welcome everyone to the meeting. Alcoholics Anonymous is a fellowship of men and women who share their experience, strength, and hope with each other that they may solve their common problem and help others to recover from alcoholism. The only requirement for membership is a desire to stop drinking. There are no dues or fees for AA membership. We are self-supporting through contributions. AA is not allied with any sect, denomination, political group, organization, or institution. Does not wish to engage in any controversy, neither endorses nor opposes causes. Our primary purpose is to stay sober and help other alcoholics to achieve sobriety," he said, looking up from his paper and taking his seat.

It sounded so official. Another man stood up and read something called "How It Works," barely looking down at his paper while he spoke. Then a woman read the "Twelve Traditions" and another man read through the "Twelve Steps." It was a lot to take in. I felt like an outsider in some secret club. Robert stood back up after everything was read.

"Now is there anyone here today counting days?"

I knew that it had been twenty-one days since I'd had any drugs in my system. Illegal drugs, that is. I raised my hand and sat in silence. I didn't think I was supposed to say anything.

"Hi there," said Robert. "What's your name and how many days?"

"Oh, I'm sorry . . . My name is Lynn and I've had twenty-one days without drugs . . ." I said.

"Hi, Lynn," the room chimed back at me. I wasn't prepared for the applause that followed. I smiled, looking down at my feet.

"Congratulations, Lynn. Come up here and get a coin."

Applause and money? I got up out of my seat and walked over to him. He handed me a thin silver coin. "Thank you," I said. It was about the size of a fifty-cent piece with the words "One day at a time" written on both sides. He gave me a hug before I walked back to my seat. I was shocked by how warm I felt inside. I had a genuine sense that I was supported by this group of strangers.

He went on to ask if anyone was having an anniversary. An older man with a tanned wrinkled face raised his hand. He looked like a farmer.

"Fifteen years," he said.

The room filled with applause once again. I was beginning to like this place. Fifteen years? I was amazed. I thought twenty-one days was a long time. It was for me. Would I be able to say "fifteen years" one day?

The meeting continued on with people raising their hands and sharing their lives. I didn't speak, I just listened. Everyone in the circle was addicted to alcohol, except me. I drank, but drugs were my thing. It didn't matter, though, our problems were still the same. Broken relationships, lost jobs, hospitalization, broken dreams, lost hope . . . it was the first time that I felt I wasn't alone since coming back to Pennsylvania. There were people like me in this world, struggling to make sense of their lives. When the meeting was over everyone stood up and held hands.

"God grant me the serenity to accept the things I cannot change, courage to change the things I can, and the wisdom to know the difference," the group chimed. My hands then began bobbing up and down in the air. "Keep coming back, it works if you work it, so work it, you're worth it . . ." More applause.

Before I could leave, strangers came up to me, giving me hugs. They congratulated me and told me to come back. It all felt so undeserved.

I got outside and began walking up Bloom Street. Not another person in sight. No one walked anywhere in this town. No pedestrian culture. Since I had no car I was about to change all that. The weather was incredible. More hours of daylight, warm sun, cool breeze, and the smell of green permeated my nostrils. I didn't realize how deprived I was of clean air living in the city. After a few years, I got used to the cement, cars, and fumes. That concrete jungle became home to me. This was a nice change, though. No one pushing me out of the way so they could get to the subway before me, no homeless man calling me a "cheap bitch" because the dollar I gave wasn't enough, no more taxi rides, no more streetlights, no more sushi, no more midnight movies, no more street vendors, no more. Suddenly I felt a sense of panic. Would I ever be ready to go back? The city was out of reach. It was no longer my home and neither was this town. Where did that leave me?

My life was moving fast and I didn't feel like I was the one steering it. Some other force had control of the wheel. I was glad that I went to the AA meeting, but I couldn't live in that church. How was I going to feel warmth and support living in my house when everything was in such turmoil? As I approached my drive-way I stopped and stared at the FOR SALE sign that stood in the front yard. As much as I hated this house, it was my last safety net. I pulled the coin out of my pocket. *One day at a time . . . one day at a time.*

I got inside to find my mother sitting at the kitchen table with piles of papers surrounding her.

"That looks fun," I said.

She wasn't amused. "I'm trying to figure out how I'm going to keep this house up and running until it's sold."

"Well, Dad's going to help you, right?"

"I'm not counting on your father for anything . . . he's a friggin' asshole," she said, throwing down the pen that was in her hand. The venom hung in the air.

"Mom, it's gonna to be okay . . . we can do this . . . I'll help any way I can," I said.

"I know . . . I don't mean to blow up at you. I've been staring at these bills too long," she said. In typical mom style, she turned around and asked if I was in the mood for shrimp.

That's what I loved about my mother. She could never stay mad for long.

"Shrimp sounds great . . . whatever you get is fine."

My mom smiled as she grabbed her purse, gave me a hug, and headed out the door.

I went downstairs to the basement. Stacey had set up her com-puter down there. I signed onto the Internet and began surfing. I didn't know what I was looking for, I was just looking. I went to Google and typed in the word "ecstasy." I clicked on the first thing that came up. Ecstasy.org. It was a website all about the drug. I clicked on the word "Experiences" and a page came up with the headings *Relationships, Positive Experiences, Personal Development, Creativity, and Spirituality.* There were stories and testimonials under each category. "Empathy through ecstasy" . . . "I saw the world in a new light" . . . "World peace, I have a vision, cannot be obtained through religion, but can be resolved chemically, there is a God called XTC!" I wanted to puke. I must have been the only one in the world to have a bad experience with this drug. I was the only psycho that became painfully addicted to a fucking love drug. I continued searching the web for other horror stories like my own. It seemed everything that I read was written by proponents of the drug. People loved it. I found some scientific information that called the drug dangerous and neurotoxic, but most of it was written in a language that I didn't understand. I wanted to find something, anything, written by someone my age, someone like me, who was feeling like shit, that was sick, that was damaged, that was confused, that was searching . . . I came up empty and decided to forget about it. I checked out MTV's website, I don't know why, maybe to see what the cast of *The Real World* was up to these days, or what celebrities were hanging out at the summer beach house. I saw the word "casting" written on the top of the screen. I clicked on it and was greeted by the word "Ecstasy" written on a pill in bright pink letters. I thought that I was seeing things and then I read the words below it: *"Tell us your story . . . we want to know."* Without even giving it a second thought, I clicked on the address and began writing a letter.

> *Hi, my name is Lynn Smith and I am a twenty-two-year-old female from a tiny town called Danville, which is in Pennsylvania. I don't know what made me browse the casting sight that was posted, but for whatever reason I did, and here is my all true and disturbing story.*
>
> *I had been a "recreational" user of the pill, X, E, Nikes, Mitsubishi, whatever their candy-coated name may be, I was popping them like they were candy.*

The story began when I moved to New York City 3 years ago to study acting and pursue a career in the Performing Arts. Ecstasy use for me was a sit at home with my acting friends kind of thing in the beginning, but as my friends changed and I changed, I found myself popping up to 4 or 5 pills and raging each weekend at one of the many clubs in NYC. I got sucked into the world of dancing, raving, and even bragging about how many clubs and pills I consumed each weekend (which seemed to be extended each week). My moods were uncontrollable. I went from feeling great one second to wanting to rip my own skin off the next. I was pushing away my friends, family, and pushing myself into an extremely dark and lonely place.

Three weeks ago today I found myself in my apartment completely paranoid, afraid, not trusting of my friends or my boyfriend, and scaring everyone around me. By the grace of God I called my "Guardian Angel," my mother, and told her that I needed to get out of the city. I thought that I was dead. Of course worried and concerned, she jumped in her car at five A.M. and rushed to the city to come to my rescue. By the time she arrived, I was so extremely paranoid and in and out of reality (mainly out) and not even believing that she was my mother. It was the most hellish nightmare that you could imagine and I was living it. She drove three hours to our family hospital, holding me down as I was crying, screaming, because I felt like I had already died and was in hell. My own self-made hell.

I could go on and on, but for two weeks I had to be in a psychiatric ward where I was scared, heavily medicated, and praying to God to get me out of the huge mess that I had made for myself. If I would not have had the support of my mother and sisters I would never have made it through. I've been out of the hospital a week and a half, each day is a step in the right direction . . . I think. I had a brain scan while in the hospital and haven't gotten the results yet, but will soon. I'm scared. I know that I'm damaged because of my drug abuse. My doctor is hopeful and pleased with my progress already. I guess the whole point of me writing this to you is that if I can change the mind of one person to think twice before using ecstasy or any drug, for that matter, I will feel a little more complete. You never think it can happen to you until it does. Thank you.

Lynn Smith

I didn't reread it or spell-check. I clicked SEND and it was done. My hands were shaking as I sat back in the chair. It was like I was channeling the words. Like I was a medium coming out of a trance. I was electrically charged. I didn't even remember what I had just typed or why I had sent it. It was out there now. Tortured pieces of my life flying through cyberspace. I didn't know if it would be read, but something inside of me told me that it might.

I went upstairs and put paper plates and plastic cups on the table. My mom hated cooking and washing dishes. My father had always prepared all the meals. I guess we were going to be eating out a lot now. I remember setting this table countless times before. My father would make a hearty meal, usually some kind of meat and potatoes. He would even bake an apple pie or chocolate cake to top it off. He cooked thousands of meals during my eighteen years living at home, but he didn't eat a single one with us. He prepared the meal alone in the kitchen and then disappeared when it was time to gather around the table. I never understood it.

With my father gone, the air in the house was shifting. I wasn't sure which way it was turning, but I was praying that it was going to get better. It had to. I walked into the living room and looked out the front window at the FOR SALE sign. "House for Sale, Dad Gone." It sounded like the title of a country-western song. I went out the front door and sat down on the brick steps. The air was cool and familiar. I stared up at the old oak tree. In a few months the green would turn brown again and leaves would cover the ground. Would

I still be here in the fall? Would any of us? I thought about the change that was taking place, not only in my life, but also in the lives of everyone I loved. I couldn't help but think that my going mad and coming home acted as some kind of enema for my family. A truth laxative that was flushing out all the dirt, dust, and demons. But when all was said and done, what would be left?

Hello, Operator?

Walking through the Colombia Mall, I was reminded once again why I hightailed it out of this town. Ames and Sears were the biggest stores and Arby's was the only restaurant. Let's just say this wasn't Fifth Avenue. Given that I left the city in my pajamas, I couldn't be picky. I was desperate for clothes and my mom offered to buy me a few new things. Walking through this mall was like taking a walk back in time. We passed a woman with brown permed hair. Her bangs were shellacked in the shape of a triangle. I couldn't believe people were still getting perms. Blue eye shadow and acid-washed jeans were spotted more than once . . . the eighties lived on. The only store I thought I could possibly find something in was The Limited. I held out hope. My mom and I walked in and were greeted by two smiling blondes.

"Hi there, could I help you find something?" they said in unison, like Siamese twins.

"No thanks, we're just looking," I said, moving past them.

There was no one else in the store. I started searching through the racks of shorts. The smallest size I could find was a six. In New York, a six was a plus size, women snatched up all of the zeros and double zeros. I made my way through the store, grabbed a few pairs of shorts, pants, tank tops, and made my way back to the dressing rooms. My mom was busy digging through the sale racks in front of them.

"Did you find some things?" she asked.

"I think so, I'm gonna try them on," I said, opening one of the doors.

"Good, I'll be right out here if you need me," she said.

I stood inside the dressing room. The overhead lighting was awful. I looked like I had a beard. I could just imagine the headline of the local newspaper: "DANVILLE GRADUATE, TURNED DRUG ADDICT, MOVES HOME AND GROWS A BEARD." I slipped my pants off, my legs were pale and hairy. God, did I need some work. I unclipped the black linen pants from the hanger and sat down on the small chair. In that moment someone turned the volume up in my head. The loud bass and electronic beats were pounding. The lights were flickering above me. Every muscle in my body tightened and my thoughts began to fly backward. I pictured myself in the center of a crowd, everyone was dancing, the strobe lights made it hard to see anything. Sweaty bodies were all around, pressing against me, tighter and tighter. I was having trouble breathing, melting, drowning . . . I gasped for air.

When I came to, I was sitting on the chair. I looked in the mirror, there was no color in my face. I was a ghost. The music was still playing and my heart was racing. My breathing was heavy and I felt trapped. I wanted to run out of the tiny cage in my underwear. I thought I was going crazy, again. I wanted to yell for my mom, but she couldn't see me like this. *Breathe, Lynn . . . just breathe . . .*

"What's taking so long in there?" my mom asked, knocking on the door. "Did anything fit?"

"Ahhh . . . yeah . . . I'll be right out," I said.

My voice must have sounded shaky because my mom asked, "Are you all right?"

"I'm fine, Mom . . . give me minute, I'll be right out," I said.

I put my gray pants and flip-flops back on. This was my new uniform. I grabbed the hangers from the hook and headed out the door.

"So do they all fit?" she asked, staring at what I was holding.

"Yeah . . . I like them a lot."

"Great, now you can wear something besides those old pants of Stacey's," she said, taking the hangers out of my hands.

I followed her to the register, my head still reeling.

"Mom, I'm going to wait out there for you," I said, pointing toward the door.

I didn't give her a chance to respond. I just sped through the store until I was outside.

"Thank you for shopping with us today," the voice rang behind me.

I sat down on a bench. The earth was swallowing me up.

"Hey, what's going on? Are you okay?" my mom asked as she walked toward me.

"Yeah, I'm fine, I just needed some air."

She handed me the bag as we walked outside. "Thanks, Mom . . . thanks for getting me all of this stuff . . . you didn't have to, but I'm glad that you did," I said, holding her hand.

My mother was my hero, the only stability in my life. Her house was up for sale, she just told her husband of twenty-seven years to leave, and she was the one holding us all together.

I stared out at the passing mountains and green fields. I couldn't stop thinking about my life and where I was headed. I missed Mason more than anything, but thinking about him meant thinking about the city, which meant thinking about the drugs, which meant thinking about the friends, which meant thinking about how fucked-up and broken my world truly was. It was easy looking back at the past, connecting the dots, and seeing where it all went wrong. I wished it was that easy to make sense of the here and now or my future. The morning meds took over and then it was hard to think about anything. My head fell back, my mouth hung open, and I was gone.

When we pulled into the garage, my mom shook my arm. "Wake up, sleepyhead . . . wake up. We're home," she said before slamming the car door.

My eyes shot open. These meds could sneak up on me and knock me out at any time. I guess that's why the doctor told my mom I shouldn't drive, until I get used to them. It was scary to think I could get used to being catatonic. I climbed out of the car and walked into the house.

My mom was reading a note on the counter.

"What's that?" I asked.

"Your father was here to pick up some tools and he also wants to put a fresh coat of paint on the walls in his room so you can have it."

"Great, so he's still the maintenance man around here? It's so weird, he acts like everything is normal. What planet is he from?"

"Who cares . . . let him paint if he wants to. The entire house needs to be repainted before it's sold. I'm not going to do it," she said, turning to walk downstairs. "There's another note on the counter for you." Her voice trailed down the stairway.

I picked up the yellow Post-it. *Lynn, Gini called for you. She's a producer at MTV???? 212-555-4563.What's going on? Stacey*

I almost forgot that I had written that letter a few days ago. Oh my God. I guess somebody did read my e-mail. I began pacing around the kitchen. My stomach was churning. I was excited, curious, and scared.

I went into Stacey's room and closed the door. I picked up her cordless phone and sank into her bed. I stared up at the yellow square of paper in my right hand. Why was I so nervous? I didn't know what to expect and that scared me. I pushed the talk button and took my time dialing. Each time I heard the *beep* of the button, my stomach turned upside down. It was ringing. I sat up in bed.

It was Saturday, maybe no one was in the office, but she called me from this number today, so . . .

"Hello, MTV news and docs?" a female voice said.

"Hi, Gini please," I said, looking down at my paper.

"Sure, who's calling?"

"This is Lynn Smith, I'm returning her call."

"Right, hold on," she said.

Was I really calling MTV? Maybe this was some kind of twisted flashback. At this point, anything was possible.

"Hi, Gini," she said.

"Hi Gini, my name is Lynn Smith. I got a message that you called today."

"Yes, hi . . . how are you?"

"I'm great," I said, still unsure if this was real or my imagination.

"Well, someone on my staff forwarded your e-mail to me and I have to say it was truly moving," she said.

I stood up from the bed, trying to remember what I had written. "Thank you," I said.

"It sounds like you have been through a lot . . . and are going through a lot, too. I was surprised when I read it because you sounded so eloquent in your speech and you wrote that you've only been out of the hospital for about two weeks . . ." I heard her rustling through papers.

"Yeah, that's right, I'm a free woman now . . ." *Free woman?* I had no idea what I was saying.

"Let me tell you about the project I am producing, Lynn. It's for a show called *True Life*. Ecstasy is garnering so much attention right now, we wanted to do a special on it. We're calling it, *True Life, I'm on Ecstasy.* Right now I'm looking for interesting stories to include in the documentary and after reading your e-mail, I knew that I had to call you. Yours just stood out," she said.

I didn't know what else to say, but "thank you."

"So did you take most of your ecstasy in New York City?"

"All of it. I moved there three years ago . . . coming from a tiny Pennsylvania town, it was quite the change. I was a kid in a candy store. I could order any drug, like ordering a pizza, free delivery and all."

"Incredible," she said.

I felt like I was channeling again. I told her about the pills, the clubs, the friends, Mason, the nightmares, the psych ward, the prescription drugs, the meetings, my parents, Danville, my house . . .

it was freeing. By the end of the conversation, Gini knew my shoe size.

"Wow, my God . . . unbelievable . . ." she said.

"I'm sorry if I went off, I didn't realize how much I had to say, it all kind of flew out."

"Please, don't apologize, that's what I needed to hear. I wanted to know about your life and how it changed after using this drug. You are a strong young lady," she said.

"I'm learning. I mean, what's the alternative, you know? I was surfing the Internet the same day I wrote you. I was looking for information on ecstasy. I wanted to hear from someone who had been through it. I couldn't find much, it made me feel even more crazy and alone . . . so when I came to your website and saw the word 'ecstasy' flashing across the screen, I knew I had to send something."

"Thank you, Lynn. I'm glad that you did. I'm sure you're not the only one that's been affected by ecstasy. That's why I want to do this show, and I want you to be a part of it. Of course, it's up to you."

Silence. My life was going to be a show . . . on MTV? I didn't know what to say, it was too much to process. "Yes, I want to do this," I said. The words escaped my mouth without permission.

"Wonderful, I'm so thankful. I'm going to let my staff know and someone will call you to go over some things. We definitely want to get footage of you in Danville, in your house, with your family, and with your doctor. You talked about going to meetings and starting outpatient therapy, maybe we can follow you to one of those. Also if you're going to be visiting New York, I'd like to include that. I'll come up with a shooting schedule and go over it with you. I know this is probably a lot to take in, but don't worry about a thing. Well, I have a meeting to get to, so let's plan on talking within the next couple of days."

"Okay . . ."

"Thanks, Lynn . . . I'm really excited to meet and work with you. Have a great weekend. 'Bye."

I sat back down on the bed. Time stood still. I wasn't blinking, just staring down at the black speck of lint on the cream carpet. I couldn't believe that Stacey missed it with her morning vacuum. The phone began making sounds. I held it up to my ear, it was ring-ing. . . . *Please hang up and try your call again, if you need help, hang up and dial your operator . . .*

I wished it were that easy.

Tomorrow, Tomorrow

A few minutes after my conversation with Gini, Mason called to ask if he could take a bus to Danville. He wanted to leave the city the next day and stay with me for a few nights. I was ecstatic. I told him about the e-mail and the phone call from MTV. He was in disbelief. I had to repeat myself a couple times before he absorbed it. Just telling him sent me back into a state of shock.

When I hung up with Mason, I went downstairs to my mother's bedroom. She was lying on her bed, reading a book. She looked up when I entered the room.

"What's up? How are you feeling?" she asked.

Since I'd been home from the hospital, my mom always looked worried when I entered the room. I think she was afraid my head was going to start spinning and green foam would trickle out of my mouth.

"Don't worry, I'm fine," I said, sitting down at the end of her bed.

"Good," she said with a smile.

"I wanted to ask you something," I said.

She sat up. "Well . . . go ahead."

"Mason called me and he wants to know if he can visit. He wants to take a bus here tomorrow. I didn't give him an answer yet. I really want to see him, but I wanted to talk to you first," I said. I was thirteen again, asking if I could go to a sleepover.

Her eyes began to squint. Her face told me that she was weighing her words. "Why do you want to see him? I mean, Lynn, didn't you get your drugs from this kid? How long have you known him?"

I understood her concern, but she didn't understand. "Mom, I know you think you know him, but you don't."

"And you *do?*" she interrupted.

"Can I talk for a second? Listen, he's not a bad person, or if he is, then I am, too. What we did, we did together, he never forced me to do anything. It was my choice and it's not his fault. We are both cleaning up our acts, we want to get better, together. I love him, I really do."

My mom put her book to the side and moved her legs so she was sitting Indian style. "Lynn, you can't expect me to just accept him with open arms. You're a big girl and I can't force you to do anything. But this is my house and right now I don't want him staying in it. If he wants to come here, fine, but he can stay in a hotel, not here. I'm sorry if that's not what you want to hear, but—"

"Don't apologize. I wasn't going to have him stay here anyway. I just wanted to let you know that he was coming. I know that I've put you through hell, Mom, I'm sorry . . . but I need to see him."

"Lynn, it's your life, the choices are all yours."

"I know . . . thanks, Mom," I said, leaning over to give her a hug.

"I'm going to make a cup of tea, want one?"

"Sure," I said, following her out of the room and up the stairs.

I lifted myself up and sat my butt on the kitchen counter. My father used to scream at me all the time for doing this. "I need to talk to you about something else."

"What?"

"The other day I was on the Internet trying to find some information about ecstasy. I didn't find what I was looking for and out of nowhere I came across this MTV site that was asking people to send in their stories about using ecstasy. I typed up an e-mail and sent it," I said, watching my mom pour the hot, steaming water into the mugs. "Someone from MTV called me."

"What?" she said, stirring in a Sweet'n Low.

"A producer, Gini, called and asked me a little more about my life. I told her everything . . . everything. She wants me to be part of a documentary they are doing about ecstasy. I told her yes." I took a swig of the hot tea.

My mother just stood there staring at me. I knew it was coming . . . "What?" she asked.

I told her again, only slower.

"Oh, well, have you thought about this, Lynn? You already told her yes, but is this something you really want to do?"

"I think so. I guess. It just feels right for some reason."

"What exactly does this entail?"

"Gini is calling me with a shooting schedule. She wants to come here and interview me, follow me around, I guess, I don't know all the details yet."

"Come here? MTV is coming here?"

"Yeah . . . you don't have to do anything . . . just me . . ." I said.

"This is unbelievable. I mean, I don't know what to say. I'll support you with this, I just want you to know what you're getting yourself into."

"It's going to be fine, Mom." She looked exhausted.

We finished our tea in silence.

"I'm going to bed, I'm tired," she said, turning to walk down the stairs.

I stayed on the cold countertop for a few minutes. On the one hand I was certain that this was something good that was happening, and on the other I had no clue what I was doing. I jumped down to the floor and picked up the cordless and dialed his number.

"Hello?"

"Mason, it's me."

"Hey, babe."

"Pack your bags, I'm going to make a hotel reservation for you at the Pine Barn Inn, it's down the street from my house."

"Did you speak to your mom?" he asked.

"Yeah, she knows. She's okay with it, as good as to be expected. We're a couple of star-crossed lovers."

"That we are . . . oh my God, I can't believe I'm going to see you tomorrow."

"I know, me, too," I said. "What time does your bus get in?"

"Twelve-twenty. Should I take a cab?"

"You can't be serious. We don't have cabs in Danville. Maybe you can rent a horse, or maybe I'll have a cow pick you up," I said, laughing. It felt good to laugh, really laugh. It had been too long. "No, I'll find a way to pick you up, don't worry. It's not far, nothing is far in this town."

"Good, I have to pack a few things and get to bed. I have to be at Port Authority by seven A.M."

"Yikes . . . Okay. I love you and can't wait to see you. I hope you recognize me," I said.

"I will, don't worry. 'Bye, Lynn."

"Good night, Romeo . . ."

I hung up the phone and went into the living room. One by one, items were mysteriously disappearing. My father had taken the big couch that was against the window. The room looked empty. I laid down in the center of the carpet and closed my eyes. I couldn't believe I was going to see Mason. What would it be like sober? I wondered if he was asking the same question.

Fun, Food, and Fantasy

I looked up at the cloudless sky, summer was right around the corner. Good old Susquehanna Trailways was coming down the hill. The windows were tinted, but I could see his outline moving toward the front of the bus. Before I knew it, there he was, standing across the street. We were both frozen in our places, staring, smiling at each other. I waved him over.

"What are you waiting for?" I yelled.

He crossed the street. "You're jaywalking," I said as he got closer.

He came straight at me and wrapped his strong arms around me. He smelled like Mason. It was Mason. His stubble brushed the side of my face as he squeezed me tightly, breathing into my neck. I felt his warm tears on my bare shoulder.

"I've missed you." His words danced down my neck.

Neither of us wanted to let go. We pried ourselves apart. I touched his beautiful face.

"Is it you?" I asked.

"It's me . . . I'm here," he said with the widest smile. His teeth were perfect. I never noticed how straight they were, or maybe I'd forgotten. "You look amazing, healthy . . . your cheeks are rosy."

"My makeup is running down my face, I look wonderful."

He leaned in and kissed me. It was perfect. I knew I was home.

We held hands as we walked to the car. "My mom let me borrow her car."

"That was nice of her."

"So are you ready to see this huge metropolis?"

"Hell yeah. Let's do it."

I drove down Mill Street. "This is like Danville's Times Square," I said, laughing. "On your right we have the post office. Up here on your left is the shoe repair man, Doc. And right there is the only restaurant in Danville, BJ's."

"You're an amazing tour guide," said Mason.

"The Pine Barn is right up here. I used to be a waitress at this place when I was younger."

"Really," he said, not taking his eyes off me.

"Yeah, there is a little restaurant next to the inn. I used to deliver room service orders."

"Room service, yum . . . we're going to have to get some of that," he said, putting his hand on my leg.

"Slow down, big guy," I said, parking the car.

They called it "barn" for a reason. It resembled an old wooden barn.

The same old woman was still working at the front desk. I thought she recognized me, but I pretended not to know her. Our room was surprisingly cozy. Everything wooden and rustic. There was a television, telephone, and air-conditioning. We never had to leave the room. Mason threw his bag down and pulled me onto the bed. We hugged each other. I was relaxed and calmed by his presence. He kissed me on the neck and then he began pulling down the strap of my tank top.

"Not right now, please, just lay here with me for a while," I whispered.

I just needed him to hold me. I wanted to feel safe and protected. I wasn't ready to have sex yet. "I love you, babe . . . God, do I love you," he said.

When I woke up, Mason was lying next to me reading a book. "How long was I asleep?"

"A couple of hours."

"Hours? You should have woken me up, God."

"You looked so peaceful, I couldn't do it," he said, putting his book down.

"Yeah, that's because I was semicomatose. This medicine I'm taking knocks me for a loop, I hate it."

"You're probably catching up on all of the sleep you were deprived of in the city. It will take a while to get used to it," he said.

"Thank you, Doctor. I don't want to get used to this. I just want to be normal, whatever the fuck that is," I said, curling up to him.

"You're going to be fine, you're doing great," he said, rubbing my shoulder.

I wondered why Mason wasn't curled up in a ball next to me, pumped full of antidepressants and mood stabilizers? It didn't make any sense, he gorged himself with the same amount of drugs that I did, probably even more, and he was fine, stopped cold turkey, just like that. Life just wasn't fair.

"Are you hungry?" I asked.

"I'm always hungry . . . you know that," he said.

"I have an idea. There's this amusement park about twenty minutes away. Knoebal's Grove. There are some decent rides and there's also pizza, ice cream, funnel cakes."

"Stop, my stomach is growling," he said, patting his. "Sounds perfect."

"I haven't been there in years, why not," I said, getting up to use the bathroom.

I left the door open while I peed. "How are you for money?'

"I got us covered, don't worry," he said.

"I am flat broke, my next project is to find a job in this town . . . God help me." I looked into the mirror. My little pimples were still there. They'd become a permanent fixture. I quickly switched the light off.

"Are you ready?" I asked before breaking out into song. "Fun, food, and fantasy, the most magical place you'll ever be . . . Knoebal's amusement resort! Thank you, thank you very much . . . please don't forget to tip the waiter on your way out."

Mason stood up laughing. He grabbed me and pulled me closer. "I love you."

"Enough of this mushy stuff, let's hit the rides," I said, pulling him out the door.

The car ride through the mountains was amazing. "Beautiful . . . beautiful," Mason said over and over.

The park was nestled in the center of the woods. It was surrounded by trees and green. There were no crowds. School was still in session so the timing was perfect. I was a little girl again, running from ride to ride. The wooden roller coaster was better than I'd remembered. We laughed on the bumper cars, we screamed in the cheesy haunted house, and we kissed in the dark tunnel on the train ride around the park. We gorged ourselves with treats. We started with ice cream and ended with pizza. I didn't want the day to end. I forgot what good, old-fashioned fun felt like, without drugs. Seeing the world with clear eyes was nice. I fell in love with Mason all over again. It sounds corny, but it was true. I sat on Mason's lap in the photo booth to freeze the moment in time. *Flash.* Goofy smiles. *Flash.* Tongues out. *Flash.* Rabbit ears. *Flash.* A kiss.

By the time we got on the road it was dark. I called my mom from Mason's cell. The reception was bad.

"Hi, Mom . . ." I said.

Her voice cut in and out.

"Mom, I'm on my way home, the signal is bad," I said before losing her.

When we pulled into the driveway the mood had changed. I was anxious and I could tell Mason was, too.

"It's okay. I'll just give her the keys and then we'll walk back," I said, grabbing his hand.

We entered through the garage. My sisters and mother were sitting at the table playing Scategories. They all looked up.

"Hello," my mom said. Her voice sounded as uncomfortable as I felt.

"We went to Knoebal's. I haven't been there in years," I said.

Complete silence. Stacey got up and went back into her room.

"Okay . . . well, this is Mason. Mason, this is my mom and my younger sister, Stephanie," I said, moving in a little closer to the table.

Steph looked at him and smiled. "Hi," she said before staring back down at the board.

"Hi there," my mom said, looking at me. "I need the car tomorrow."

"I know, here are the keys," I said handing them to her.

"Thanks. Do you want a ride to the Pine Barn?"

"No, we can walk, it's so close," I said, squeezing Mason's wet hand.

"Well, be careful," she said.

We turned around and walked through the kitchen. "'Bye," I said before closing the door.

We got outside and both of us let out a sigh. We walked up the dark street holding hands. "Well, I think they really liked you."

Walking Through a Spiderweb

Within a week of Mason's departure there was an MTV camera crew in Danville following my every move. I had an appointment scheduled at Geisinger Hospital and they were going to film it. My mom was working at the hospital. She was going to meet me in Radiology. Today was the day. The results were in and I was about to find out the true meaning of "This is your brain on drugs." Gini was great. She made me feel comfortable, like I was talking to an old friend. Her long brown hair and poised, professional demeanor reminded me of my high school drama teacher, Cynthia Cronrath. I trusted her.

I walked through the automatic doors in the front of the hospital with a mike clipped to my shirt, and a cameraman walking backward in front of me. People stared as I walked through the hospital. Danville had never seen this much excitement. I couldn't believe that this was happening. I moved to New York City to find my "closeup" and it took coming back to Danville to get one. This wasn't what I'd had in mind. No script or character to hide behind, it was all me—uncut. I was nervous enough about getting the results of my scan, but having a camera in my face recording my every expression didn't help. I made my way through the hallways and into the elevator with my entourage. The cameraman took a break and began chatting with the sound guy.

"So how are you feeling? Are you nervous to get the results?" Gini asked me.

"Yes, extremely. I have no idea what to expect," I said as the elevator door opened.

My mother was standing in the lobby outside the clinic. I walked over and gave her a hug. The camera was up and rolling again.

"Hi, Kathy. I'm Gini, pleasure to meet you," she said, shaking my mom's hand.

"Nice to meet you, too." She looked at the camera and glanced at me. Her smile was one of disbelief. "I think they're ready for you in there."

"Okay, here we go," I said, leading the way through the door.

I held my mom's hand as we went back to the room where I first had the scan done. The same nurse was there.

"Hi there, Lynn, how are you?" she asked me.

"I'm doing well, I guess, a little nervous," I said. I wanted her to give me a hint, a secret signal. She had to know the results.

A doctor was standing over by the computer station in front of the machine.

"Hi there, I'm Dr. C.," he said, shaking both of our hands.

"Nice to meet you," we said in unison.

Gini directed the cameraman to a corner where he could get all of us in the shot. I sat up on the table and my mom stood next to me.

"Well, Lynn, as you know, we took a scan of your brain a couple weeks ago . . ." he said, looking past me. I think he was playing to the camera. "Today I want to show you and your mother the results of this test."

The nurse took a seat at the computer and began punching away at the keys. "First, Sherry is going to pull up the scan of a normal person," he said, pointing with his pen at the screen.

A normal person . . . give me a break.

A few seconds passed before a green 3D image of a brain appeared on the large monitor. "Now you can see here that this one is plump and full . . . and now we are going to pull up the image of your brain next to it."

Drum roll, please . . .

I blinked and there it was. My stomach fell to the floor. I heard my mother quietly gasp in my right ear. I couldn't take my eyes off the screen.

"As you see here, Lynn, all of these dark areas—Sherry, will you please rotate the image," he said.

I watched my brain move in a circle around the screen. I could see right through it. Pieces were missing. Swiss cheese came to mind. That couldn't be good. No . . . no . . . no.

Pointing to the screen with his pen. "Your brain looks like a cobweb, almost moth eaten. These dark spots are areas of inactivity, they look like holes, but they're not. These are areas of inactivity, lack of blood flow. Memory, decision making, mood, depth perception, all of these things are effected. Lynn, how old are you? Eighteen? Twenty?" he asked.

"Twenty-two," I said.

"Looking at your brain image, I would say that this was a sixty, sixty-five-year-old woman who has had multiple strokes . . ."

And the hits just keep on coming. Everything disappeared. The camera, the doctor, my mom . . . all I could see was my brain. My poor brain. It was real. In that moment, it all came to a head. Literally. This was something tangible that couldn't be denied. I knew that I had done some damage, that there were consequences to pay, but this was concrete proof. A neon sign flashing in my face telling me that I'd fucked up, this wasn't the end of the battle. I gave myself brain damage. I had a friend, Adam, die in a car accident when I was in high school. He suffered from severe head trauma, all internal. He had no choice. I did, and what did I do with my head? I looked over at my mother; her signature red hives were breaking out on her neck.

"Let's look on the positive side," Dr. C. said.

"Yes, please." I needed something, a glimmer of hope.

"You're young and that means your brain is, too. The brain has amazing ways of rewiring itself. It can find alternate pathways around things. Since ecstasy is a fairly new drug, we don't know much about long-term damage, I can't guarantee that somewhere down the road this won't affect you."

It was affecting me already, there was no doubt of that. My mother put her arm around my shoulder. I watched the doctor's mouth move, but I had tuned him out. I had heard all that I needed to. I managed to thank the nurse and the doctor, it just seemed like the right thing to do. They left the room and Gini came over to me.

"Oh my God, was that really the first time you saw that?"

"Oh yes," I said looking over at my mother. She was as red as a lobster.

"I can't believe it. I mean, I look at that brain and then I look at you, it just doesn't make sense," said Gini.

"It all makes sense to me now, I'll tell you that," I said as Gini gave the cameraman a look to continue rolling. "I didn't think anything like this could ever happen to me, you know? I never heard anything bad about it, about ecstasy. Of course, everyone I was hanging out with was doing it, too." I turned toward the black screen. The image wasn't there, but I could still see my brain. I would always see it. "I'm not going to let that image tell me who I am. I'm going to make better choices now, live the life that I was meant to live."

As she wiped her eyes, my mom leaned over and hugged me. She was boiling hot. "I love you, Lynn. You're going to rise above this, you will."

The Truth Sucks

It had been two long months since I'd left the city kicking and screaming. I decided that I needed to go back to Brooklyn to get my things. It had to be done. I hadn't talked to any of the old gang except Mason since I'd left. It's funny how that worked, when I was high in a club I was surrounded by friends. They hugged me, massaged me, hell, they loved me . . . all for one, one for all. Where were they now? I guess when the chips fall, you find out the truth. I was nervous to see them and that dingy apartment. If music playing in a store could set me off, what would this do?

One evening after my mother returned from work, I told her my plan. I followed her downstairs to her room.

"What's up?" she asked as I shadowed her through the basement.

"I want to go back to New York, to Brooklyn. I need to get my things. All my clothes, my bed, everything is still in that apartment and I can't just leave it there."

She kicked her heels off and began pulling down her nude panty-hose. "Well, I guess you have to, if you want to keep that stuff."

"Want to keep it? It's everything that I own. My books, pictures . . . of course I want to keep it. We'll have to rent a van or something, your car is too small to fit."

"I can't go. I can't take any more time off of work right now, you're going to have to do this alone, or maybe Steph will go with you," she said, hanging up her skirt in the closet.

I couldn't believe what I was hearing. "Why won't you go with me? I want you to go, you know Steph, she won't. Besides I need you," I said.

"Lynn, I'm sorry, I'm not going to that city with you. I don't want to see that apartment. I don't want to see any of it," she snapped.

I stood there in silence for a few seconds, staring at her scurrying around the room. "Mom, you don't have to do anything. I'll drive. You can sit in the car—"

"Lynn, No. I'm sorry," she said, pulling a T-shirt over her head.

"I can't believe this, what am I supposed to do? I don't want to do this by myself." Blood was rushing to my face. I could feel myself ready to spew words that I'd regret. "Thanks, thanks a lot," I said, stomping out of the room and up the stairs.

I walked outside. I hated that there were no sidewalks. I hated that there were no people out. I hated that I felt this way about my mom. She was all that I had. The only person I could depend on and she was turning her back on me. The whole process would go quicker if she helped me, plus I had no money to rent a van. I felt all alone . . . fuck it. I didn't need anybody's help. I could do this. Fuck the friends. Fuck my mom. And fuck this town. This small, sheltered, tractor-lovin', corn-growin' town. I marched down Bloom Street and crossed the road to go to the Uni-Mart. I bought a pack of Big Red and marched right back out.

When I got home, my mother was quietly sitting at the kitchen table by herself.

"Lynn . . ." she said in a soft tone.

"Yes, that's me," I said, opening the fridge.

"Don't be smart. I wanted to tell you that I'll rent a van for you."

My heart was lightened by her words.

"But . . ."

Don't say it.

"I'm still not going to the city. I'll help you out with the van, but I can't go," she said.

"You mean you won't go. There's a difference."

"Lynn, this isn't easy for me. I have a lot going on in my life, too." She sounded so vulnerable.

"I know, Mom, I know." I didn't want to upset her. "Thanks for helping out with the van . . . I really need it."

"We can go in the morning before work. I think it opens early, that way you can leave at a decent hour and come back in the evening."

"All right, Mom, okay. Fine. Let's do that."

"Why don't you call Mason, I'm sure he can meet you and help you out."

"Yeah, I will . . . I'll figure it out. Thanks for your help," I said, walking down the stairs.

I knew what had to be done next.

I picked up the phone and dialed my old number. Kelly answered.

"Hello?"

"Hey, Kelly . . . it's Lynn . . ." I said with my stomach churning.

"Oh my God . . . what's going on? Where are you?"

I wanted to say, *Remember what happened, remember me bouncing off the walls a few weeks ago and you telling me to have a cigarette before going to bed? Remember I left the city to go to a hospital? Remember you never called?* Instead I just said, "I'm at home in Pennsylvania."

"Why don't you ever call? I mean, you just disappeared."

I wanted to fucking scream. "Well, Kelly, I just got out of the hospital not too long ago, a lot has happened, it hasn't been too easy."

"Vinnie and I didn't know what to do. I mean, we got this apartment thinking that we were going to split the rent," she said.

I couldn't believe her. No "how are you feeling? What happened?" She was worried about the dirt cheap rent. "I'm sorry, Kelly, I didn't exactly plan for this to happen, you know? I paid you for May's rent anyway before I left. I didn't live there the whole month. Mason also told me that Jake was moving in with you guys."

"Yeah, he might, did you hear about him and Sandra?"

I didn't fucking care about Jake or his girlfriend. "No, Kelly I didn't. Listen, the reason I'm calling is to let you know that I'm coming to the city tomorrow to get my stuff. I'm renting a van and I'm gonna ask Mason to help me move my things out."

"Tomorrow? Okay. I don't work until four so I'll be here. Vinnie should be here, too."

"Good. I'm leaving early so I'll be there by eleven or twelve, depending on the traffic."

"Are you staying over? You should, maybe we could all go out."

I was talking to a brick wall. Clueless. "No, I'm not staying over and I don't want to go out."

"What? You're done going out?"

I couldn't take it. "Kelly, listen, we'll talk tomorrow. I still have to get things ready for the drive. See you then."

"Okay, see you soon. I love ya," she said.

The words slapped me in the face. Love? She couldn't be serious. "'Bye," I said before laying back on the floor. I wanted to vomit.

I had changed. When I heard the word "love" it all became crystal clear how fake my existence truly was. Tricking myself with pills, creating an instant intimacy that disappeared when we weren't all high. We wanted to feel "the love"—skip all the messiness, be one with God, what a fucking joke. I wished that I could have laughed, but nothing about this discovery was funny. My whole life up until this point was a scam and a lie. The truth was becoming apparent and it was anything but beautiful.

Memories

As I approached the city my stomach began to tighten. I saw the Empire State Building in the distance. I was close. The traffic was mild. I had just missed rush hour. I felt like I had been away for years. So much had happened in the past month that it was difficult to gage the passing of time. When I turned the sharp corner to approach the Lincoln Tunnel, I saw it. The skyline. The beautiful, wonderful, terrible skyline that held so much meaning for me. It was the symbol of my dreams and nightmares. So many ghosts, so much unfinished business. I wasn't ready.

I entered the orange-lit tunnel. The music in the van turned to static. The bright lights and the sound of the radio made me feel like I was about to be transported to a galaxy far, far away. I was right. When I emerged from the tunnel it was everywhere. The noise, the cabs, the sirens, the traffic, the city . . . my home. Sitting bumper to bumper on Thirty-fourth, I decided to call Mason on the cell phone my mother had lent me. She had also given me sixty bucks. I knew that she felt guilty. I dialed his number.

"Hello?" he answered.

"Hey there . . . so I am here."

"Where are you at?" he said, sounding groggy. With no job and free room and board at his parents' house, he could sleep all day if he wanted.

"I'm sitting in god-awful traffic, did I wake you up? It's eleven."

"I know. I have to jump in the shower. Call me when you get

close so I can be outside waiting. There's no place to park," he said.

"Okay, see you soon."

I continued at a snail's pace and made my way through Herald Square. Passing Macy's, the Gap, and countless other stores made me think about the Colombia Mall and the lack of shopping opportunities in Danville. It didn't matter anyway, I had no money to spend. I turned down Second Avenue and the path was wide open. I hit every green light all the way to Seventeenth Street. Maybe that was a good sign. I called Mason and gave him the heads up that I was double-parked outside his building.

I also called Gini, as promised, and told her that I was in the city. She asked for the address in Brooklyn and told me she was going to send a cameraman over there right away. She sounded so determined, I couldn't bring myself to tell her that I didn't think it was a good idea.

Mason opened the door and climbed up. "Oh my God, this is a school bus, babe," he said.

As Mason and I drove across the Brooklyn Bridge, shivers went up and down my spine. I remembered the last time that I crossed it. I was in a cab with Mason staring at the sunrise, completely out of my mind. I kept my eyes straight ahead. My heart began to race. *Not now, not here,* I thought to myself. *Breathe, Lynn . . . breathe.* Mason put his hand on my leg.

"Don't worry, babe, this is going to be fine, we're in this together," he said, rubbing my leg.

He knew just what to say and when to say it. I loved that about him. "Thanks," I said as we exited the bridge.

We began driving through our neighborhood. I turned left onto St. John's Place. I couldn't believe that this street was named after a saint. It was dirty, dark, and sad. Satan's Alley might have been more appropriate. When I pulled in front of the building, there was a white couple standing outside holding camera equipment. I knew it had to be the MTV crew. We got out of the car and walked over to them.

"Hi, I'm Lynn, and this is my boyfriend Mason."

"Nice to meet you, I'm Tara and this is Dan," she said, pointing to the young guy behind her. "What's the plan?"

"Well, my plan is to get my stuff from the apartment, that's about it," I said, glancing at Mason.

"Do you think it would be okay if we followed you in?" she asked.

My body tensed up. I could just picture it now. *Surprise, guys! I'm here, oh, and you're on MTV!* "I don't think that's a good idea. I haven't seen my friends since I left the city and they have no idea that I'm doing this. There's no way they want to be on TV."

"Okay, we can get some footage of you bringing stuff out and putting it in the van, we'll figure something out. Here, we have mike packs for both of you."

I clipped mine on my back pocket and slid the wire up under my shirt. Mason followed my lead. He was silent. I knew that he was as freaked out as I was.

The camera was up and rolling. Mason and I went to the door and pushed the buzzer. We waited. Mason pushed it again.

"Hello?" Kelly said. I could tell we'd woken her.

I looked at my watch, it was noon. This was early for them. "Hey, Kelly, it's Lynn and Mason," I yelled into the intercom.

I pushed on the door, it wasn't locked. We walked into the building, it was even grimier than I remembered. "This is awful, Mason." He grabbed my hand. We walked up the stairs. Each step made my heart beat faster. How did I ever live here?

"I put a lot of your stuff in boxes after you left, it shouldn't take too long," Mason said.

"Good. I want this to be as quick as possible." When we approached the door, it was ajar.

I pushed on it and walked in. The fucking smell of cigarettes assaulted me and I began to hack. This house was haunted. I walked past my room with Mason's hands on my hips. I couldn't look in. We entered the living room and Kelly was sitting on the couch in her pajamas, smoking away. She shoved her cigarette into the over-flowing ashtray. The room was so dark. The covers on the windows were exactly how I left them.

"Hey mama," she said, running over to me and giving me a hug. "You look so tan."

I wanted to say, *You would be, too, if you ever saw the daylight.* "Yeah, I have been outside a lot in Pennsylvania."

She moved around me and hugged Mason. I looked into his eyes while her arms were around him. We both wanted out.

"Vinnie is still asleep, we were out late last night," she said, walking into the kitchen. "I made something for you."

She turned around and was holding a silver cake pan. I looked inside and saw an uneven brownie with the words "welcome home" written in green gel. "Thank you, thanks, Kelly," I said, trying to force a smile.

"I was going to make pot brownies, but Vinnie told me not to," she said, setting the pan down on the cocaine-encrusted coffee table.

I was speechless. "Well, we are going to start moving my stuff down to the van," I said.

"Okay, I'm going to lay back down with Vinnie," she said, walking back to her bedroom and closing the door behind her. "I love you, mama."

Mason and I stared at each other. I was shaking my head as he guided me toward my room. I entered it. Thank God Mason put most of the stuff in boxes. The room was coated in ashes. There were dust bunnies bigger than New York City rats in the corners. My stereo had melted wax on it, as well as inside of it.

"Well, looks like I'm leaving this here," I said, pointing to it.

"I haven't touched the closet. Everything is on hangers, though. We can just carry those down," he said, lifting up a box.

I looked around. I had a lot less than I thought. I sat down on my bed, which felt like mush. I stood up and pushed aside the dirty green blanket. *This isn't my mattress.* This was Kelly and Vinnie's.

They'd switched theirs with my brand-new, superior, deluxe plush, pillow-top bed.

"Mason, look at this crusty, old mattress, this is theirs, not mine." I was fuming.

"Lynn, calm down, we need to get moving. Grab a box, come on."

I followed him out the door. We got outside and the camera was in my face.

"How is it going up there?" Tara asked.

"Okay, I guess. I just want to get out of here."

"Do you think we can come up? Have you changed your mind?"

"No," I said, following Mason back through the front door.

We made a few more trips. It took less than an hour. The van looked empty without the bed, but there was no way I was getting my mattress back. I didn't really want it anyway. I looked around my vacant room. My blue curtains were still covering the window. They reeked of my past. We went into the living room. Some of my CDs were scattered on the floor by the stereo. Bad Boy Bill, Aphrodite . . . I didn't want them, either. I never wanted to hear electronic music again. Kelly and Vinnie shuffled out of their room. They were ghosts, pale and tired. Vinnie gave me a hug. He had no shirt on. My arms could have wrapped around him twice.

"Hey, girl," he said, rubbing his eyes and taking a seat on the couch.

Seeing him made me want to cry. I'd always had a strong connection with Vinnie. I knew that he was full of potential. He'd had a rough life and it showed. He looked like a feeble old man and he was only twenty-one. The drugs have eaten right through him. Kelly ran back into her room.

"I have something for you, Lynn," she yelled from behind the wall.

Something told me that I should brace myself. She came out with a purple book in her hand.

"Here you go. I made this, so you could always remember the good times," she said, handing me the book.

It was a small photo album. On the front written in gold letters was the word MEMORIES. I held my breath as I opened it. The first picture was of Kelly and me. We were holding onto each other, both of us looking up at the ceiling. Our eyes were crossed, not intentionally. We were rolling. Pictures flew by like a movie. In each one I was higher than the last, all of us were. I closed the album and I knew that she was staring at me.

"Thanks, Kelly," I said, swallowing my disgust.

She was a child that didn't know any better. I wasn't mad at her. It was like I was seeing nude photos of myself years after I had posed for them. I couldn't take it back. They were frozen in time.

"We have to get going," Mason said, speaking through the uncomfortable silence.

"Hey, guys, you can't stay any longer?" Kelly asked.

"No, I have a rental van that I have to take back to Pennsylvania."

They walked us to the door.

"'Bye. Call us next time you're in the city. We can all get together," Kelly chimed.

Vinnie didn't say anything.

"'Bye, guys," we said, closing the door.

I couldn't walk fast enough out of the building and there was once again a camera in my face. I walked around the van.

"So how did it go? Did you say good-bye?" Tara asked from behind the lens.

"Yeah . . . we told them good-bye," I said, looking down at the photo album. "They were our best friends, you know? It's strange . . . but it's over . . . done."

"What do you think you're learning from this?" she asked as the camera moved closer.

"I'm just glad I came out of it alive."

Naked Blue

I drove my things back to Danville and that was that. In one day I said good-bye to the friends, the apartment, and the city. The show was over. It was official. There was no longer a question in my mind where I lived. The cameras stopped rolling and I was right back where I started from. Life was unraveling. Our house was on the market, my father was gone, I had no friends, no money, and the love of my life was three hundred miles away. I had never felt so alone.

I turned my father's room into my own only after burning about a thousand Glade candles to mask the stench. I took my time putting everything in its place. What was the use in rushing? My mother bought me a new bed. I think it was out of guilt for not going to New York with me. I didn't care, I was just glad that I didn't have to sleep on the floor. I went to Wal-Mart with Stacey one evening, hoping that I could find a few cheap things to spruce up my new living quarters. With twenty dollars, I was able to buy more candles, white Christmas lights, new sheets, a journal, and a Picasso print. Most of the posters were of dogs, cats, rainbows. I almost opted for the teddy bear with the words "bear with me" written above it, but just then I was saved by a beautiful naked woman sitting with her legs curled up against her. You could only see her back. I knew that she felt as vulnerable and exposed as I did.

It was strange to inhabit the space that was once my father's. His spirit still lived in the house long after he was gone, reminders of

him hiding around every corner. Old Spice aftershave lotion left in
the bathroom, a pair of his white socks in the laundry, snow boots
in the garage. He moved just a few blocks up the street from us. He
invited my sisters and me up to his apartment one Sunday afternoon. Stacey and Stephanie went, but I couldn't play the game.
They came back pissed off, telling me how excited Dad was to have
his own place, his bachelor pad. He was cooking for his friends and
entertaining all the time. He acted like a teenager who had moved
away to college, not like a father and husband who had just lost his
family. I thought once he was gone that everything would magically
clean itself up and get better. I was wrong. Now that he was gone,
none of us had anyone to blame for our own misery.

The hours crawled by in that house. With my mom at work and
Stacey in grad school, it was lonely as hell. I had no car and even if
I had, there was nowhere to go. I was becoming bitter, pacing
around the house like a zombie, trying to figure out what to do
with my life. I called Mason every hour, pleading for reassurance.
I wanted to be with him, but there was no way I could handle or
afford going back to that city, not yet. But being in Danville didn't
seem any easier. I sank deeper into self-pity. Wondering, *Why?*
Why me?

My mother worked all day and searched the classifieds at night
for a second job. She would walk through the door carrying her despair with her each day. All of her rage was directed at my father.
"That asshole, do you want to know what that shithead did?" She
had a new name for him each day, which really didn't boost family
morale.

We never sat down as a family, a new family, to discuss anything.
It was obvious that things had changed, but there was no period of
mourning. My mother just kept pushing on. *Get up and dust yourself*
off. Dust it under the rug, was more like it. I wanted answers and
reasons. Why didn't you leave years ago? I knew that my mother
couldn't take anything back, but I wasn't going to let her off the
hook that easy. I was full of venom, ready to attack.

I had no road map or compass to point me out of this bottom-less pit of despair. I stopped talking to my mom and began ignoring her. Passive aggression was an old talent of mine. I stopped going to AA meetings, I was sick of wallowing in sorrow with a bunch of old geezers. I could do that on my own. Most nights I would slap on my Walkman and flee the house. I would walk around outside in the dark for hours, listening to Fiona Apple or Alanis Morissette . . . young, whiny bitches that understood my pain.

One night after one of my excursions my mother cornered me in the kitchen.

"I need to talk to you. Sit down," she said, moving to the dining room table. It was the first time we had spoken in a while.

I took my headphones off and sat down. "Okay?"

"Listen, have you thought about looking for a job?" she asked with her hands folded in front of her.

I wanted to pounce on her like a lion. "Yes, I've thought about getting a job. I'm just trying to figure out where. I guess I could chop meat or be a welder."

"Lynn, don't be smart with me."

"Mom, I'm not being smart. There aren't too many opportunities in this town, if you haven't noticed."

"Well, I need help with some bills. I can't support everybody and keep this house running all by myself."

You should have thought about that before choosing a husband. "I know, I don't think anyone is asking you to," I said, staring out the back window.

"By not helping with anything you are asking me to," she said, turning an even brighter shade of red. "Anyway, there is a woman that I know from town who needs someone to stay with her mother, Ruth. She has a mild case of Alzheimer's and she lives all alone in Riverside. I can't do it during the day, but I could do overnights, and I thought that you and Stacey could share the days."

Things couldn't get any stranger. I was going to be a nurse for an elderly woman with Alzheimer's? Come again. "What?" I asked.

"She will pay us ten dollars an hour, cash. We just have to prepare her meals and make sure she takes her medicine. She is a sweet old woman," my mother said.

Ten dollars an hour sounded good, especially for this town. I was flat broke and it was better than *Welcome to Wendy's, can I take your order?*

"I guess, if I have no choice. I'll do it." I could just see it now, me and the old lady sitting side by side, taking our meds together. God help us.

"You do have a choice, Lynn. I'm not forcing you to do anything," she said.

There was a tight cord connecting my mother and I.

"Okay . . . whatever Mom," I said, getting up from the chair. Lightning began crackling outside. The evening sky was turning black. *Not a good sign.*

"Sit down," my mom demanded.

I could feel the cord about to snap. I was shocked by her tone. My mother never yelled at me, we never argued. "What?" I asked, hearing the downpour outside.

"I said, sit down. There is something else I want to talk about," she said, pointing to the chair.

I did as she said. "I'm all ears."

"What is your problem? You've been walking around this house with a stick up your ass. You're ignoring me and your sisters."

"I talk to Stacey and Steph . . ."

"Okay, fine—me. You're treating me like shit. Why? What have I done to you?"

This was a side of my mother that I had never seen. She was confronting an issue. I would have hugged her if she was confronting someone besides me. "I'm not treating you like shit. I'm just trying to work through some things."

"Are you using drugs again?"

Her words flew out of left field and hit me in the gut. "You can't be serious. There is no way you just asked me that."

"And why not? Like I don't have reason to," she said with her lips getting tighter and tighter.

"No, you *don't* have reason to," I yelled, pushing my chair away from the table. "Don't you think it's a little late for the questions? Give me a fucking break, now you're trying to be mother of the year?"

Her eyes began to well up with tears. "You're the one that did this to yourself, not me. These were your choices, Lynn, not mine. You're not the only one in pain. What happened to you has affected all of us."

"Oh, great! Now you're going to blame me for everything. You don't have Dad anymore, so you're coming at me. Pain, you say I've caused pain," I said, standing up from the chair. "Look around. You talk about choices, look at your choices. You chose to live with an alcoholic and raise your children in this poor excuse for a home. Your choice, we didn't get one. Believe me, if I did . . ." I was stabbing her in the heart.

"STOP!" my mother yelled as I paced around the kitchen. She was moaning like a wounded animal. The tears were pelting down her face. The storm wasn't only raging outside the house that night.

I stared at her with her face in her hands, listening to her gasp for air. I didn't care. I walked down the hallway into my room, my father's room. It was the changing of the guards. I fell face-first onto my bed. The pillow and the thunder muffled my screams. I came up for air and grabbed my journal from the dresser.

Tears flow from her eyes like the heavy rain raging from the sky.
Why do you act this way? What have I done? You have caused pain.
Are you still using drugs?

A little late for the questions, a little late for concern
A little late to repair this bridge that we've burned
I will leave you alone

I will pay everything back
Soon I'll be gone
I'll cause you no slack
This picture's not perfect
This smile is strained
Look closer and closer
You can see all the shame
You say I've caused pain
You say that I've lied
I've learned this from you
This you can't hide
A family without honesty
Your lies and pretending
But still I could see
Ignore all the years
Ignore all the tears
Protect so you thought
But now you've been taught
I am sorry that I'm such a mess
I am sorry that I've come home
This monster that you've created
Will continue to roam
Far away . . .

Tick Tock

There was no resolution with my mother. She went her way and I went mine. All I could think about was saving money to leave. I didn't know where I was going, but I was determined to get out of that town. Putting on our "happy" faces, my mother, Stacey, and I went for an interview and took the job at Ruth's.

The house was right across the river from Danville. A tidy, modest, two-floor home with a nice backyard. I wasn't sure if sitting with a senile woman was good for my health, but I had no choice. I was desperate. Her daughter Kate answered the door. She was a short woman with a thick waist and sandy brown hair cut in the shape of a bowl.

"Hi girls, I'm Kate, Ruth's daughter . . . come on in," she said, holding open the screen door. "Mom, you have some visitors," she yelled.

"I do?" I heard a voice say from the other room.

"Why don't you all have a seat on the couch in there. Do you want anything to eat or drink?"

"No thank you," we all said in unison before entering the living room.

The inside of the house was impeccable. Pressed, white curtains covered the windows. Lace doilies were placed neatly around the room. The blue wall-to-wall carpeting was pristine, but as clean as the house was, you could tell that it was lived in. It smelled like an old person. Stale and musty. It was an odor that I remembered from my Gram Witmer. I saw Ruth sitting on a chair by the window and to my surprise she wasn't the frail, little old lady I was expecting.

"Well, hello there," she said to us as if we were her long lost friends.

My mom went right over and extended her hand. "Well, hello Ruth, I'm Kathy Smith and these are my two daughters, Stacey and Lynn."

Her smile was sweet.

"It's nice to meet all of you young girls. My, I can't believe that you're old enough to have these daughters."

My mother began gushing. "Oh, that's sweet of you to say, I'll pay you later," she said, laughing.

Oh, please.

"Kate, make them something to eat," Ruth ordered.

"Mom, I already offered. They're just here to pay you a visit and talk about keeping you company."

"Oh no, I don't need that," she said, straightening the doily on the table next to her chair.

It must be hard for her, I thought, *to be losing control of her life and having total strangers coming into her home.*

"Mom, we talked about this. The doctor told you that you were going to need some assistance if you wanted to stay here."

Ruth quietly stared at the floor.

I wanted to cry. I thought about my own life and how scared I was to have no control. I felt empathy for Ruth. Your mind can leave you at any age and there's nothing to do but wait until the body decides to go with it.

Kate went on to tell us all about her mother. Her medicine, her disease, her daily routine, her favorite snacks, her cat Bing, her mail, et cetera. All the while, Ruth sat there like a child whose mother was filling the new babysitter in on the details. I was sad, but I needed that job. It seemed pretty simple; I mean, how hard could it be to keep a sweet old lady company? Kate hired us with-

out too many questions, thank God. She liked that we were working as a family. We were warm and friendly and she trusted that we
would be kind to her mother, even though I couldn't find it in my
heart to be kind to my own. We said good-bye to Ruth, went home,
and worked out a schedule among the three of us. We were business
associates. The next day I would take the first shift.

I woke up with a sense of purpose, knowing that I had a responsibility that day other than moping around in my misery. I was working toward my goal. I had tunnel vision. *Save money and leave, save
money and leave.* Each day I was that much closer to freedom. I had
a skip in my step. The end was in sight, or so I thought. I had no idea
where this road would lead. I got dressed, put my journal, book,
and lunch into a bag. I washed down my morning meds and was
ready to rock. Stacey dropped me off at Ruth's at seven-thirty in
the morning. I was greeted by Kate.

"Hi, sweetie, I left a note in the kitchen with emergency numbers. I'm sure everything will be fine, though. I have to get to
work. 'Bye, Mom," she yelled before rushing out the door.

I walked into the living room. The *Today* show was on without
any sound. Ruth sat staring at the television, sipping on a cup of tea.
"Hi there, Ruth, I'm Lynn, remember me?"

She looked up and smiled. "Don't be silly," she said, "Get yourself a cup of tea and sit down."

I opened a few cabinet doors until I found a mug. I filled it with
water, a Lipton tea bag, and put it in the microwave. No one had
heard of green tea in this town. I stared at the cup rotating in circles
inside the glass. Yes, ladies and gentlemen, this is my life. *Ding.* As I
took the hot mug out of the microwave something moved across
my feet. I jumped up, spilling the tea on my shirt, and looked down
to see a set of bright green eyes staring back at me. *Meow.*

"So you must be Bing," I said, rubbing the spot on my shirt.

The cat followed me into the living room. I sat my tea down on
a coaster that was waiting for me. "Ruth, do you mind if I turn the
volume up on the television?"

"Oh, I don't care," she said, waving her hand in the air. "I have no idea what they're talking about anyway."

I took that as a yes, it was okay, and knelt down by the huge wood-paneled television. It was more like a dining room table than a TV set. The cat rubbed up against my body. I wanted to throw it out the window, but instead began scratching behind its ears. I wanted to be polite and show Ruth that I cared about her furry friend.

Ruth stared at me and then the cat. "Is that your cat? What's his name?"

I was confused. I was sure that Kate said her mom had a cat named Bing, who she adored. "This is your cat, Ruth, not mine. His name is Bing," I said, continuing to pet the feline.

She sat up straighter in her chair and adjusted her thick glasses as if she wasn't seeing clearly. "Oh no, that's not mine. I don't like cats. Well, if it's not yours, it shouldn't be in here. Go on, get out of here, caddy, I mean kitty, get out!"

Bing ran out of the room. I stayed frozen on the carpet. I was in an episode of *The Twilight Zone*.

"Drink your tea before it gets cold, I think I'm going to lay down. I'm a little tired," she said, pushing herself up.

I stood up and helped her lay down on the couch. "Will you please get me a blanket, dear? They are in my room upstairs in the closet."

"Sure, I'll be right back."

I walked through the dining room and up the stairs. There were two bedrooms and a bathroom. I went into Ruth's closet and the smell of mothballs slapped me in the face. I held my breath as I pulled down a brown, crocheted blanket. I closed the door tightly and let out a sigh, as something caught my eye on her dresser. It was a black-and-white photo of a young man and woman with their arms around each other smiling. It had to be Ruth and her late husband. They looked to be my age, in their twenties. It was beautiful. I thought about the photos of Mason and me from Knoebel's.

Someday this would be me, old, frail, and gray. Would I outlive my husband and friends? I couldn't imagine depending on strangers to take care of me. Eighty-four years of life and the only proof that I was once young and in love would be a picture on my dresser.

I took the blanket downstairs and covered her sleeping body. Her mouth was open and her breathing was slow. I gently removed the glasses from her face and sat them on the table. It was hard to believe that this tired, confused old woman was once a young girl. That she had dreams and aspirations. That she danced with her husband and played with her children. It made me even more focused on moving forward, spreading my wings, and finding my path. I didn't want to die without going for it, whatever "it" was. The clock began ticking in my head. I pulled my journal out of my bag and began writing. Thank God I had a pen and paper, it was my only escape from the *tick tock*.

Big Brass Bed

Days turned into weeks, weeks into months, and before I knew it summer was over. The excitement that I'd once had for my new job wore off. The reality sunk in. I wasn't going anywhere. I was stuck in Pennsylvania, sitting in an old lady's house day after day. I prepared simple meals for her, helped her dress, and listened to her snore. Ruth took lots of naps. The television kept me company. My only visitors were Jerry Springer and Ricki Lake. Occasionally Montel stopped by, depending upon my schedule. I was trapped inside a monotonous routine. Each day was a carbon copy of the last. The *tick tock* that once was a clock in my head turned into a time bomb. The countdown was on.

My mother and I only spoke about work. *How was Ruth today? Do you want to pick up my overnight shift this Saturday?* Other than that, we were strangers that shared an address and that was even changing since I was picking up every unwanted shift. I needed someone to blame for my misery and my mom was the easiest and closest target. *If she would have left my father years ago, my life would be just fine* . . . at least that's what I kept telling myself. Anything to avoid taking responsibility. I was only home to change clothes and pack my bag. Ruth was my new roommate. The mother that was once my best friend became the knot in my stomach and the pain in my heart. I shut her out and wallowed in victimhood. All that I had left was Mason and his daily phone calls to keep me going.

"Lynn, everything is fine . . . this is all going to be over soon, hang in there."

Every conversation between us was the same, a broken record. I cried, unleashing my pain and frustration on Mason. Mason reassured me day after day that it was going to get better. He promised me that we'd be together again very soon. I wanted to believe him, but I was losing hope. He was still living at home with his parents, I was living with an old lady with dementia, he didn't have a job, and I had no money saved. This seemed like a lost cause. I couldn't see through the thick black cloud that was wrapped around me. I hated the person I was becoming. My depression grew like a deadly fungus. It was harder and harder to get up in the mornings, finding no good reason to face the day. Brushing my teeth was a daily struggle. The two things that fueled my existence were writing in my journal and drinking coffee. Without them I would have jumped off the Riverside Bridge. When I had a mug in one hand and a pen in the other, I was awake and alive. When I didn't, I was a medicated failure.

I decided that I needed to get out of Danville, even if it was just for the day. I took a bus trip to the city to see Mason. We spent the day holding hands and walking around downtown. Summer was over, but the air was still warm. Broadway had the best little stores. I could only afford to window-shop, but at least there were windows to look in. The smell of roasted nuts filled the September air. The crowds moving up and down the sidewalk reminded me that people were living their lives. I wanted to be one of them, but I was the girl in the bubble. I could observe the outside world, but not join in. Look, but don't touch. It was a bittersweet afternoon. I loved being back in the city with Mason by my side, but knew I only had a few hours before my carriage turned into a pumpkin.

We rode the A train up Eighth Avenue toward Port Authority. I stood in the crowded car, holding onto Mason swaying back and forth. I used to hate being packed into the smelly subway, but not that day. I savored it, stank and all. *I never appreciated this city while*

I had it. I never thought that my life would end up this way. I watched the passengers get on and off at each stop. They lived and worked here. They were New Yorkers, while I was just a visitor passing through.

Mason walked me to gate 14. There weren't too many people on the bus trip. Most natives of Danville were afraid of New York City. Even my relatives thought I was crazy for moving there when I was nineteen. At every family gathering they would poke fun at me, making jokes about criminals and bums. I took no offense because I thought they were even crazier for never traveling outside the county lines.

"I love you," Mason said, wrapping his arms around me.

I loved how his broad shoulders made me feel safe. "I love you, too, thanks for spending the day with me. . . . I don't want it to end . . . please, don't make me get back on that bus," I said with tears running down my face.

"Just be strong, it's going to get better. I promise you. Soon we'll be together, living out our lives the way we want, blazing our own trail," he said, picking me up off the ground.

My tears became laughter. I squeezed him even tighter. "Promise?" I moved my face in front of his.

"I promise you, Ms. Lynn Marie Smith, I love you," he said, kissing me. I melted into the floor. "Do you need a bottle of water or anything?"

"No, I have some goodies in my bag. I'll be fine."

"Can you call me when you get home?" he asked, taking tiny steps backward.

"I will," I said, running over and giving him one last hug.

"You're never going to leave if we keep this up," he said.

"That's the plan," I said, kissing him on the cheek.

"'Bye, babe. See you again soon," he said, turning to walk away.

He got on the escalator and turned around. We smiled at each other as long as we could and then he disappeared from sight. I looked at my watch, I had twenty minutes to kill. I didn't want to sit on the cold, dirty floor and wait. There were stores and magazine stands upstairs. I rode the escalator up and made my way over to Hudson News. There were too many magazines to choose from. Britney Spears, Gwyneth Paltrow, and Michelle Pfeiffer plastered the covers. *There are way too many skinny blondes in this country.* I left the stand empty-handed and walked into the GNC.

I liked being inside a health food store, they had a way of making me want to get fit. I touched my stomach. I was thin and flabby. My butt was like a pancake from sitting over at Ruth's all the time. I perused the shelves. The energy boosters caught my eye. Stackers . . . a natural energy booster and fat burner all in one. *Perfect.* The pills were the brightest shade of yellow. That should have told me something. *CAUTION, CAUTION.* I skimmed over the label. A lot of Chinese herbs I couldn't pronounce. They had to be healthy, I mean, this was GNC, not a crackhouse in Hell's Kitchen. I purchased the bottle and headed down to my gate.

I gave my ticket to the bald, overweight bus driver and hopped on. The farther back I went into the bus the more it smelled like urine. I took a seat somewhere in the middle. There were only about ten other people on the bus. I unzipped my bag to get my Walkman. Music was the only thing that could take my mind off the stench and my destination. I saw a white piece of notebook paper folded inside. I pulled it out to see that Mason had written me a letter. I put my bag down on the other seat and leaned back.

I wrote this while you were in the hospital. I never sent it to you. I just stumbled across it and I figured I should give it to you since it still holds true for the most part.

Dear Lynn,

I find that I am blaming myself for your present situation more and more everyday. I often feel that you would be in much better shape had you never met me. It is part of what drives me to succeed now. I hate it. I hate that because of me your life is a mess. I know

that it's not all my fault, but a lot of this would not have
happened had I not been introduced to your life. I know that you
still have it in you to be the best you can be. No matter how hard
it seems now. We are in this for the stretch. I don't just mean our
relationship. I mean life. Yes, we reaped what we had sown. But we
will be reaping again soon. There is good stuff ahead, we just have
to work for it. When the demons show their faces in an attempt to
stop us, we can tell them to go back to hell, because we've been
there already and they can't beat us a second time. They have
nothing on us because we have nothing to hide. Nothing. Our
lives are as open as can be. All our evil is gone. It is time to fight
the world and anyone who stands in our way for what is rightfully
ours. Our freedom. Our freedom to live our lives the way we know
is right for us. So be patient, the stretch awaits, and it has never
looked so good.

Love, Mason

I watched the paper soak up my teardrops. I folded it and put it
back in my bag. I wiped my eyes as the bus began to move. Mason
was the only person who understood me in this world. He knew
me at my worst, and still loved me. I knew it couldn't be easy, but
I was grateful that he was sticking by me. Now I had to work on
loving myself. It sounded simple enough, but I was my own worst
enemy. I knew I couldn't blame Mason or even my mother for
where I was in my life. I hated myself for all the times that I said yes
instead of no, for all the times that I didn't speak up, for all the
times that I lied to myself and others, and for all the times that I
didn't ask for help. I wanted to forgive myself, but I didn't know
how. I did the crime, now I had to do the time. It was payback and
my life was the penance.

We exited the tunnel and everything turned black inside the
bus. I could see the bright city skyline disappear as we continued
down the dark, windy highway. I wanted to reach out and pull it
closer. The days were getting shorter and shorter. Soon we would

turn the clocks back. I wondered how much longer I would have to stay in Pennsylvania. Would I be there to see a snowy winter? When would I see Mason again? How long would I have to work at Ruth's? I slid my headphones on and turned up the volume. I closed my eyes and rested my head against the cold window. *Lay, lady, lay . . .*

Take Two, and Call Me...

September became October, Halloween passed, leaves turned orange, and I remained on the inside looking out. The days became shorter, and the darkness took over. The Stackers did the trick. They gave me the energy to keep going. I had a hard time sitting still, though. I would run up and down Ruth's stairs for exercise while she took naps on the couch. I tidied her house, washed her dishes, prepared meals, baked cookies, did her laundry, and sorted the mail with ease. Things appeared clear to me at first, I was in a focused routine. But as weeks went by, that began to change. I paced around the house anxiously, looking for something to do. I needed to have a task to keep me sane. I rarely stopped to eat, my daily nutrients came from a few grapes and gallons of coffee.

One day I hopped on the scale in Ruth's bathroom. I'd always weighed somewhere between 130 and 135 pounds, which seemed perfect for my five-foot, eight-inch frame. The orange arrow pointed just below 120. I thought it was broken. I hadn't noticed that fifteen pounds of my body had disappeared. Apparently nobody else had, either. My mother and I still weren't speaking. Stacey and I would exchange a few words when I was at home or when she was relieving me from a shift, and I never saw Stephanie. It was just good ol' Ruth and me. Two gals losing their marbles together.

At that point I didn't realize that the Stackers were pushing me to the brink again. If I did, I didn't care. I just wanted to survive, get through the day, and if that meant swallowing two fluorescent yellow horse pills, I would. As I got more agitated, so did Ruth. We spent so much time together that we were becoming linked, like women that lived in the same house and got their periods at the same time. Each day I was having to remind her of her sanity while I was slowly losing mine. She would wake up from an afternoon nap wanting breakfast or change back into her pajamas after lunch.

All I could do was write to keep my mind occupied during the day. Notebook after notebook was filled with thoughts, poems, sketches, and cries for help. There was so much crammed into my head that it needed another place to hide. There was no room left. I was a hamster on a wheel unable to jump off. I thought about Mason, the city, school, acting, my mom, my dad, and on and on. Each one led back to the same place. I felt dead inside. I was alive, but not living. Watching Ruth was like looking into a mirror. In my mind, we were both old and senile. It didn't matter that she was sixty years older than me. I was twenty-three and my cards were played. My life was over.

One desperate morning I decided to call Dr. P. His secretary put me right through.

"Hi, Lynn."

"I don't know what's happening, I feel worse and worse each day . . ."

"Listen, Lynn, I'm glad you called me. It could be that we need to adjust your meds."

Am I a fucking thermostat? Just turn me a few degrees cooler and I'll be fine. "Okay," I muttered while Ruth snored on the couch.

"Remind me what you're on again," he asked.

"Um . . . I'm taking Resperidol and Clonapin. I was taking them two times a day, but you cut them down to one." I didn't mention the superenergizing fat burner called Stackers. I mean, they were from GNC, the "live well place."

"Well, I'm going to start you on something else. I want you to stop taking the meds that you're on. I'm going to write you a prescription for something called Paxil, it's an antidepressant. A lot of my patients are finding it extremely helpful. I think it might work for you, too. The prescription will be waiting for you at the pharmacy by the end of the day, all right?" he asked.

"Okay, I'll pick it up there. Thank you for your help."

"No problem, Lynn, why don't you also call to set up an appointment with me, we can talk about what's going on."

I wanted to say, *If I had insurance I would,* but instead I said, "I will, thanks."

"Take care, Lynn. I'll see you soon."

"'Bye."

I sat on the chair and thought about how simple it was to call a doctor and have him dish out more pills. *Paxil, hmmm* . . . I remember seeing a commercial for it on TV. *Are you uncomfortable in crowds . . . not feeling quite right?* There was a pill for everything nowadays. One ad after another. *Swallow this if you have nail fungus, pop this if you urinate a lot, take this if you sweat . . . if you cough . . . if you're fat . . . if you're tired . . . if you're alert . . . if you have red fucking hair!* Talk about mixed messages. We have "Just Say No" commercials running along side "Swallow This" commercials. It didn't make any sense, but I wasn't about to ask questions. I was going to follow the doctor's orders.

The side of my shiny, new orange bottle of pills read *Warning, may cause nausea, loss of appetite, and sleeplessness. Perfect,* I thought as I washed them down. *This should be good.* The first couple weeks didn't feel any different than the last. I was still taking Stackers along with the Paxil. It was hard to imagine that it could get any worse, but it did. I was off the wall and couldn't even sit still to write. I paced around the house, looking out windows, and washed my hands several times an hour. I still performed my daily duties with Ruth. Feeding her, helping her dress, letting the cat in and out. But once she started sleeping during the day, all day, I was alone.

At night, I would lay in the bedroom across from hers with my door open so I could hear any movement. She never had a problem sleeping before, but she was starting to get up more and more. I was the mother of a newborn, barely closing my eyes before I had to be in the other room quieting things down. The one time that I dozed off, I was woken up by the sound of a closing door. I ran into Ruth's room to find her bed made and her pajamas folded on the chair. I rushed downstairs and checked the rooms, she was nowhere to be found. I ran out into the cold, predawn air, barefoot. This wasn't New York City where there were always streetlights shining. The only thing that I could see was my breath. It was dark and cold as I ran around searching for her.

"Ruth, Ruth . . ." I yelled out.

There was no response as I made my way to the front of the house. Nothing. I ran down the street and heard movement. I was waiting for a bear to jump out from behind the trees and maul me, but my wish didn't come true. There she was with her coat on and her purse around her arm, out for a Sunday stroll.

I held onto her arm. "Ruth, what are you doing, it's three in the morning?"

"Oh . . . I'm going to see my sister Claire."

"Ruth, Claire died. Remember, we've talked about this, Claire doesn't live down the street anymore," I said, turning her around.

"She doesn't? Well, by golly, I guess I forgot. I just wanted to see her again, I miss her," she said as we walked back in the house.

"I know you do," I said.

I helped her change into her pajamas again and tucked her in. "Now if you need anything or want to go anywhere, just come over to my room across the hall. I'll help you with whatever you need, all right? Good night," I said, turning to walk away.

"Thank you Lynn. Thank you for being so nice to me," she said yawning. "Ahhh . . . I'm tired, so tired."

That was the first time she had called me by name. I closed her door and went into the bathroom. I splashed cold water on my face and looked into the mirror. I had bleached my hair white, my skin was pale, and my bones were noticeable. Someone who didn't know any better might think that I was the patient and Ruth was my nurse.

I Used To . . .

I used to take ecstasy,
Now I take Paxil.

I used to have friends,
Now I have doctors.

I used to spend all night dancing,
Now I spend all night pacing.

I used to have clear skin,
Now I have acne.

I used to try to forget,
Now I desperately try to remember.

I used to have drive,
Now I have depression.

I used to control my thoughts,
Now they control me.

I used to fear death,
Now I fear life.

Snow Falling

I was sitting in the middle of the living room floor with my note-book open and pen in hand. Ruth was in her usual horizontal posi-tion on the couch, arms folded and mouth open. A chill passed through me. I inhaled deeply and filled my head and lungs with oxygen. A sense of calm lifted me to my feet. I walked through the dining room into the kitchen and stared out the window into the backyard.

An invisible force was pulling me out into the cold air. I took a deep breath, reached my arms out to the sky, and closed my eyes. I felt soft kisses covering my face and opened my eyes to see the first snow of the season falling all around me. I was transported to a dif-ferent world. I was an angel dancing in heaven. A sense of peace captured my soul and I was one with God. I was in ecstasy.

I wanted to share my treasure with the world. I ran inside and closed the door. The sense of peace melted along with the snow on my sweater. It was replaced with dread. I looked at Ruth laying on the couch, her snoring getting louder and louder until it was all I could hear. Everything started to move faster. I paced around the kitchen, in the dining room, and up and down the stairs. It was hap-pening again. I went into the living room and began packing my bag. I didn't know where I was going.

"Are you okay, dear?" Ruth asked, sensing my confusion.

"It's my head, something is wrong with my head, please, no, no, no . . ."

"Why don't I get you an aspirin," she said, standing up.

"No, Ruth, I can't . . . I have to call someone," I said, picking up the phone.

"All right, you do that."

"Hello, Business Services, this is Kathy speaking, may I help you?"

"Mom . . . it's me." I hadn't called her at work in months. I hadn't had a conversation with her since summer. "I'm at Ruth's, something is wrong."

"Lynn, what happened? Is she okay?"

"Ruth's fine . . . it's me . . . it's me . . . it's me," I said, crying into the phone.

Her worst nightmare all over again. Another phone call, another desperate plea for help. "Lynn, stay right there, don't leave. I'm coming over there, okay? Listen to me . . ."

"Okay. Okay," I said, looking up at Ruth, who was staring at me.

"Don't leave Ruth, stay with her. I'll be right over."

"Why don't you go home, I'll be fine here by myself," Ruth said. "You need to rest."

"No . . . my mom is coming, I have to wait," I said, turning on the TV.

The smiling news anchor was yapping away. He was made of wax. Fake, plastic, and shiny. I began biting the skin off my cuticles. I was gnawing at myself like a rabid dog. I couldn't sit still, I stood up and looked out every window in the house, starting downstairs and working my way up. I was moving inside a snowflake. Everything was white, the walls, the blankets, the carpet. The falling snow was like watching static on a television. I prayed to God once again to save me. *Make it stop . . . please, make it stop . . .*

Talking to the Dead

The squeaking of the windshield wipers were like nails across a chalkboard. I closed my eyes and covered my ears.

"Lynn, what's going on? What happened at Ruth's?" she asked, moving my left hand off my ear.

"I don't know . . . I was writing . . . I felt good . . . peaceful, and then it changed. I saw the snow, something was in the snow."

"Lynn, I think I should take you to the hospital."

"NO, please, no," I begged. I pictured the emergency room, the pills, the psychiatric ward. I couldn't go back there. "I just need to go home, I want to sleep."

"Okay, but if you feel worse, we need to see a doctor."

I think she was relieved in a sense, knowing that I had no insurance to pay for another hospital stay. I would just have to keep this under control. It would pass.

We pulled into the driveway. Everything was blanketed in white.

I rushed back to my room and climbed into bed. I rolled up into a fetal position and moaned into my pillow. I could feel my brain sizzling and overheating like a racecar. I was waiting for smoke to shoot out of my ears. My thoughts were fragmented and fast. It brought everything back, six months ago I was in this exact same position in my Brooklyn apartment. Was this going to keep happening? I shuddered at the idea. My mother entered, carrying my Tigger mug.

"Are you okay? Do you want to talk about anything?" she asked.

I wanted to scream at the top of my lungs that I was in hell again. That I needed her to get me out of this, to make it stop. "No, I think I'm tired . . . I've been at Ruth's too much." I was biting my tongue, holding my breath underwater.

"Well, I'll let you get some rest. If you need anything, I'll be right out here."

"Okay."

I let out a loud breath as she closed the door. I stood up and paced around my room, lighting my cinnamon Glade candles and pulling a random book from the shelf. It was the blue Bible. "See you around, Dollface" was written on the inside cover. I took it as a sign, a foreshadowing of events; I was going to end up back in the loony bin, I knew it.

My room became solitary confinement. I was on lockdown. I stared out the windows, scribbled in my notebook, and read quotes from the Bible. As the hours disappeared, so did I. My mother came in to check on me a few times and I struggled to keep it together, hiding my torment. I forced myself to eat some soup, and saltines. I wasn't used to anything in my stomach, I wanted to vomit. I deserved an Oscar for my performance. I don't know if my mother believed me, but she acted the part, both of us playing our roles to protect ourselves from the truth.

I could hear them talking outside my door. *Is she okay? What's going on?* The words "hospital . . . medicine . . . doctor" echoed inside my head. I crouched down by the door and put my ear to it like I used to, listening to my mom cry after my parents fought. Then the conversation got even louder, turning into a roaring cackle. Like the witches at the beginning of *Macbeth*. I heard laughing and then they started to call me names: *idiot, psycho, crazy, damaged.* The words lashed against me like a whip.

I was wide awake long after everyone else was asleep. The dead silence made me feel even crazier. I was ready to burst apart into flames. I tore open my door and went into Stacey's room.

"Stace . . . Stace . . ." I whispered into the black room.

"What? What's wrong?" she asked, turning the light on. "It's four in the morning."

"I can't sleep, I don't know how, will you help me, please?"

She got up from her bed, wrapping her blanket around her. "I'll come to your room."

For a split second I thought this might help. If I had a sane person lying next to me, I could fall asleep and all this would cease. She climbed into bed next to me. When we were little, Stacey and I used to sleep together when my mother worked night shifts. I was scared, knowing that my father was the only one in the house, so Stacey would always invite me to sleep in her bed. So here we were again, eighteen years later. Little Lynn reaching out to her big sister.

"Are you afraid of me, Stacey?"

"No, why would I be afraid of you?"

"Because I'm like this . . . crazy."

"You're not crazy, Lynn." I could tell she was trying hard to believe that.

"Do you think about death?"

"Lynn, I can't do this right now, try to sleep."

I lay there with my mind and thoughts reeling. My body was still, but my insides were racing. A few minutes of silence passed. I couldn't do it. My mouth started to move a mile a minute. Babbling about life, death, the Bible, our childhood, the snow.

"Stop, Lynn. I have to be up in a couple hours. I need sleep. I'm sorry."

"It's okay . . . good night," I said as she left my room and closed the door.

I stared at the stereo on top of my dresser. Music, that's what I needed. I put in my *Mozart for Meditation* CD and pushed play. The noise inside my head was too loud, so I turned the volume up all the way. My walls began to shake as I danced around the dark room. My door swung open.

"Lynn, what is going on here?" my mother asked, trying to find the power button on the stereo.

The silence was back. "I couldn't sleep . . ."

"Well, other people are trying to." She stared into my eyes. "Come down to my room, grab your pillow."

I followed her down the stairs and into her bedroom. I laid next to her and she wrapped her arms around me.

"You're all right, I'm right here," she whispered into my ear.

I started crying and couldn't stop. A dark, lost, tormented child calling out for help. "Oh my God . . . oh my God . . ." I repeated over and over.

I stayed in my mom's room, keeping her awake with my questions about life and death until morning began to rear its ugly head. The room was getting brighter and I hadn't slept at all. I remember taking ecstasy, partying all night, and never resting. I thought it was fun. *Now look at me, look what I've become.* I wanted to push stop or rewind, but I couldn't. This wasn't a fucking movie.

I got out of bed and staggered upstairs, my mom shadowing my every move.

"Lynn, we have to go to the hospital. I don't know what else we can do. Why don't you come back downstairs with me while I get dressed?"

"No, I'm going to lay right here until you're ready. I need to sit still."

"Okay . . . I'll be right back. Don't move."

When I heard her footsteps going down the stairs, I jolted up off the couch and rushed back to my room. I slipped into my black Converse sneakers, ran back through the kitchen and out the back door into the snowy yard. I didn't care that it was below freezing outside. I had no jacket on, just fleece drawstring pants and a yellow T-shirt with the words GIRLS KICK written in black across the front. I was in a marathon, huffing my way down to the creek. I stepped through the water and climbed up the snowy hill that led to the cemetery.

I could hear my shoes slapping against the wet road. I weaved in and around the tombstones, searching for something, anything to help me while reading the names and dates of the dead that surrounded me. My Gram Witmer was buried somewhere up there. She could help me find my way. I was on a hunt, wiping the cold snow off random headstones, praying to the spirits to help me find my gram. I came to a large tombstone and rubbed off the white. JULIA AND HARLON WITMER. She and my great-grandfather were buried side by side. I got down on my knees.

"Hi Gram, it's me . . . I need you . . . please, help me . . . I don't know what to do . . . show me the way . . . please . . . please," I pleaded, pressing my face against the cold stone. "I know you can hear me . . . meet me . . . take me to where you are . . . I want to be with you."

My tears were freezing on my face. I had never been so desperate in all my life. I was the only one on earth. The wind was blowing through the naked trees and I looked up and saw a black bird flying above. Maybe that was her. I stood up and began running under it, following its every move. I was at the top of the hill and lost sight of it. I began sliding down the hill, branches crackling under my shoes and twigs and burs sticking to my pants. I worked my way down the hill and through the brush. I was a wild animal trying to find its way to safety.

I came to an open field and stared up at the sky. The bird was gone, along with all hope. I collapsed on the ground and laid back with my face toward the gray clouds. The ground was frozen and hard underneath me. I wanted to die. This dead corn field could be my grave. I closed my eyes and willed my departure from the world. I opened my eyes to see that I was still trapped in this warped reality.

I stood up and began to run toward the road. I crossed the street and entered a circle of houses that looked exactly the same. I read the sign: THE MEADOWS, A RETIREMENT COMMUNITY. *Great, this could be it, maybe my gram would be here waiting for me.* I started to open mailboxes at the end of each house, reading through the names. An old lady with pink rollers in her hair came out of a house.

"Can I help you with something?" she asked.

"Do you know where Julia Witmer lives? She's my great-grandmother."

"No, I don't think I know her. Did she just move here?"

"Well, she died when I was . . . seven, so she's been here a long time."

The old lady just stared at me. I could tell that she had no information. I dropped her mail on the ground and ran in the other direction. I saw a pickup truck parked along the road in front of one of the houses. No one was in it, but the engine was running. People did this all the time in Danville. I opened the door and hopped in front of the wheel. I was about to kick it into drive when I saw a maroon Toyota Camry a few feet ahead. I thought it was Stacey, it was her car. I jumped out of the truck, slammed the door, and ran toward Stacey's car.

There was an older woman walking toward it with her keys out.

"Wait," I screamed.

She looked up at me as I approached her car. "Are you okay, honey, do you need some help?"

I was angry that this strange woman had stolen my sister's car. "You're not my sister, this is her car."

"This is my car, sweetheart. What's your name?" she asked, moving toward me.

I moved a few steps back. "Lynn, why?"

"I'm just trying to help you, you seem lost."

The gold cross dangling on her necklace caught my eye. A sense of calm came to me. "I am lost. I'm looking for my great-grandmother, Julia Witmer, she's going to take me to heaven."

"Well, Lynn, my name is Isabel. I'm going to help you," she said, putting her arm around me.

I trusted her. "Let's go down to Maria Joseph Manor, that's where the nuns live. We can call someone for you there."

"I don't want to go in your car," I snapped. *Don't get into a car with a stranger.* I could lay on graves, go through an elderly woman's mail, get into a running car, but there was no way I was taking a ride from a stranger.

"Fine, we can walk. It's only right down the hill," she said, pointing to the large brick building below.

We walked hand in hand down the hill. She was several inches shorter than me and smelled like lilacs. "Now do you have other family here in Danville?"

She was a smart woman. "Yes, lots of family."

"What's your grandma's name?"

"Kate Bennick is my grandmother, she lives close to Mill Street."

"Oh, I know her. She's a nice lady. Volunteers a lot for the church and the Red Cross," she said as we approached the building.

She opened the door and I followed her in. My body began to defrost and the warm air stung my frigid skin. Old, decrepit nuns were everywhere. Some were being pushed in wheelchairs, others were walking with canes. I didn't want to be there, it smelled like rotten flesh, and I was already plotting my escape. A tall nun approached us.

"Hi there, can I help you ladies with something?"

Her face felt like it was pressing against mine. She had very masculine features. I thought she was a transvestite playing a nun. Isabel pulled her to the side and I could hear their whispers. Mr. Nun came over to me and grabbed my arm.

"Let's go into a room and relax, all right?" she said, pulling me toward a hallway.

I had flashes of being locked in a room with a transvestite nun as she beat me with a ruler. *I don't think so.* I looked at the large, wooden cross around her neck and pulled myself away from her. "No . . . you are evil . . . you shouldn't have that cross around your neck. I'm not going with you, sister," I yelled as I turned around and ran for the door.

"Wait, Lynn, wait, " Isabel yelled as I escaped outside.

I started running back toward the road. A police car pulled up next to me, forcing me to the side.

He rolled the window down. "Lynnie, it's Jay. Your mother is looking for you, get in."

This was a small town, everyone knew everybody else. My grandfather used to be the chief of police. Jay was at my graduation, family gatherings, and birthday parties. "I'm not getting in," I said as I looked straight ahead and continued walking.

"Fine, I'll just follow you then, make sure you get there," he said, driving slowly next to me.

On the other side of the road came my younger sister driving down the hill. She jumped out of her car and ran over to me.

"Lynn, what are you doing? You're freezing! Get in the car, I'll take you home."

I started to cry. "I can't . . . I'm sorry . . ." I said as Steph walked with me.

"I'm your sister, I don't want to see you out here."

I raced away, sprinting up the hill toward Bloom Street. I walked out into the middle of the road and started running on the yellow lines. Cars passed both sides of me and then traffic came to a standstill. I walked in between the cars, staring straight ahead. I heard sirens behind me, I was numb. I wanted a truck to hit me and break me into a million tiny pieces. I was ready for it to end. My mother came running over and pulled me off the road. We were in front of my house.

"You're frozen solid," she said, holding onto me for dear life.

I was shaking with fear and exhaustion. My mom wrapped a blanket around me as Jay came through the front door.

"Lynnie, that was not a smart move. Listen, if you don't go with your mother to the hospital, I'm going to have to handcuff you and take you in my police car. I don't want to do that. Okay?"

I nodded my head. I went back outside and got into the car with her. Jay pulled out of the driveway after us. I leaned my head against the window. There was nothing left for me to do.

"You're going to be fine, Lynn, I'm right here with you," she said, rubbing my shoulder.

Nothing mattered anymore. I was hanging onto life by a thin thread. I was as transparent as water. We went into the emergency room and I told the doctor about the Paxil and the Stackers. My mother's eyes widened. She had no idea. The young doctor told me that he wanted to give me something to calm me down. I didn't even realize that my hands were bleeding until I saw him glance at them. I was eating away at my skin and I didn't even know it. I couldn't feel. He told me that I had to make a choice. I could either swallow two pills or get a shot in the ass. I bent over and dropped my drawers. I was through with pills . . . for good.

Sticking Together

The room became quiet. I lifted my head up. It was a bowling ball. I got a glimpse of a fat man sitting in a chair by the door. He was wearing a brown uniform. My head fell back down with a thud.

"Help me, please . . . help me," I said, slipping away.

"I am praying for you right now . . ." said my guard.

Outside I could hear my mother's voice in the hallway, along with my father's. I heard the doctor. He was the teacher from *Peanuts. Waaah . . . Waaah . . . Waaah.* I was out.

When I woke from my sedation I was lying on a twin bed in a strange room, wearing hospital attire. There was a black stamp on my gown that read PROPERTY OF BLOOMSBURG HOSPITAL. Blooms-burg was the town right next to Danville, ten minutes away tops. I stood up and looked out the barred window. I could tell by the dark blue color of the sky that it was early morning. I was a little groggy, but other than that felt normal. I knew where I was and what had happened the day before. It wasn't like my last "episode," when I woke up confused and disoriented. Strange to think that a stay in the psychiatric ward could be as normal as sleeping at a Best Western. The door opened and a young nurse entered.

"Good morning, Lynn, I'm Julie. I'm a nurse on the ward. Do you know where you are?"

I pointed down at my hospital gown. "Bloomsburg Hospital?"

When she smiled she looked even younger. "That's right. I

wasn't sure if you remembered. When you were admitted you weren't lucid," she said, looking down at her chart.

"How did I get here? I mean, I know how, but who brought me?"

"Well, I know you were transferred in an ambulance from Geisinger, their psych ward was full. Your mother, and I believe your sister, were with you."

I was thankful that the psych ward in Danville was all stocked up. I don't think I could have faced the same nurses and the same setting. I was relieved to be somewhere different, where I didn't have a track record.

"Well, I'm sure you want to change into your clothes," she said.

I was waiting to see what hoops I had to jump through first. "Yeah, that would be nice, although I think the open-back dress is quite flattering," I said, laughing. I couldn't believe that I was making jokes. Wasn't I supposed to be ripping my hair out and crying?

"Well, the doctor here has prescribed something called Zyprexa. Have you heard of it?"

I wanted to say, *Yeah, all my crazy friends and I get together and compare medications.* "No."

"I'm going to get your dose and bring the bag that your mother left for you," she said, smiling as she left the room.

It was weird to feel this normal. Like I just woke from a long, horrible dream. No racing thoughts, no delusions. I just wanted to see my mom and sisters. Julie entered the room again, carrying two tiny cups.

"Here you go, Lynn."

One had water, the other had two pink pills. I put them on my tongue and washed them down. "Ahhh . . ." I said, lifting my tongue before she asked me to.

Her smile told me that she knew that this wasn't my first time on a ward. "Thank you. I have to ask one of the other nurses where your bag is. It might be locked somewhere, I didn't check yet. I'll be right back."

As much as I never wanted another pill to touch my tongue again, I knew that I had to cooperate. I knew the drill. I wanted to be out of there as quickly as possible. I had to play the game by their rules. I sat down on the hard bed and thought about the past couple months. None of it seemed real. *Had I really been living with a senile woman? Did I really think that mixing antidepressants with Stackers was a good idea?* I knew that I had fucked up, again, but I wasn't about to bleed from the same scars. I had a sudden sense of strength and calm just knowing that I was alive. Julie emerged again, carrying a plastic shopping bag.

"Here you go, Lynn. After you get changed, come out to the nurses' station. I want to show you around the ward and get some food in your stomach," she said, turning around to walk away. "Oh, and Happy Thanksgiving."

I had no idea that it was Thanksgiving. The past couple months had melted together to become one long day. I had lost all sense of time. I opened the bag to find my favorite red hooded sweatshirt and a pair of jeans. I craved a shower, but I wasn't about to ask a nurse to assist me. I slid out of the blue pants and gown and looked down at my body. My ribs were jutting out and my skin was hanging off my bones. I was shocked by how thin I was. I was a prisoner of war, starved and held against my will. I pulled the warm sweatshirt over my head. I was comforted and overwhelmed with emotion and tears started to dance down my face. I climbed into my baggy jeans and knelt down on the cold floor. I placed my elbows on the bed and let my head fall into my hands. *Thank you, thank you for saving me again. I promise you that I won't ruin this chance like the one before. I'm ready . . . I love you, Lynn.*

My mom and sisters came that evening and brought Thanksgiving dinner. We celebrated the holiday together on the psychiatric ward. There were only four other patients besides myself on the floor. There were no group activities that day, everyone just kept to themselves. There were other families there that evening, but we were the loudest—jabbering away like we were in the privacy of our own home. There were no forks or knives allowed on the ward, so all of us were trying to cut our turkey with a spoon. We laughed out loud at the absurdity of it all. I raised my cup of ginger ale for a toast.

"I want to thank all of you for putting up with my shit these past couple months. I know it hasn't been easy, but I'm planning on making some changes. Mom, thanks for seeing through my ugliness. Stace, thanks for doing my laundry and cleaning my room, and Steph, thanks for playing hard to get," I said, leaning over and kissing her on the cheek as she pushed me away.

"That was a beautiful toast, Lynn," said my mom, taking a drink from her plastic cup. "Now I want to say something."

"Great, here we go," said Stacey, smiling and rolling her green eyes.

"The four of us are a family; it might not have turned out the way we wanted it to, but this is it. I can't take anything back, but I can apologize to each of you," my mom said as tears began to well up in her eyes. "All we have is each other now and I am so grateful for that. It's easy to snap one stick in half, but when you have four bunched together it's much harder to break them."

I stood up and walked around the table and wrapped my arms around my mother. "I love you, I'm so sorry for the way I've acted."

"What did mom say about sticks?" I heard Stephanie ask Stacey.

"I love you, I'm sorry, too." Stacey said.

We might not be the Bradys or the Cleavers, but we were a family. A group of women standing together. When I was younger I never understood the meaning of Thanksgiving. Each year, I watched my relatives stuff their faces and sit around with their pants unzipped, watching the football game. But that day I understood. It wasn't about the turkey, the pumpkin pie, the tablecloth, or even the utensils or lack thereof. It was about coming together and being grateful. It was about understanding and forgiveness. It was about lifting our plastic cups to the sky and smiling.

part 5

*

coming clEan

Ashes

I was released the next morning. In and out. I signed my name on a piece of paper, a nurse gave me a few pamphlets, and I was on my way home. Even though I didn't want to get my new prescription filled, my mother insisted. I was determined to lead a drug-free life and that included all pharmaceuticals. But I wanted to ease her worries, so I decided to give them another whirl.

The day after I arrived home I received a phone call from New York City.

"Hi, Lynn, this is Gini."

"Hi there, how are you?"

"Great, I wanted to call and give you an update. The show is complete and it is set to air next week, on the thirtieth at ten P.M."

It had slipped my mind. I had forgotten all about MTV and the *True Life* special. "Oh, wow. Good, I'm excited to see how it all turned out," I said, still in shock that I was going to be on TV.

"I think you're going to be pleased, Lynn. Your section is really moving and I want to thank you. Thank you for being so open and vulnerable and allowing us into your life. I know it wasn't easy."

"You're welcome. I'm sure you did a great job and I look forward to seeing it."

"Well, we'll definitely talk after the show airs. Take care of yourself, Lynn."

"I will, thanks, Gini. 'Bye."

I sat down at the dining room table and looked out at the gray sky. I couldn't believe that the ugliest part of my life was going to be viewed by millions. *What was I thinking?* The first time that I was out of the hospital back in May, I jumped right in without giving it much thought. Now here I was once again and it was showtime. I had no idea what to expect. I was nervous, excited, and scared thinking about the next week.

Over the next few days I became jittery and it wasn't from nerves. The Zyprexa was taking hold and I was on edge. My hands were shaky and I had trouble sitting still. My thoughts began to race and I knew that I had to stop. There was no way that I could go down this road. I never wanted a pill controlling my life again. I didn't care what the doctor ordered, I threw the one-hundred dollar bottle of pink pills in the garbage, then went back into my room and pulled the colorful hospital pamphlets from out of my closet.

One of them was about Zyprexa, describing its benefits and how it could "give me my life back." The others were about mental illness, depression, and "what everyone should know about anxiety disorders." But my favorite one was "what you should know about schizoaffective disorder." The cover was bright orange with a confused man standing with his hand up to his mouth. Above his head floated a dark gray cloud with two pictures inside of it. One was a spaceship and the other was a tombstone. I gathered them up and put my shoes on. I grabbed a box of matches from the kitchen drawer and went out into the backyard.

The ground was hard and crunchy under my feet. I shivered as I crouched down and struck a match against the box. The wind blew it out and I tried again. On the third try I shielded the match with the pamphlets and one of them caught the small flame. The wind was on my side as the papers began to burn. I held on until the heat reached my fingers and I had to let go. I wrapped my arms around my legs and stared as flecks of ash flew away with the wind.

I knew that my health, happiness, and freedom were never going to be attained by reading a pamphlet or swallowing a pill. I was going to have to do it the old-fashioned way: work hard and earn it. *I might be sick, but I'm not schizophrenic or psychotic.* I was a young woman struggling to find strength in a broken life and the cure for my disease was not a prescription. It was acceptance. I don't know exactly how it happened, but the shame, guilt, and pain that had been my existence were disintegrating, along with the pamphlets. I had stopped resisting my life. I was a drug addict. My father was an alcoholic. My family was fucked up. And it didn't matter anymore. I stood up and walked back to the house. The wind whistled in my ear and the cold air passed through my body. I was charged with hope.

Put on a Little Makeup

We all gathered around the television. The room was silent as we watched it unfold. There were old pictures of me from high school, smiling, with long, wavy hair. I was young and innocent. My mom had also given MTV some home videos. Watching myself on stage singing and dancing made my eyes well up with tears. I was so vibrant and full of possibility. I felt sad and hopeful at the same time.

I'm not going to lie and say that I wasn't upset at myself for not putting a little more effort into the way I looked. A box of hair dye and a little makeup couldn't have hurt. But overall I was touched by my own words. I had forgotten most of what I had said to the camera months ago. It was like picking up an old journal and reading through it. The "old" you teaching the "new" you a thing or two about life. I was proud of myself for being open and honest and letting all of the ugliness and pain come through. There was no more hiding.

After the show was over I looked around the room. My mother's eyes were wet with tears. Stephanie and Stacey seemed to be filled with disbelief as they sat staring at the TV. None of us had had any idea that it would affect us as much as it did.

"I'm tired, I have to be up early tomorrow," Stacey said, cutting through the silence and standing up. "Good job, Lynn, good night."

Stephanie followed her up the stairs and it was just my mom and me left sitting on the carpet. "That was incredible, Lynn. What did you think?" she asked, grabbing a Kleenex.

"I don't know . . . it's a lot to take in," I said, picking up a piece of brown fuzz from the carpet. "I can't really wrap my brain around it right now. I'm still in disbelief."

"I know I say this to you a lot, but I mean it. I'm so proud of you . . . for everything," she said, leaning over to hug me.

"I know I don't say this enough, but I'm proud of you for everything, too. For choosing to turn your life around," I said, holding onto her. "I love you."

That night I stayed awake thinking about the show. It was liberating to know that I was no longer full of fear or shame. It became clear to me that night what I had to do. I was ready to move back to New York to tie up all the loose ends that I had left behind. Pieces of my heart and soul were scattered throughout the city streets and I needed to go back to reclaim them. I knew that I could do it. There would be more demons waiting for me, but I was ready to slay them and this time I would bury them . . . for good.

A Phone Call

The morning after the show aired there was a knock at the front door. A man handed me a vase of two dozen beautiful red roses. I set them down on the dining room table and inhaled their fragrance. The tiny card read, *You inspire me to be a better man, I love you and miss you, Mason.* I put my nose up to the soft petals and closed my eyes. I was touching his cheek.

That sweet-smelling gesture was then followed by some stinky ones. I received several phone calls in the days after the MTV show aired. Old acquaintances and a couple ex-boyfriends resurfaced like worms after a rainstorm. *What's going on with you? I thought you were studying acting? You looked horrible.* It was strange talking to people that hadn't seen me in years. It's not like I had landed a commercial or was on a new sitcom. I exposed the darkest part of my life for everyone to see. My fellow classmates and everyone in my town certainly knew what I had been up to since high school. It was front-page news. "DANVILLE GRAD TELLS HER STORY OF ADDICTION ON MTV. LYNN SMITH'S STORY OF ECSTASY AGONIES." I couldn't even go to the grocery store to buy a box of Cocoa Puffs without someone staring at me and whispering behind my back. At first it bothered me, but then I found the humor in it. I got a kick out of putting Danville on the map the way I did.

Another call came my way one afternoon in early December. It was from a man who worked at North Central Security, a juvenile detention center close to our house.

"Hi, Ms. Smith, my name is Michael Farrell. I work as an instructor and guard at a lockdown unit for young men between the ages of twelve and eighteen. Most are from the inner city, Philly and New York. Most of their crimes are drug related. I saw your special the other week and I knew that you lived close to North Central. I think my guys could really benefit from you coming in and talking to them, if you would be willing to."

I had no idea how to respond. I mean, what was I going to tell a group of inner-city guys? What did I know about anything? How could I help them? "Um . . . I guess I could. I haven't ever done anything like that before, but . . . yeah, I'll do it."

"Great. Let's set something up for next week. Better that we get you in here before the holiday. How is the fifteenth at nine A.M.?"

Since going back to Ruth's was out of the question, my schedule was wide open. "That's fine. Do you have a VCR that I can use? If I could, I would like to show a clip of the show?"

"No problem. It's a smaller room, only about twenty guys. We can wheel in a TV and VCR for you. I really appreciate this, Lynn. I would love to pay you, but we don't have much of a budget."

Money had never crossed my mind. "That's okay, I just hope they don't throw tomatoes at me," I said, laughing.

"Believe me, they'll be on their best behavior, and there will be guards in the room. You'll be safe."

I was making a joke, but this was serious. These guys were prisoners, not schoolgirls. "Thanks. So I guess I'll see you next week."

"Thank you," he said. "I look forward to next week, Lynn. God bless you."

"Thank you. 'Bye."

I stood in the kitchen, thinking about speaking in that jail. Would I prepare a speech? Or maybe I would write my thoughts down on note cards? Yeah, right, I could just see me staring down at my hands while a bunch of brutes rolled their eyes and shifted around in their seats. Prepared speeches were never my thing. My strongest skill in acting school was improvisation; I would just have to wing it and hope for the best.

I went back to my room and stared out the window. I'd watched spring turn into summer, summer to fall, and now the ground was covered in white. My life was changing shape along with the seasons. I had been back in Danville for eight long months. I needed to get out while I still had it in me to leave. I'd rather move away and fall flat on my face than sell out on my dreams. The new year—2001—was approaching fast and I had only one resolution. *New York City, here I come.*

Hi, My Name Is . . .

Neil Diamond woke me at seven-thirty in the morning singing "Cracklin Rosie." I shot up out of bed, the butterflies were already flying around in my empty stomach. It was the first day of school, a blind date, and opening night all rolled into one. *Why am I so scared? What's the worst thing that can happen?* The only thing that calmed my nerves was knowing that no one could get up and walk out in the middle of my presentation.

I decided to sport my red hooded sweatshirt with the word "Independent" written across the front. I also wore a pair of baggy jeans, although they weren't nearly as baggy as they had been a few weeks earlier. I didn't want to look sexy and made up. I wasn't trying to impress or find a date . . . *But what am I trying to do?*

My mouth was as dry as a bone by the time we pulled into the parking lot. It was a dark, frigid morning. The wind was howling through the barren trees. Barbed wire covered the windows of the old brick building that stood on top of the small hill. The closer we got, the more I wanted to turn around and run the other way. I was in the movie *Psycho* walking toward the Bates Motel.

"Your going to be great, Lynn. Don't worry," my mom said, rubbing my back as we entered a set of double doors. I let out a gasp, realizing I was holding my breath. There was a large, bearded man standing inside. He towered over my mother and me like a giant.

"Hey, Lynn, I'm Mike," he said, reaching out his massive hand.

"Hi there, nice to meet you," I said as my hand disappeared inside of his.

"I really appreciate you doing this for us, Lynn. Follow me and I'll get you into the room before we bring the guys in. I warned them if they gave you any shit today they would have to answer to me. No one wants to deal with me."

His laugh was as gigantic as he was, bouncing off the bare walls and vanishing down the long hallway. This place looked like an abandoned school. The air inside was stale and cold. I looked up at the barred windows and was reminded of my stays in the psych wards. I took in a deep breath as we entered a room filled with wooden desks. Each desk had a chair attached to it. There was a TV and VCR on a metal cart in the front of the room. A woman in a uniform sat in a small glass room off to the side, drinking a cup of coffee.

"So this is it. I don't know if you have to set anything up," he said, looking around the room.

My mom pulled the tape from her purse and handed it to me. "I just have to pop this in the VCR. I'm just going to show a portion of it, its pretty long," I said, feeling my palms begin to sweat.

"You can have as much time as you like," he said, turning on the TV.

I stared at the blue screen. His words made my heart beat even faster. I had no idea what I was even going to say. "Okay, that's good to know."

"I'll be back in a few," he said, walking toward the door.

My mom took a seat at a desk in the back of the room. She smiled and winked at me. My body was heating up. I wished that I hadn't worn such a bulky sweatshirt. Maybe I should have squeezed into a tiny tank top, then maybe they would stay interested, even if they were just staring at my boobs. I stood at the front of the room, took in some stale air, and said a silent prayer to God. *I have no idea why I'm here, but I think you do. Please help me find the right words, guide me* . . . My prayer was interrupted by the sound of feet marching down the hall. I wanted to pee my pants as the footsteps got louder.

They filed in, about twenty of them, each one looking younger than the last. The majority of guys were black and Hispanic. Their piercing stares and blank expressions made them look hard. I was standing in front of a firing squad. My giant guard, Mike, made his way toward the front of the room. I could tell he demanded respect, but something in his brown eyes told me that he was really a teddy bear.

"As you have been told, today we have a special guest here to talk to you guys. Her name is Lynn Smith. I saw her on MTV last week talking about her drug problem and how it almost destroyed her life . . . *Alan,* eyes up here," he ordered the boy sitting near my mother. "I want you all to give her your undivided attention. She was nice enough to come here this morning. Don't give her any shit. And I don't want you to be afraid to ask her any questions. . . . Lynn," he said, looking over at me.

What an intro. The room was silent. "Hey, guys . . . my name is Lynn . . ." Each word was like thick mud coming out of my mouth. "I wanted to come here today to show you guys something. I was on an MTV show called *True Life, My Agony with Ecstasy.*" Some sat up a little straighter in their chairs. "I'm going to show you some of that show today and then I'm going to talk to you about it . . . and hopefully get a conversation started," I said, turning around and pushing play as quickly as I could.

Mike turned a set of lights off as I sat down at an open desk in the middle. The boy next to me glanced over. I smiled and he did the same and immediately turned away. The show started and I could feel the energy in the room shift. These guys were watching and listening. It was only the second time that I was seeing it, so it was still new to me. When images of clubs, raves, and people rolling appeared, there were several laughs and whispers bouncing around the room. They knew this scene, some of them were in here because of this scene. I started to relax as I peered around the darkened room. I knew that I could do this. You could hear a pin drop when the image of my brain flashed onto the screen. Then there were a few gasps and whispers. I stood up and made my way to the front. The lights came on as I turned around to face the group.

"So there you have it . . . some of it, I guess. I grew up in a small town, the same one that you find yourselves in today. After high school I had my sights set on the Big Apple," I said, looking around the room. I wasn't afraid anymore. Everything was there, ready to come out and fill the space. I told them about my life, about growing up in an alcoholic home. I told them the worst things that happened to me because of choosing drugs, the psych wards, the meds, the depression. I stared into their eyes, they weren't hardened criminals, they were just kids. Kids that were lost, confused, and broken, like me. Kids that needed a second chance, kids that didn't know any better, kids that wanted to be loved.

"I might be a white girl from a small town, but I know how you feel. I know how it feels to be locked somewhere, to lose everything you have. I just got out of my second psychiatric ward. I know what it's like to have no freedom, to have no hope," I said as tears snuck out of my eyes. I looked over to see Alan, the boy next to my mother, with tears streaming down his face. My mother had her hand resting on his back. I had never felt so connected to other people in my entire life. Time stood still as I went on to speak to them about life and choices, my choices.

"Every time I snorted a line or swallowed a pill, I lost a piece of myself. Giving up my power, giving up my control, and losing my mind in the process. I know you probably feel pretty shitty right now being stuck here. It's a waiting game. I know how awful it is to watch days pass by and life becomes a countdown. Please don't think that because you're locked in here, you are the only ones that feel this way. The only reason I'm not in here with you is because I got lucky. Each of us, everyone on this planet, feels hopeless at some point. Not everyone commits a crime, but believe me, we all do our time in one way or another." I glanced up at the clock on the wall, over an hour had passed. I couldn't believe it. "Well, I want to wrap things up by saying . . . that I love you guys . . . I truly mean that. Hopefully you have some questions or comments for me now, thank you."

The room was silent for a split second and then applause filled the air. A loud roar of hands slapping together. I knew that this was far from Broadway, far from the place that I had dreamed about when I was little. I was nowhere near the lights of the big city, but I had found home. I was being myself, authentically connecting to every person in that room.

Hands started to rise one by one. They asked me questions about ecstasy, about Mason, about acting, about the city. "What are we supposed to do when we go back to our homes, most of us live in cities. How do we stop?" "How do we say no when it's all around us?" "How do we say no when our parents sell it . . . snort it . . . do it, too?" The questions shot out of their mouths like bullets. They were scared and angry. They wanted answers to some tough questions, some questions that didn't have any answers.

"You know what, guys . . . I don't know. I'm right there with you. Those are all good questions. I'm planning on going back to New York City and I'm going to have to deal with the same things. Saying good-bye to the clubs, the friends, the drugs . . . it's not an easy choice. It's the hardest one we'll ever have to make. I'm willing to try, I'm willing to fight for it. If that means being alone, living by myself, having no friends, reading a book instead of going out, then that's what it means. I want to live, I don't want to be locked in a psych ward or in a jail. So I say to all of you, make that choice right here and right now. Promise yourself that you will do what it takes. Stay away from the stoops, stay away from the corners, stay away from your family, if that's what's going to keep you alive." The words flew out of me. As I was telling them, I was telling myself. Believing that I could create a better life. "Don't let people tell you that you can't. Don't let people judge you because you're black or Hispanic or because you did drugs or because you were locked in here. Each day we have a fresh start. Use it."

I looked back at my mom, her eyes were wide and present. The guards were dumbfounded as the guys got up out of their seats and came to the front of the room. I hugged each and every one of them. They inspired me as much as I did them. Their expressions were softer and more vulnerable as they smiled at me and walked out the door. I will never forget those faces. Mike walked over to me and wrapped his strong arms around my shoulders.

"Amazing . . . amazing," he said, letting go of me. "When I asked you to come here, I thought that it might be helpful. I've never seen these guys respond to anything like they did today. Some of these boys never speak. I couldn't believe some of the questions that were coming out of their mouths. I learned a lot. I had no idea what you were going to do today, no idea," he said, shaking his head.

"Neither did I, believe me. Neither did I."

Are You Ready?

As Christmas approached I still had no definite plan. I was determined to move back to New York City, but I had no clue what I was going to do once I got there. I had eight hundred dollars to my name and that wasn't enough to get my own place. Living with my old friends was out of the question. Mason offered to ask his parents if I could stay with him in their house until I was on my feet again, but I declined. I knew that they would say no and I didn't think that the situation would work. I was becoming desperate. I felt like my time was running out, and then one afternoon the phone rang.

"Hello?"

"Hey, stranger, how are you?" the voice said.

"Oh my God . . . Jill? Is that really you?" I squealed.

"Yes, I just got into town. I'm home for the holiday."

"Great," I said. Just hearing Jill's voice made me happy. We met in summer Bible school in fifth grade and became best friends that same day. We stayed close throughout middle school and high school. We were in plays together, skipped school together, even dated brothers together. We laughed, listened, and understood each other.

"Dude, I can't believe that I saw you on MTV, what the hell is going on? I had no idea. I was sitting in my apartment and your face appeared on the screen. I almost passed out!"

"I know, it's pretty crazy. I guess a lot has happened since we last talked. Are you still living in Manhattan?"

"Manhattan, no. Queens, yes. But not for long. You remember Nick, my boyfriend?" she asked.

"I think so . . ."

"Well, he just went out to L.A. He's landed some acting jobs out there and I'm moving out with him," she said.

"It figures, just when I start to get my shit together, I'm moving back to the city and you're moving to another coast. Great timing," I said, wiping my eyes with my free hand.

"You're coming back to New York City? When?"

"I don't know, soon. I have no idea where I'm going to live or what I'm going to do, but I'll figure it out. I just need to get out of here. I want a fresh start, you know?"

"Well, I don't know how you feel about this, but I'm not planning on moving to California until February. Nick's gone, so I'm all alone in a big two-bedroom apartment in Astoria. Come live with me. I know it's only for a month, but it could buy you some time. January's rent is already paid."

My whole body was lifted off the chair. "Jill, I can't believe this. I'm accepting your invitation. Yes . . . yes . . . yes!"

"Hey, we always wanted to be roommates, didn't we? This is going to be great. Let's get together soon. I can't wait to give you a big, fat hug."

"Me, too . . . me, too. Thanks, Jilly, I'll see you soon."

I was frozen in my chair. This was a sign that things might just work out. *Where there's a will, there's a way.* Now I had to break the news to my mother. She knew my plans, but I'm not sure that she believed I would follow through with them. It wasn't going to be easy. I knew that my mother hated the idea of me living in that city again. Deep down, she blamed the big rotten apple for transforming her little Snow White into a drug-crazed lunatic. It wasn't entirely untrue, but I knew that it was just a place, just a city. I'm sure that I would have found trouble in Oshkosh, Wisconsin, turned into a cheese addict or something. If I had to give my mom a spiked glass of eggnog to make the news go down easier, I would, but I had to tell her.

"What's in this?" she asked.

"Oh, it's just eggnog," I said, taking a seat across from her at the table.

"It tastes a little funny," she said, setting the cup down.

"The Little Drummer Boy" was playing in the background. "I want to talk to you about something . . . " *Pa-rump-pa-pum-pum* . . .

My mother quickly lifted the cup to her lips. "Ummm . . . I like it."

"I talked to Jill this afternoon . . ."

"Jill Farley?" she said, glancing up at me.

"There's only one Jill, Mom," I said, resting my hand on top of her tapping fingers. "She called because she saw the MTV special. I filled her in on a lot of what happened and told her that I was planning on moving back to the city, and she offered me a room in her place until I figure out what I'm going to do."

She lifted her head and stared straight into my eyes. "Lynn, do you think you're ready?"

"I don't know. But I can't sit around here and wait. I have to do this, Mom."

"It's your decision, Lynn, and as scared as I am, I'll support you. If you need to do this, then do it. When are you planning on leaving?"

"Jill's going back for New Year's, but I want to stay here with you guys. I thought that I would leave after the holiday." Even as I was saying the words I couldn't believe it. This was for real. In a little over a week I would leave Danville for good.

"Maybe I could take you."

"Mom, I know that you don't want to go back there and I don't blame you. I'll take the bus. I know it hasn't been easy. I haven't been easy. I could never have made it through this without you . . ."

My mother put her cold hand on top of mine. "I want you to

know something. I think this has been a blessing in disguise. You coming home, being in that hospital, put everything in perspective for me. I don't think I would have ever told your dad to leave. I would have probably stuck it out and been miserable for the rest of my life. I'm thankful . . . I'm just so happy you're alive," she said as tears streamed down her face.

I walked over to my mom, sat on her lap, and leaned my head against her shoulder. "Thanks."

"You're welcome," she whispered into my ear.

Welcome Home

I remember packing, and saying good-bye. I wrapped myself up in my wool peacoat. I layered up with a thermal shirt and sweater for the blistering conditions. I heard my mother's footsteps approaching from downstairs. The scent of her Spellbound perfume entered the room before she did.

"Are you all set?" she asked, sliding her arms into her long coat.

"Yeah, my stuff is in the car and I said my good-byes to Stace and Steph," I said, moving toward the door. *I remember my mom, Stacey, Stephanie, and me holding on and starting over.*

"The bus is at seven-thirty, so we should get moving," she said, flipping the kitchen light off and opening the door.

I turned around and looked at the darkened rooms. The smell of Christmas still hung in the air. At the end of the hallway the door to my father's room, my room, was open. *I remember my father and the smell of his breath.* I could see her hanging on the wall. *I remember looking at Picasso's* Naked Blue *and seeing my own pain.* I had to leave her behind. There was no room for her where I was going and I knew that she understood.

I closed my eyes and whispered, "Good-bye." I knew that my mom would sell the house soon and that I would probably never see it again. I was right. *I remember the FOR SALE sign and the sound of his van pulling out of the driveway for the last time.*

I closed the door behind me and braced myself for the frigid air.

The garage door was open and my mother was already sitting inside the running car.

"Do you want to stop and get anything to eat or drink to take on the bus?" she asked, backing out onto Bloom Street. *I remember walking down the middle of Bloom Street, feeling cars brush past both sides of my body.*

"No, it's too early to eat. . . . I don't think I could anyway . . . I'm a bit nervous," I said, turning around and watching my house get smaller.

"I'm nervous, too, are you sure you want to do this?" *I remember telling my mom and the fear in her eyes.*

"Mom, don't go there . . . please," I said, looking out my window. *I remember thinking the clouds were never going to lift, but praying they would.*

We drove to the bus stop in silence. I felt like a little kid on my way to the first day of kindergarten. My mother parked in the same spot where I waited for Mason's bus to arrive back in June. *I remember the way his words soothed me, how his eyes loved me, and how meeting him saved my life in the strangest way.* The tree on the corner was bare. We both stared up at the snowy hill, unsure of what to say. I switched the radio on and Tom Petty's voice, singing "Free Fallin'," filled the car. I leaned back in my seat and smiled.

I saw the bus turn the corner and make its descent down the hill. *I remember swallowing a pill, one after another, trying to fill the holes, but only making more.* My mom turned the radio off and opened her door. Slipping my coat on, I followed her lead. The bus pulled over as we crossed the street. *I remember feeling worse after I stopped.* I looked up at the tinted windows and couldn't see any shadows or outlines of people. The bus driver stepped off and opened the storage space below.

"Where are you two ladies going today?" he asked as he put the suitcases in and shut the door.

"Oh, it's just me. I'm going to New York City," I said, looking at my mom. She forced a smile.

"Round trip?" he asked, reaching into his pocket.

"Nope, one way," I said in disbelief. *I remember missing the city, feeling her pulling me closer.*

"That's going to be thirty-two fifty," he said, handing me a pink slip of paper.

Before I could even reach into my bag, my mother flashed money in front of him. "Keep the change," she said.

"I never get tips. I thank you kindly, ma'am," he said, stepping onto the bus.

My mother wrapped her arms around me. "I love you, be careful. I love you," she said. I could tell by her voice she was holding back tears. *I remember never being alone, yet always feeling lonely.*

"I love you, too. I'm going to be fine, Mom, I promise you. I've got to go," I said, pulling away and stepping up onto the bus.

The door closed behind me. *I remember the darkness, the music, and the smell of the bathrooms.* There was one person sitting in the front, no one else was on the bus. I took a seat toward the middle and looked out my window. My mother was sitting in the car, waving. I pressed my hand up to the cold glass as we pulled away. "'Bye, Mom," I said as tears flooded my face. I could smell her perfume on my coat. Pressing my nose against it, I took a few deep breaths. *I remember wanting to disappear, break free, and stay frozen in the moment forever.*

I watched the landscape change as we went through the mountains. The bus made a lot of stops in small towns along the way. Picking up one or two more people each time. *I remember waking up in a fluorescent room wearing a blue gown.* I knew this drive so well, but this time I took notice of every tree, every turn, every sign, knowing that each mile that passed was a mile closer to my destination, to my new life. *I remember blaming everyone, especially myself.* We made two stops in Jersey, one in Somerville and one in Newark. When the bus driver announced "next stop, New York City," my heart skipped a beat. *I remember feeling myself dissolve into a ghost.*

I began to see signs for the Lincoln Tunnel and then there it was, straight ahead, standing in the distance. The Empire State Building. *I re-*

member feeling scared, nauseous, and unsure. This was it. In that moment I wanted to vomit, pee my pants, clap, jump up and down, and scream at the bus driver *to turn the fuck around.* I thought about the first time my mother brought me to the city. It seemed like a lifetime ago. I remember the sense of anticipation that I had that cold winter day. *I re-member the first time, the last time, the old life, the voices, the memories.* That same feeling was back again, but it was different. I knew who I was, what I had been through, and what kind of life I wanted to lead.

I remember seeing the city skyline break through the darkness. We got closer and I saw it burst through the gray clouds. That beautiful sky-line. There was nothing like it. It gave me a great sense of pride and possibility. *I remember the dreams and the nightmares.* I knew that my life was in there . . . somewhere. I was going to find it, reclaim it, and rebuild it. I knew that I could make this work. I was no longer paralyzed with fear. *I remember feeling death at my door and welcoming it in.* I was floating in the middle of a tranquil ocean. *I remember the night that I died.*

We entered the Lincoln Tunnel. The birth canal that I was ripped from months ago. *I remember losing everything.* The orange lights surrounded me and twinkled like a warm fire. I could see the opening ahead getting larger, we were moving toward the light. *I remember talking to God and seeing an angel.* I closed my eyes for a few seconds and when I opened them, I was in the city. We turned onto Forty-second Street as I watched some fat, dirty pi-geons gathering around an overflowing garbage can. They were pecking at the rotten food lying on the sidewalk. It was a beautiful sight. *I remember being told to swallow more pills.*

We pulled into Port Authority and the inside of the bus dark-ened. The driver slid into gate 14 as I stood up and grabbed my bag. *I remember having nothing and everything.*

"For those of you who are just visiting, enjoy your stay, and for those of you who live here . . . welcome home." *I remember seeing my life in front of me. I remember smiling.*

*

aftErword

Dear Everyone,

Since that fateful night a few years ago, a lot of people have asked me how I did it, moved back to New York City, started over, and remained drug-free for four years (and counting). I don't think there is any easy answer or easy way. I just did. The day I saw my brain scan was a major turning point for me. I realized how destructive I had been to myself, my body, my soul . . . something inside me finally clicked. I knew I had been given a second chance and that's not something everyone gets. I had a choice to make. I could either go back to my old ways and end up institutionalized, in jail, or dead, or I could try a new road. A road where I would have to fight my way back to some kind of life, some kind of normalcy. Basically I could be a victim or victor. It wasn't an easy choice and still isn't some days. That was just the beginning of my long and arduous road to recovery. I was truly blessed to have a wonderful support system behind me; Mason, my mother, and sisters. I know not everyone is lucky enough to have that.

I felt a lot of guilt and shame after I got out of the psych ward(s). How were people going to treat me? How could I have let this happen? Would I be shunned or looked down upon because I was an addict? It was scary and I felt very much alone. But the best decision I have ever made was to share my pain, my life, with others. The more I talked about what was going on inside of me, the less fearful I became. I receive thousands of e-mails from people all over the country and world. Mothers, fathers, teachers, and countless young people, all sharing their own stories of pain and agony. I now realize how "not" alone I am. All of us fuck up, make mistakes, and pay the consequences. I believe it's what we do with the "fuckups" that make us or break us. You always hear that saying, "Don't worry, time heals all wounds." I don't buy it. I think it's what we do with that time that heals.

Today I live a completely different life than the one you have just read about. I find joy and ecstasy in the small things. Waking up on a cool morning and sitting on my patio with a cup of coffee, traveling around the country and talking with young people about addiction, sitting on the beach and watching a California sunset. I know I must sound like the biggest cornball right now, but it's true. I am high on life. So I guess I will leave you with this . . . those of you out there who feel like your life is over, that you have nowhere to go and no one to turn to, I know your desperation. I lived it. I want you to know there is a way out. Sure, you'll have many rocky mountains to climb, but what awaits you on that other side is beautiful, fucking amazing. I promise.

Love always,

Lynn

*

rEsources

Expert Contacts
and Informative Websites

The Partnership for a Drug-Free America (PDFA)
www.drugfreeamerica.org

For Parents
www.theantidrug.com

Sex, Relationships, Drugs, Advice
www.drdrew.com

Scot Anthony Robinson, Vision Warrior
www.visionwarrior.com

Information on Drug Policy
www.whitehousedrugpolicy.gov

**Substance Abuse and Mental Health Services
Administration (SAMHSA)**
www.health.org

**For a referral to a treatment program near you, call the
Center for Substance Abuse Treatment's National Drug
and Alcohol Treatment Referral Routing Service at**
1-800-662-4357

For questions about ecstasy:
1-866-XTC- FACTS

ACKNOWLEDGMENTS

I would like to thank . . .

Christy Fletcher and Greer Hendricks, for believing in me. George Greenfield and Beth Quittman, for making my voice even louder . . . who knew? Mary Steinborn, AKA "Structure Queen," for her support, creativity, kindness, and sweet-ass watermelon. I couldn't have done this without you. MTV, Oprah Winfrey, and the Partnership for a Drug-Free America, for giving me a sturdy platform to stand upon.

My beautiful sisters, Stacey and Stephanie, for putting up with all of my shit over the years; you're the best. Pap, Nan, and all of my nutty, wonderful, relatives in Pennsylvania, for never letting me take life or myself too seriously. Max Greene, for loving me, even when I didn't love myself; you saved my life in so many ways. Jill, Kevin, Brad, Kate, Christian, Scot Anthony, Artie, Loung, Rebekka, and Mr. Warren G, for the friendship, inspiration, support, advice, laughter, and sass you all bring to my life. James, Anne, Josie, and Mollie, you will always be my New York City family. Sandy, Sophie, Gustav, Uloo, and Barney, my San Clemente family, thanks for the food, shelter, and love.

To all of the jails, middle schools, high schools, and universities that I've been invited to speak at over the past three years, I love you guys! The thousands of people who email me, your words lift me up and fuel my fire to keep on keepin' on. New York City, without her there would be no book. David Hazen, what to say, what to say? You're crazy, hilarious, amazing, and unsurpassable. I'm lucky that I get to share my life with you (thank you, James). Lastly, to the lovely Kathleen Diane Smith, you are my angel, hero, mother, and best friend. I love you . . . all!